Survival at Sea

Survival at Sea

A practical manual of survival and advice
to the shipwrecked, assembled from an analysis
of thirty-one survival stories

Dr Bernard Robin

translated and edited by
Richard Simpkin

INTERNATIONAL MARINE PUBLISHING COMPANY
CAMDEN, MAINE

©1981 by International Marine Publishing Company
Library of Congress Catalog Card Number 80-85442
International Standard Book Number 0-87742-141-2
Printed and bound by The Alpine Press, Stoughton,
Massachusetts

Published by International Marine Publishing Company
21 Elm Street, Camden, Maine 04843

First published in France in 1977 by Editions Chaix. First
published in Great Britain in 1981 by Stanley Paul & Co., Ltd.,
an imprint of the Hutchinson Publishing Group.

Contents

Introduction to English edition

I was particularly pleased to be invited to translate Bernard Robin's book, since I have devoted a fair amount of attention to safety and survival in my own writings on sailing. While controversy still rages about Alain Bombard's views, he undoubtedly sparked off new thinking about survival at sea; but American and British officialdom and industry have perhaps led in specifying and providing the equipment needed to implement this more positive approach.

This unusual blend of historical accounts with analysis and practical conclusions brings home to me five key points of general application:

Yachtsmen can no longer count on merchant ships maintaining a visual lookout; this reinforces my own view and has implications going far beyond rescue.

Inshore sailors can very rapidly become ocean-going survivors; any boat that puts to sea needs the same level of survival equipment.

Given modern knowledge and equipment, those who go to sea in small boats can have a really good chance of surviving shipwreck.

One prerequisite for enjoying this chance is training; survival techniques should be just as much a part of the syllabus of any sea-going qualification for yachtsmen as are seamanship, navigation and so on.

The second prerequisite is modern equipment in good condition.

The report on the 1979 Fastnet Race[1] brings out very well the potential and the limitations of modern life-saving equipment. Perhaps the key points relevant to this book are the importance of not abandoning ship prematurely (*see* Chapter 30), the need for annual testing and servicing of inflatable life-saving equipment, and the value of teaching and rehearsing emergency drills.

1. *1979 Fastnet Race Inquiry*, carried out and published jointly by the RYA and the RORC.

The results of the Fastnet storm also highlight the question of cost – the cost of rescue equipment and of services alike. The lesson the historical chapters of this book, the Fastnet Report and other recent studies combine to drive home is that good life-saving equipment, properly maintained and used, not only reduces the risk of loss of life but also simplifies the task of the rescue services and diminishes the degree and duration of danger to which they are exposed. It cannot be right that a yachtsman's chances of survival should depend on his bank balance, or that disasters to poorly equipped yachts should lead to avoidably hazardous and expensive rescue attempts. Perhaps the Royal Yachting Association, the Royal National Lifeboat Institution and the insurance companies could come together to find a solution that would reduce both the avoidable risk and the real cost of rescue.

Finally, there is the problem of conflicting medical opinion. Valuable as Bombard's hypothesis may have been in stimulating thought, authoritative medical opinion in Britain and elsewhere, and I believe the weight of general French medical opinion, remain diametrically opposed to it. The author very fairly opens up this issue, and it is of such – literally – vital importance that I have included a note on it.

I should like to record my deep indebtedness to the Dean of Naval Medicine for the great trouble the staff of the Institute of Naval Medicine has taken to analyse and comment on these various physiological, biochemical and physical aspects; and to Captain Peter Young, a senior member of staff at Leith Nautical College whose responsibilities include the running of the College's survival course, for his comments on the nautical and general sides and his help with documentary research. My warmest thanks to the Cruising Secretary of the Royal Yachting Association for guidance on, and help in providing, documentation.

Richard Simpkin
Elgin, July 1980

Note to English edition on some medical aspects of survival

Perhaps it is the irony of suffering and death from thirst and/or hunger when surrounded by water rich in food that makes these hazards the most dramatic facets of survival at sea. In focusing on them the author may possibly have diverted attention from two other factors that are often even more critical – cold and over-exertion.

Since heat causes the body to lose water and cold makes it lose heat, there is no 'ideal' set of climatic conditions for survival – simply an optimum balance that varies with the circumstances of each survival situation. Even in temperate climates in summer the body will tend to lose heat progressively without the subject's even being aware of feeling cold. The effects of exposure are now widely known and understood under the term *hypothermia*. Once this condition sets in, it develops insidiously but rapidly, soon affecting alertness, rationality, power of decision and above all the will to live. Quite apart from its direct effects, this lowering of efficiency leads to stupid mistakes and acts of desperation or even folly. Unless there is a clear-cut need to protect oneself against the effects of high ambient temperature and sun, the first priority is normally to keep warm.

No less important – perhaps more so because it flies in the face of all a healthy individual's accepted ideas and habits – is the avoidance of exertion. It is, of course, essential to keep the muscles flexed and, if possible, to change position every now and then; but any physical effort beyond this has a rather dramatic effect on the time for which the organism can cope with survival conditions, and thus on the chance of ultimate rescue. Since one thing a survivor has plenty of is time, it is always worth performing tasks very deliberately and working out ways to save and share out effort. Briefly, exertion accelerates both heat loss and dehydration, the survivor's worst enemies. There is a happy mean between repose and exercise under any given set of survival conditions, but finding it requires a fair amount of knowledge and some cool, hard thinking.

We now come to the nub of the problem. As a yachtsman and a reasonably informed layman, I find myself faced with a head-on clash. On the one hand, we have Bombard's experience and recommendations, and many of the expedients used by actual survivors ancient and modern. On the other lies absolutely solid and authoritative international medical opinion backed by rigorous scientific proof. Since all the protagonists in this controversy and most of the modern survivors at least are persons of intelligence, integrity and goodwill, they can be assumed to be telling the truth as they see it. In any event there is too much similarity between accounts widely separated in time, space and circumstance for the common ground to be false.

So there has to be an unknown factor. Most probably this is the quantity of rainwater collected and consumed; even where the amounts are logged at the time or recorded in retrospect, this data may well be incomplete or incorrect. Further, we have no means of knowing whether those who drank seawater and/or ate fish when dehydrated and survived might not have been able to survive for longer, or might not have been in better condition when rescued, if they had abstained from these.

This whole problem hinges on two basic and seemingly indisputable physiological facts which the author – perhaps naturally in a book written by a doctor for laymen – does not explore and which Bombard presumably questions or rejects. One is that despite the kidney's remarkable ability to concentrate salts 'uphill' by transferring them from fluid with a lower content (blood) to one with a higher (urine) there is a limit to this process. In fact, the maximum concentration of common salt attainable in the urine is only rather over half that in seawater. The organism can only get rid of this 'extra' salt by passing more urine; and in the absence of fresh water the fluid for this additional urine is drawn from fluids already in the body. Thus the end result of drinking seawater is inevitably a net loss of fluid from the body – in other words, a worsening of the degree of dehydration.

A roughly analogous argument applies to the drinking of urine, particularly as this is likely to occur only when dehydration has become severe. Here there is a second factor too. Urine contains urea which is a poisonous substance. This urea has to be re-excreted by the kidneys, a process which draws off even more of the precious body fluids.

Urea is in fact the link between the dangers of drinking seawater and of eating fish when in a dehydrated condition: for fish is protein, and urea is one of the end products of the breakdown of protein in the organism. Thus eating fish causes a build-up of urea which has to be excreted, yet again at the cost of the stocks of fluid already in the body.

Finally, we come to the related question of the use of colonic irrigations of seawater as a means of making fresh water available to the body (as practised by Lynn Robertson). It is beyond question that water administered in this way is absorbed through the bowel; but there is no scientific evidence to suggest that the bowel wall shares the kidney's special property of concentrating salts. Since seawater has a higher salt content than the body fluids, there would seem to be a risk that the net effect of introducing seawater into the bowel would be to *increase* the concentration of salt in the body fluids, thus indirectly aggravating dehydration.

I see two linked problems here. One is that, as Bombard himself strongly emphasizes, the decision to drink seawater has to be taken straight away, before dehydration sets in. No one disputes that it is disastrous for a dehydrated person to drink seawater. The second is that the drinking of seawater (or even urine) does produce subjective short-term relief by temporarily increasing the amount of *extra*cellular body fluid (i.e. the fluid *outside* the actual cells of the organism). Unfortunately, there is irrefutable evidence, outlined above, that it does this at the expense of the *intra*cellular fluids which determine how long a person can survive dehydration. In some ways this controversy resembles the one about seatbelts in cars. Just as there will always be the isolated case where wearing a belt results in a death that could otherwise have been avoided, so there may be the isolated case in which the temporary relief obtained from drinking seawater might enable some critical decision or action to be taken. In neither instance do these cases alter the hard fact that wearing a belt or abstaining from seawater offers by far the better chance of survival.

Foreword

by Alain Bombard

Life is the object of man's presence on earth. From the day he is born he must be taught two basic principles – to love life and to prepare for death. Living and dying are the only two things we can be absolutely sure of; but if every child should be prepared for death and every man face it calmly as the one inescapable certainty, love of life and a fierce resolve to preserve it as long as possible must also guide man's thoughts.

Among the living are ordinary people threatened by every kind of danger – natural dangers like illness, and accidents and natural disasters such as volcanic eruptions, floods and earthquakes; man-made dangers – the fruits of progress, civilization and human cruelty – like road accidents, bursting dams, pit disasters and murder. From these known hazards which may bring sudden death I single out shipwreck.

I tried to combat the fatality rate from shipwreck by countering the four physical shocks which kill the victim before his forces are spent: drowning, which kills in minutes; exposure, which kills in hours; thirst, which kills in days; and hunger, which kills in weeks. When I had done this, I found a fifth threat that could also kill in hours, helped by exposure and brought on by the terrible shock of shipwreck – fear, panic, distress, the crumbling of morale. This is why I had to practise what I preached and submit to the law of shipwreck with '*l'Hérétique*'.

Many others too have undergone, voluntarily or otherwise, terrible ordeals in the face of hostile terrain, adverse seas or desert. It is these human lives, all of them distinguished by the desire to live, the will to conquer death (or, if not to conquer, at least to say to it 'Not today, thank you') that Bernard Robin has brought together in *Survival at Sea*.

I read these pages avidly. I knew some of the tales, while others were new to me. But the sum total of these struggles showed me man's extraordinary capacity to battle against fate. Morale, of course, is the common denominator, the prime mover in every battle we read of against death. Claudel wrote 'Remember, man, that you are spirit', and every page of this book tells of the conquest of mind over matter.

We owe a great deal to this book and to its author for having shown us, by stirring tales of devotion to life, that at the end of the struggle men are driven by spirit and morale. We see victory over death – a passing victory to be sure, and gained with the last ounce of strength – and at the end of the tunnel of trial and suffering we see the light of hope bringing us that most precious of gifts, *life*.

Introduction

However interesting the characters in a novel, however skilfully the author has assembled them and whatever words he has put in their mouths, the reader almost always has a slight reservation about allowing himself to be moved by imaginary misfortunes. The real way to grip him is to place before his eyes heroes who actually lived.

EYRIÉS, Histoire des Naufrages (1854)

Find me the sailor who in the heart of a storm has not thought with horror of the possibility of shipwreck. Again, find me the sailor who, lying peacefully in port, thinks of nothing but preparing for shipwreck. This paradox is an age-old one. It dates back to the time when man first launched himself on the waters, entrusting his life to craft – better and better craft admittedly, but we tend to forget that the fury of the waves takes little account of these improvements. These are two sides to a strange paradox that will be with us for a while yet. The aim of this book is not to lose sight of it altogether but simply to make sailors realize that they owe it to themselves to think about survival at sea.

When we read the stories of those who have managed to force themselves into adapting to this terrible condition, we are bound to be struck by astonishment and dismay at the deprivations and major mistakes which make up these tales. Alain Bombard, who must have read everything on this subject, writes:

> I am now convinced once and for all of the need to think about books for the victims of shipwreck – tips on navigation, signs of nearness to land like floating pieces of wood, butterflies just above the surface, gossamer and various insects or birds. The authors of *Raft Book*[1] must not be upset if I say that although the frigate bird may not spend the night at sea it goes as far as 1500 miles out. They also say that this bird rarely fishes for itself; yet I have seen with my own eyes frigates catching on the wing the same flying fish that my dorados[2] were hunting in the sea.

Experiences like this on a whole variety of topics cropped up constantly as I leafed through thousands of pages. In this way there gradually took root in my mind the idea of giving sailors a unique experience based on hard fact, the experience of all those who have *actually known shipwreck and survived*.

True, most of the victims who have told their tales have re-created for us the pang of thirst and hunger, the horror of storms, the loss of a companion in suffering, the desperation when a ship fails to see them. Very few have given us accurate comments on how their raft behaved or the resources they drew from the sea. Yet in all these tales lie little pieces of information, a host of small details. By comparing one with the other, one can assemble a considerable mass of data. Computer-like I have tried to process this data and extract some general rules without getting involved in science or bringing in technical laboratory studies on the subject.

The book is in two parts. In the first part I have tried to summarize thirty-one stories of shipwreck, chosen for the information they yield on all aspects of the question I was exploring. The informed reader is bound to know some of them already and may be surprised not to see others which I rejected. I rejected them because despite appearances they in fact duplicated information; I must ask forgiveness for not including everything. In the second part I have rearranged in rather longer chapters all the information that might improve the lot of those who may one day suffer shipwreck.

---

1. An American survival manual.
2. The French name suggests that these were *Coryphaena hippuris*, sometimes referred to as dolphins, rather than the mammal *Delphinus delphis*. (See also pages 79 and 107.) [Trans.]

Part One

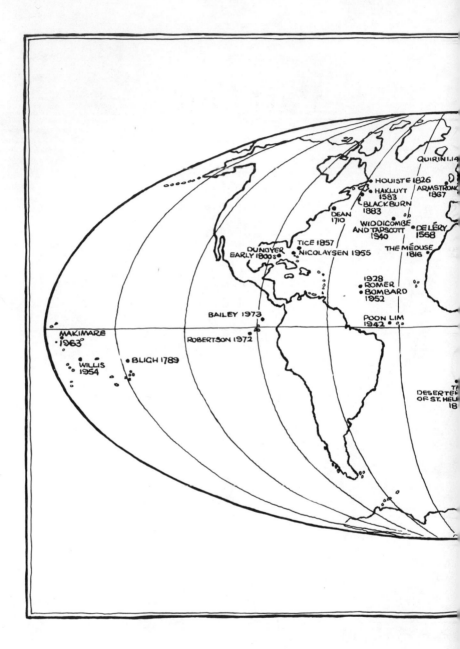

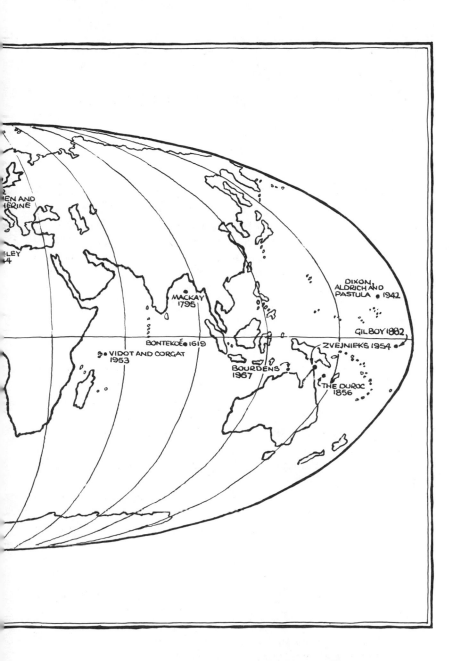

EN AND
HERINE

ELEY
44

DIXON,
ALDRICH AND
PASTULA ● 1942

MACKAY ● 1795

GILBOY 1882

BONTEKOE ● 1619

ZVEJNIEKS 1954 ●

● VIDOT AND CORGAT
1953

BOURDENS
1967

THE DUROC
1856

1
Piétro Quirini and his companions
(1431)

On 25 April 1431 Piétro Quirini, a Venetian merchant based at Candia (Heraklion) on the north coast of Crete, left port bound for Flanders. During the passage along the Mediterranean he found a leak and was forced to put into Cadiz for repairs. It was 14 July before he could set sail again. To start with he was carried towards the Canaries by head winds and problems with the rudder and did not reach Lisbon until 29 August. The damage was repaired, and on 14 September the ship headed once more for Flanders. During a violent storm the ship lost its rudder a second time and started to drift. The days went by and the stock of provisions rapidly fell; rationing was begun. The ship continued northwards and on 17 December, three months after leaving Lisbon, it was struck by yet another storm and soon started to go down. There were sixty-eight people on board. After sharing out what was left in the way of water, wine and food, forty-seven men took to a longboat and twenty-one to a gig. The two boats became separated during the night, and on the morning of 18 December the gig disappeared amid the wild waves.

For the forty-seven men packed in their longboat their life as castaways had begun. They were stripped of all provisions when, on the second day, the seas became so heavy that the boat continually threatened to capsize. In a moment of panic accompanying a particularly violent surge all the food and even the barrels of water were thrown overboard. It is not easy to tell from Quirini's account what was the worst part of the eighteen days of suffering that were to follow. The cold was typical of the North Sea latitudes in December, and the sailors were very seldom dry. Thirst, quenched to begin with by the parsimonious doling out of a barrel of wine that had miraculously survived, became so fierce that many of the men could not resist the temptation to drink seawater. Hunger was easier to bear but contributed to the general stupor; the men found no strength to try and steer the boat. Despair set in as each dawn revealed more dead. Twenty-six men had perished before the longboat with its load of frozen, dying men reached an island covered with snow on 4 January 1432.

Hope was reborn for the survivors. They crawled about in the snow, quenching their thirst by melting vast quantities of snow in their mouths. The island was deserted, except for one hut; they nevertheless managed to start a fire. Those who had not succumbed to the terrible

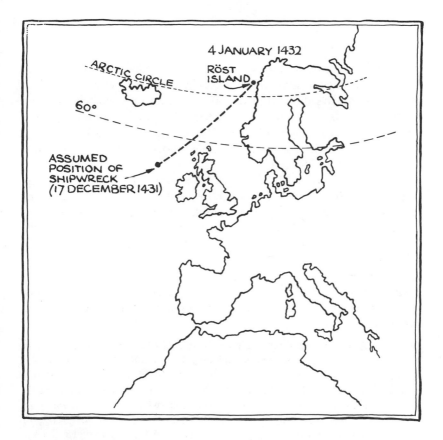

privations they had already suffered kept alive on seaweed, mussels and other shellfish until the day they found thrown up on the beach an enormous fish of 200 pounds or more. With extraordinary courage these starving men held out until 31 January 1432, when a fisherman landed on the island and told them that they were only eight miles from Röst, in the Lofoten Archipelago off the north-west coast of Norway. The rescue of the survivors was arranged without delay.

2
Jean de Léry and his companions
(1558)

Jean de Léry's tale represents a very unusual aspect of the problems raised by survival at sea, for it is a case of a crew 'shipwrecked' in their own ship. As the days went by, all the conditions that characterize shipwreck were built up one after the other, but despite everything they held the trump card of comfort – only relative comfort perhaps, but very different from the extremes known to those whom fate consigns to a frail lifeboat.

Jean de Léry boarded the *Jacques* to return to France on 4 January 1558 at the port which was later to become Rio de Janeiro. The first half of the crossing passed under conditions that could be considered favourable for such a voyage at such a time, although the whims of the wind considerably slowed the ship's progress. As the months went by, everyone on board began to realize the danger of famine intervening before the end of the voyage if the latter lasted much longer. The first steps towards rationing were taken. At this point we turn to Jean de Léry's account after three and a half months of a desperately slow crossing:

It was 16 April with about 500 leagues [just under 1500 nautical miles] to go to the French coast. Our victuals had shrunk so much that we were on half rations, but this regime was not nearly strict enough to prevent provisions running out towards the end of the month. We were reduced to sweeping the storeroom, the plastered and whitewashed room where the biscuit was kept. There we found more worms and rats' droppings than crumbs of bread; but what we did find was doled out by the spoonful in the form of a gruel as black as soot and even more bitter. At the beginning of May those who had parrots killed and cooked them. Some went to the point of eating their Morocco belts and leather shoes. We had to start thinking about hunting rats and mice. These were pursued with such a cunning variety of traps that soon there were few left. The price of a rat rose to four crowns. Water was short too. When it rained, we stretched out sheets with a weight in the middle to gather it. Finally, on 24 May 1558 the grace of God brought the sight of the shores of Brittany to the wretched men stretched motionless on the deck.

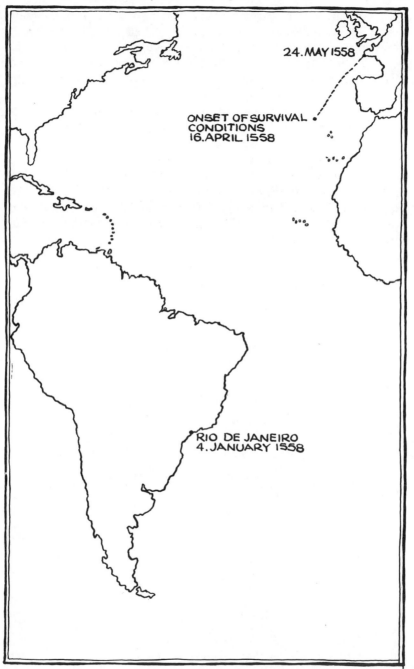

24.MAY 1558

ONSET OF SURVIVAL
CONDITIONS
16.APRIL 1558

RIO DE JANEIRO
4.JANUARY 1558

The situation on board had reached such extremes that the crew lacked all strength and let the wind drive them towards the shore. According to statements made later by the captain of the *Jacques* to Jean de Léry: 'If our situation had lasted just one day more, I had decided not to draw lots among us but, without warning anyone, to take one of us as food for the rest.'

We do not know how many of the forty-seven people who had left South America arrived. Jean de Léry simply says: 'Many died of hunger and exhaustion.' He also explains 'that a score died ashore from sating themselves too quickly'. He closes his account by analysing the numerous illnesses that arose in the days following their arrival in Brittany – oedema of the lower part of the body, the rejection of meat and wine, and above all difficulties of vision and hearing that made him fear he would be afflicted with blindness and deafness. Nothing came of this and he recovered completely.

3

Richard Hakluyt and his companions
(1583)

During a storm of 21 August 1583 the *Delight*, under the command of Captain Richard Clarke, was driven on to the shoals of Sable Island off Newfoundland. The ship sank and was lost beyond recovery, all that was left afloat being a one-ton boat only partially equipped with just a single oar. Those who could swim made their way to it, hauled themselves aboard and dragged from the water all those still struggling on the surface. Sixteen men in all were huddled in this small boat; to their horror they discovered that there was not a drop of water or a bite of food. Richard Hakluyt relates:

These men were less concerned with doing anything active than with surviving if it was God's will, for the boat was very small and overloaded and the weather was so bad that no craft could have hoisted even a stormsail. We passed two days and nights on the water and began to realize that by God's grace our boat was standing up well, although we had only one oar which we used for steering and to hold the boat head to wind. . . . Among us there was a quartermaster by the name of Hedely: "I see it is God's will that our boat rides the waves." he said to me, "and if it was not so overloaded He might bring some of us safely to shore. Let us draw lots and throw the four losers overboard, taking good care of our captain of course." I replied that we would live or die together. He then asked me if I had a clear idea of our position and I retorted that I thanked Providence for having granted me a good memory and that we were two or three days from land – in other words sixty miles or so.

On the third and fourth days the sea grew calmer. As the fear of capsize receded, thirst and hunger reared their heads. Some seaweed floating on the surface was gathered and eaten, while most of the men quenched their thirst with seawater. On the fifth day Hedely and another man died. Hakluyt continues:

On the sixth day the situation had not changed much and everyone longed for death, except for myself who tried to restore their spirits and promised them that with God's help they would soon be ashore. Yet these men remained very wretched and very doubtful of seeing land again, although on the seventh day I

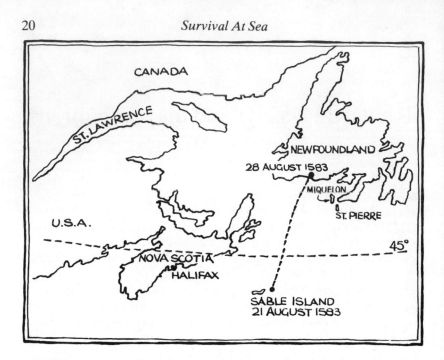

took the risk of promising them that they would see the coast soon and that if not they could throw me overboard. In fact at eleven o'clock in the morning we sighted land and at three in the afternoon set foot on it.

4
Guillaume Isbrantz Bontekoé and his companions
(1619)

Bontekoé was the captain of a vessel of the East India Company of 1100 tons, the *Nieuw Hoorn*, with a complement of 206 men. It was 28 December 1618 when the ship left Texel in the West Fresian Islands, just north of Holland, bound for Sumatra. After an uneventful voyage she rounded the Cape of Good Hope and put into the Island of Sainte Marie off Madagascar to take on water and fresh food. The *Nieuw Hoorn* set sail for the last time, headed for the strait of Selat Sunda which separates Java and Sumatra.

On 19 November 1619 with the ship in latitude 5°30' South (Captain Bontekoé does not mention longitude in his memoirs) fire broke out on board. The situation quickly assumed dramatic proportions, all the more since the whole crew knew that there were some barrels of powder in the holds. Everyone, of course, should have set about fighting the fire, but eighty-seven members of the crew piled into a large lifeboat and a gig and abandoned their shipmates to the mercy of the explosion. One hesitates whether to condemn the cowardice of these men or to acknowledge their good sense! Be that as it may, the *Nieuw Hoorn* blew up. Of the 119 crew members who had bravely fought the fire, the men in the boats, who had watched the explosion from a distance and then returned to the scene of the disaster, picked up only two, both seriously injured. Captain Bontekoé was one of these and despite his injuries he set about organizing the survivors without delay. The degree of panic had been such that no one had thought of getting supplies of water, food, charts or a compass. The men used their shirts to jury-rig sails, and the master applied all his skill to bringing them towards Java or Sumatra.

Some tropical showers allowed them to collect a little fresh water, but in the absence of a receptacle each man's ration was very small. Some drank seawater, others their urine. One night a shoal of flying fish fell in the boats; they were devoured raw, as was the flock of gulls which descended on the unfortunate men in such great numbers that they could be caught by hand. But apart from these few days of feasting, food was extremely short. There was talk of eating the weaker members when they died, and it took Bontekoé all his authority to stop these ideas being put into practice.

It was on the thirteenth day, 2 December 1619, after a heavy rainfall which had revived even the weakest men, that an island was sighted. When they had landed, their disappointment surged to the point of fury when they found there was not a drop of water. But there were plenty of coconut palms: for several days the coconuts put new life into

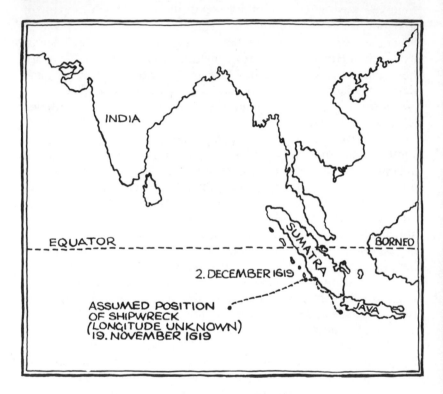

the men and gave them a chance to set off in better shape for less desolate places. On the second day of this new phase in their life as castaways, to which the coconuts they had taken on board gave something of the air of a cruise, they reached the coast of Sumatra after some difficulty in finding their way through a barrier reef. Bontekoé and his men could do little about exploring the coast, for they were set upon by a whole army of Malays. They withdrew hastily to their boats, leaving six dead on this inhospitable shore.

For day after day the survivors sailed along the coast, going ashore from time to time to replenish their stock of coconuts and gorge themselves on oysters and small shellfish. They even discovered the taste of the 'hearts' of palm trees and bamboos. The bamboos gave them the ingenious idea of making receptacles. They bored out the cores of long, strong bamboo stems, leaving only a plug at the bottom. By filling these with coconut milk they provided themselves with a reserve of 'water' that allowed them to stay afloat longer.

In this way they headed southwards, along the coast of Sumatra and across the Selat Sunda Strait, until finally they were picked up by a fleet of twenty-three Dutch vessels cruising off Java. There were fifty survivors.

5
William Okeley
(1644)

The story of Okeley and his four companions is not strictly speaking one of shipwreck but of deliberately putting to sea with extremely limited resources. The reader must form his own opinion of their decision. In June 1639 William Okeley embarked at the small English port of Gravesend in the *Mary* bound for Providence Island in the Gulf of Mexico. Six days after leaving the Isle of Wight, where she had put in to pick up some passengers, the *Mary* was captured by Barbary pirates. The sixty men of the crew and the passengers were transported to Algiers and sold as slaves.

'I spent four really terrible years in this way,' Okeley relates. So it was that when he was working in a textile factory he got the idea of building a canvas boat to escape – a folding boat which would not be assembled until the last moment to avoid giving the game away. After several months of secret work with four friends among his fellow slaves, everything was ready.

On the evening of 30 June 1644 in an isolated inlet about half a mile from Algiers the five men stretched a double skin of sailcloth thoroughly coated with tar and tallow over the wooden frame they had assembled. Putting two goatskins full of water and some provisions on board, they set course northwards and were on their way. The boat started to leak straight away, and the routine soon became tedious and exhausting. While four men rowed, the fifth bailed. On the third day of their escape, they ran out of water; and the remainder of their food, soaked in seawater, had become inedible. The heat was overpowering, and although the man bailing sprinkled the rowers, dehydration started to make them light-headed.

On the fifth day, when they had given up hope, they saw a turtle sleeping on the surface. They approached it with great stealth and managed to catch it. They cut off its head, drank its blood and ate its liver and as much flesh as they could. With their strength thus renewed, they were sated and went to sleep. On the following day, the

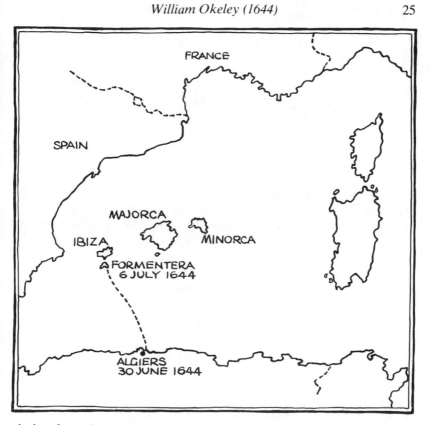

sixth, after a long spell of bailing, they took to the oars again. Rowing hard, they reached the shore of the Island of Formentera in the Balearics, where their exploits won them a splendid reception.

6

John Dean and his companions
(1710)

John Dean was captain of the *Nottingham*, a 120-ton galliot armed with ten guns. In December 1710 the ship was wrecked within sight of the North American coast. Before the ship could put about, she touched on the western extremity of a rock known as Boon Island, about thirty-five miles east of Piscataka. The *Nottingham* rapidly sprung a leak and sank. The crew managed to reach the wave-swept rocky shelf where their life as castaways was to begin. The cold was terrible. There was no question of lighting a fire, for everything was soaked; the rock was almost awash and was too constantly swept by spray to support vegetation. The best they could do was to rig up a tent with strips of canvas to protect them from the rain and the spray.

For a week the fourteen survivors had nothing to eat but the cheese they had salvaged from the wreck. When the sea went down, they built a raft with some planks which had been washed up on the island in the hope of gaining the mainland near by. But their raft was torn to pieces by the waves the moment they put it in the water. On 21 December 1710 John Dean wrote:

Soon we were reduced to the most wretched and tragic situation imaginable, with everyone dying of cold and hunger. Their hands and feet were frozen and on the point of gangrene.

They kept themselves alive with seaweed and marine vegetation along with two or three mussels per day. Their wretchedness was deepened by an obsession that a high spring tide might submerge their islet completely. There came a day when one of the men was found dead in the morning, and a gull was captured and devoured on the spot by the thirteen survivors. The one thing they had plenty of was fresh water. It snowed and rained continuously, and the water that kept them alive collected in the crevices of the rock. By the end of December only ten men were left, and it was then that the carpenter, 'a fat man of forty-seven', died. As Dean tells us:

My people begged me to give them the body of their comrade to eat to support their wretched existence. I must admit that nothing that I had experienced so far seemed to me as cruel and horrible as this revolting suggestion. Having pondered and reflected thoroughly both on the legality of such an act and on the absolute necessity in which we found ourselves, reason, conscience and all moral considerations had to give way before the arguments of a ravaging hunger. So we decided to satisfy it.

After relating a number of details too basic and repulsive to merit inclusion about how he himself was obliged to preside over the dismemberment and cutting up of the corpse, the author of this account goes on:

I assigned an equal portion to each man to avoid any possibility of argument or jealousy. After a few days I saw a complete change in the character of these unhappy men. Peacefulness and mutual affection gave way to a wild fixed stare and a fierce barbaric laugh. Instead of jumping to obey my orders as they had always been happy to do until then, entreaty and forcefulness alike became useless.

Luckily, the castaways' experience of these conditions came to an end on the morning of 2 January 1711. A sloop passing near by spotted them and was able to draw near enough to their rock to give them some victuals and something to light a fire with, as well as arranging their final rescue a few days later.

John Dean decided to abandon life at sea and settled in Ostend, where he died in 1761.

7

Madame Dunoyer

(early eighteenth century)

Mr Dunoyer and his wife had settled at Samana on Santo Domingo
Bay (in what is now the Dominican Republic). Every now and then
they sailed in their schooner to Cap Français[1] where they had relatives.
It was during one of these voyages that the terrifying experience of
becoming a castaway left a permanent mark on Mrs Dunoyer's life.
She went on board with her husband and two children, their seven-
year-old son and an unweaned baby boy. With them were their slave, a
black girl, and two Englishmen taken on to help sail the ship. During
the first night on board, with the lights of Santo Domingo Bay still
above the horizon, the two Englishmen murdered Mr Dunoyer and
took over the schooner. Thirty-six hours later, to get rid of embarras-
sing witnesses, the two mutineers put Mrs Dunoyer, her slave and her
two children in the dug-out canoe which served as a tender to the
yacht. A mother's entreaties made no impression, and the two adults,
the child and the baby were cast adrift in the middle of the Caribbean
Sea with 'a wretched straw mattress on the bottom of the canoe, four
slabs of biscuit, a pitcher holding rather under a gallon[2] of fresh water,
six eggs and a small piece of salt pork'. Darkness fell, intensifying the
anguish of the castaways. The sea got up and a wave 'washed away the
biscuit and upset the fresh water'. At dawn the situation seemed to Mrs
Dunoyer so bad that she lost consciousness. 'The care of her faithful
slave brought her back to life, but only to see all the more clearly the
abyss into which she had been cast . . . with faltering hands she offered
the child at her breast to the mercy of the supreme arbiter of our days.'

  Seven whole days and nights went by like this, 'battling with the
waves, exposed to the ravages of the air in the worst season, with
nothing to drink and nothing to eat but a scrap of salt meat'. On the
seventh day, feeling that she was about to succumb, Mrs Dunoyer

---

1. I think this may be simply Cap or Cap Haïtien. [Trans.]
2. 'Four pints', the old French pint being 0.9 litres. [Trans.]

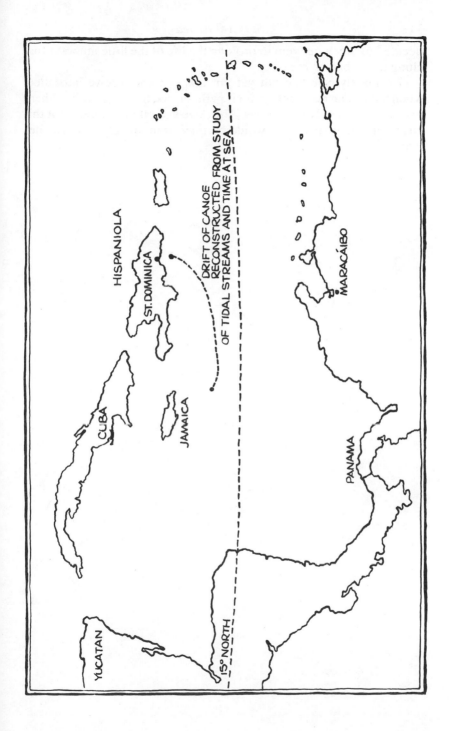

decided to 'open her vein to prolong the life of the little innocent that clung to her barren breast'.

Fortunately, she had not yet put this extreme resolve into effect when a rescuing boat crossed their path, picked them up, revived them and took them to New Orleans. The slave was publicly freed, 'but this girl replied that only death would part her from Mrs Dunoyer and her two children'.

8

Captain Bligh and his supporters
(1789)

The well-known story of the mutiny on the *Bounty* claims a place in this book not on account of the mutineers themselves or Fletcher Christian who headed them, but because of the survival of Captain Bligh and the eighteen men who remained faithful to him.

On 8 April 1789, a few days out from Tahiti, mutiny broke out on board the *Bounty*. Bligh and his eighteen companions were abandoned in mid-Pacific, crowded into a 23 ft open boat, a kind of whaler, equipped with some oars, a mast and a sail. They were given some casks of fresh water and provisions. While the *Bounty* disappeared, headed for the islands of Australasia, the nineteen men embarked on what was to be a legendary exploit – a voyage of over 3000 miles in forty-one days to reach Timor. The whole credit for this must go to Bligh himself – with his will-power amounting to an obstinate determination, his expert navigation and the extraordinary grip he had on those who remained faithful to him. Despite rationing, food and water soon ran out. The whole of the second half of this extraordinary ocean passage was made under extreme survival conditions. Yet Bligh lost only one man – an achievement just as great as the voyage itself, and likewise due to the indomitable will with which he succeeded in inspiring his shipmates.

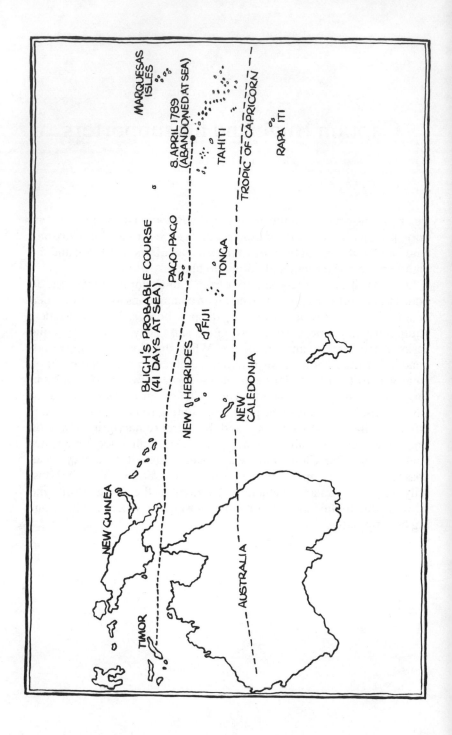

MARQUESAS
ISLES

8.APRIL 1789
(ABANDONED AT SEA)

TAHITI

TROPIC OF CAPRICORN

RAPA ITI

BLIGH'S PROBABLE COURSE
(41 DAYS AT SEA)

PAGO-PAGO

TONGA

FIJI

NEW HEBRIDES

NEW
CALEDONIA

NEW GUINEA

TIMOR

AUSTRALIA

9

John Mackay and his companions

(1795)

John Mackay was second mate on the *Juno*; the master was Alexander Bremmer who had with him his wife and a slave. The *Juno* left Rangoon on 29 May 1795, bound for Madras with a cargo of 450 tons of teak. On board was a crew of fifty-three, mostly Malays, and some European passengers – sixty-two people in all.

On 1 June during a storm a leak appeared, and 'everyone without distinction had to man the pumps to keep the ship afloat'. After eight days of continuous pumping, the weather improved enough for improvised repairs to be carried out: 'A tarred piece of canvas was nailed over the hole . . . and this expedient was completely successful.'

On 19 June high seas were running again in the Bay of Bengal. The tarred cloth tore under the buffeting the *Juno* received, and the leak became worse than before. The ship started to settle, and the mainmast was cut away to lighten her. Some of the Malays decided to make their escape in the large lifeboat and a six-oared pinnace, but 'they got into difficulties and started to ship water'.

In latitude 17°10' North the *Juno* started to sink. But once the deck was submerged an equilibrium was set up; the ship did not settle further, but soon only the remaining masts and the standing rigging remained clear of the continuing heavy seas. 'Everyone climbed into the rigging, working their way further and further up as successive waves made the ship settle a little further.' The gale went on for three days, and the sixty-two victims stayed clinging to the shrouds, battling with the incessant swaying and trying not to give way to fatigue. Some, in fact, dozed off for a few seconds and let go; they fell and disappeared in the waves which every now and then threatened to tear away the unlucky ones who had not found room at the top. Others, packed in the mizzen crow's nest, tried to swim to the foremast; they were swept away by the waves which were breaking on the kind of bank formed by the submerged hulk of the *Juno*.

On the fourth day the weather eased. Very soon the survivors, who

no longer needed to concentrate all their thought and strength on the
sole task of hanging on to the rigging, were swept by new waves of
thirst and hunger. Now the weather was clear, and the noonday sun
beat down on them. Mackay tells us:

Although the deprivations I felt, among them thirst, were very distressing, they
did not reach the violent extremes the stories had led me to expect. I remembered having read in Captain Inglefield's account that his shipmates in his
lifeboat wrapped themselves completely in blankets soaked in seawater and
that the pores of the skin absorbed the water and left the salt on the surface. I
tried this expedient out as best I could by dipping in the sea from time to time a
flannel vest I was wearing next to my skin. Several of my companions who
followed my example were also refreshed, and I am sure this trick saved our
lives.

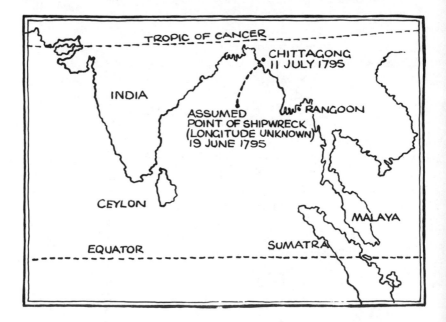

On the fifth day the most enterprising among the survivors built a
raft with pieces of wood. The reader will envisage what a task this was
with no firm support except the masts and the rigging that surrounded
them. Two of the men working on the building of what they thought
would be their way to safety fell into the water and were drowned. On
the sixth day the raft was finished. Those who still had some strength
left drove the weaker ones from it. Mackay was among those who

thought the way to safety lay on the raft, but privation and despair did not prevent his realizing that there were far too many on a wooden structure like that to offer any real chance of success. He swam back to the mizzen crow's nest.

On 27 June, after the survivors had been living in the *Juno*'s rigging for eight days, the raft reappeared, borne on the currents from the opposite side. Its occupants had been thinned out; many were dead and the rest exhausted. John Mackay, whose only resting-place all this time had been the collection of wood and cordage that was still above surface, takes up the tale again:

I abstained from salt water as long as I possibly could; but when I could no longer stand the fire which was devouring my stomach and entrails I went down and drank two large glasses or so of seawater. What a surprise! Instead of doing me harm, this nauseating drink revived my strength and my spirit. Despite this I still had no doubts about its poisonous effect and waited moment by moment for the agony to commence. . . . I felt better and better. . . .

Mackay stresses after some extremely violent bouts of vomiting: 'These drawbacks were slight in comparison to all the good it did me'.

On 28 June, while the rigging was once again laden with the unfortunates who had put all they had left into the attempt with the raft, a squall got up, accompanied by heavy rain. Everyone went about collecting this water, which was their greatest need. Clothes, converted into receptacles, had to be rinsed out several times to make sure the water stayed drinkable, but the tropical storm lasted long enough for everyone to quench their thirsts.

The slow hours of two more days laboured their way beneath the fierce sun. The survivors used their strength to take pieces of sail down to the waves and place wetted cloth on their parched bodies. By now they lacked even the strength to go down the rope ladder formed by the shrouds and dip themselves in the water and refresh themselves. 'One of the Lascars died in the cat-harpings of the shrouds, just above the crow's nest. The man nearest him tried to throw the body into the sea, but it was so entangled in the rigging that he could not free it. The body remained there two days giving forth an insufferable stench'.

On the morning of the twelfth day, 1 July, Captain Bremmer drew his last breath in the arms of his wife. One by one, the passing days swept away the last resources of all those who had lost hope. The survivors no longer had the strength to speak 'loud enough to be heard at that distance' – the distance from one crow's nest to the other. From this point on Mackay's account becomes vaguer: 'By then I could scarcely take in what was happening'. Thirst tortured them, but hunger was hardly noticeable. Their weakness was extreme. As the days went by, the shrouds were re-rigged to make life less precarious and acrobatic; by now they allowed themselves a few moments rest, which were also like pangs of death. 'I was hardly conscious of what was happening to those of our people who were not right near by me'.

In this universe of twisted wood and cordage rising from the ocean heart-rending scenes took place – acts of fellowship and friendship, or of hate, which were to be made meaningless by the death of those who performed them.

On the evening of 10 July, the twenty-first day, those perched highest in the rigging thought they saw land. After a long night of wavering between hope and fear of a mirage, the dawn finally rose on the coast that meant life. The sun rose to its zenith and sank once more behind the horizon, giving those furthest gone ample time to ponder on the problem of getting ashore when the ship ran aground. It was not until the following morning that the *Juno* drifted to a standstill in the sandy bottom. The tide exposed the deck; this was a luxury for the survivors who dragged themselves round trying to flex their stiffened joints. The bravest swam to the shore and found a river there. Soon no one was left on board but 'two women, three old men, a middle-aged man who had been bedridden for several days when the ship half sank, a young boy and I. These weak beings had borne tribulations which had carried away many men younger and stronger than them'.

Weak as he was, John Mackay could not resist the call of the land and threw himself into the water: 'A moment before, I could hardly move my joints; but I was hardly in the water when my limbs regained all their suppleness'. The narrator was then picked up by some Hindus who carried him to the river and gave him some rice. 'I took some in my mouth, chewed it a little but it was impossible to swallow.'

All those still alive when the ship grounded were rescued. They slowly regained their strength and reached Chittagong, six days on foot from the place where the *Juno* came to rest after her twenty-one days adrift.

10
The deserters of St Helena
(1810)

After several months on the island, five soldiers from the garrison of St Helena started looking for an opportunity to desert. This presented itself in the form of the very accommodating master of the *Colombia*, an American ship which put into the island early in June 1810. The desertion was arranged; as a precaution they agreed a rendezvous with the *Colombia* in a deserted creek on the island. In this way the five men would be able to board the ship in complete safety and without danger for the master.

It was on 10 June 1810 that McCannon, Brighouse, Conway, McQuinam and Parr stole a whaler, which had been neglected and was therefore in poor condition. They forced a sixth man who had surprised them at the moment of departure to accompany them and made their way to the rendezvous, taking with them a cask of water, twenty-five loaves of bread and a compass. The creek where they were to join the *Colombia* was soon reached, and their period of waiting began. This lasted a long time, and the deserters had reluctantly to admit that the master had not kept his word. On the other hand, there was no question of going back, for their desertion would inevitably have been reported. The five deserters and their prisoner put their heads together and decided to make for Ascension Island.

They rigged an oar as a mast and sewed handkerchiefs together to make a sail, but it did not take the six long to realize their total inexperience of the sea. Their boat, difficult to steer, spent most of its time at the mercy of the currents. The idea of making for Ascension was abandoned in favour of going with a set that should take them to the coast of South America. In these early days nothing seemed impossible to these determined men. The sail made of handkerchiefs was torn up and replaced by a new one made from their shirts.

On the tenth day, 20 June, there was nothing left but 'three pounds of bread and about a jugful of water'. Rationing, already strict, was tightened even further; in this way their provisions were made to last

until 28 June. On the 29th Parr, using the gaff, managed to catch a
small dolphin which had been escorting them on their way. They
managed to tip it into the boat, and gorged themselves on its blood and
its flesh for four days. Then 'hunger returned, more terrible than ever'.

   The days went by. Rain was infrequent and slight. Fishing with the
gaff proved fruitless. Gradually, each man began to watch his neigh-
bour with greed and mistrust. It was McCannon who was the first to
talk of sacrificing one to give the others a chance of survival. Despair,
thirst and hunger had reached a point where the idea was accepted.

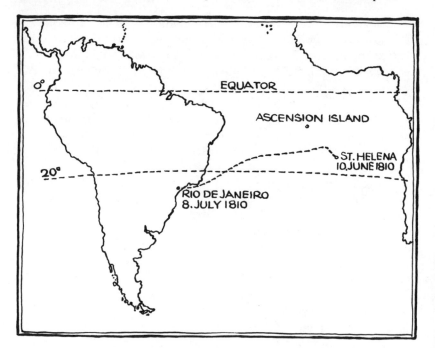

McCannon cut from the boat six pieces of wood and carved a name on each.
Shaking them in his hand he moved across to Parr and asked him to take one.
'Not me,' said Parr. Each refused to be the instrument of destiny. McCannon
went to the side and dropped the names one by one into the sea. Only one
remained, and he read it without flinching. 'It's me,' he said, 'God is calling for
my life to save yours.' Making the sign of the cross he plunged a knife into his
heart. The others gazed with stupefaction at the body stretched out at their
feet. Which of them was to make the first move? Who would be the first to
partake of this sacrificial meat? For another two hours they continued to suffer
the agonies of hunger. . . . Protected from putrefaction by seawater, the
corpse provided them with food for eight days.

As 8 July, the twenty-eighth day of their voyage, dawned, another climax was reached. Once again the five survivors started actually discussing the rules for a fresh sacrifice. But luckily the horizon was embellished with an unmistakable profile: land was near. The five gathered the last of their strength to row, and before long their whaler charged out of control into violent surf which capsized it.

Only three men reached shore. McQuinam and Brighouse met their death at the moment when rescue seemed to be at hand. The three survivors had come ashore not far from Rio de Janeiro. They settled in Brazil.

11
The *Méduse*'s raft
(1816)

The wreck of the *Méduse* is one of the best-known dramas of the sea on account both of the scenes of horror and cannibalism which accompanied it and of Géricault's famous picture which immortalized it. It is only because of the chronological sequence of this book that this story follows on the heels of the tale of the deserters from St Helena, six years earlier, which also raised the problem of cannibalism.

The *Méduse* was a forty-four gun frigate, dispatched by France in 1816 to reassume possession of the territories of Senegal restored by Great Britain under the Treaty of Paris. Under the command of Commander Duroy de Chaumareix, an *émigré* of noble birth who had just rejoined the service after an absence of twenty years, she sailed from Rochefort on 17 June. Her navigation verged on the fantastic, and on 4 July she ran aground on the Arguin Bank, sixty miles or so south of Cap Blanc and not far off the coast of northern Mauritania. All efforts to refloat the frigate having failed, Duroy de Chaumareix decided to abandon ship. Since the lifeboats had room for only 250 of the 400 on board, it was decided to build a large raft capable of carrying 200 people. It was in complete disorder and utter anarchy that in the end 147 people, including one woman, embarked on the raft and were towed towards the shore by the six lifeboats. From this point on the evidence is highly conflicting, as the inquiry held at Rochefort in 1817 disclosed.

When the convoy was a bare five miles from the hulk of the *Méduse*, the tow broke or was cut – most probably the latter, for the lifeboats drew away, abandoning the raft to its terrible fate. Completely at the mercy of wind and tide, without even a mast or a sail to return to the frigate they could still see, the 147 castaways began to drift out to sea. They had under 25 lb of biscuits, some onions and lemons, some casks of wine and several barrels of fresh water. The disorder and anarchy which had already characterized the navigation, the shipwreck and the building of the raft reared their heads once more. The crew were a mixed bag – a few naval officers, a large number of soldiers and some passengers, all of them shattered by the blow fate had struck them. No one really assumed responsibility for organizing their survival, and this lack of authority soon made itself felt.

As early as the first night the sea got up and weakened the raft's structure. Many of the castaways were crushed between the timbers as

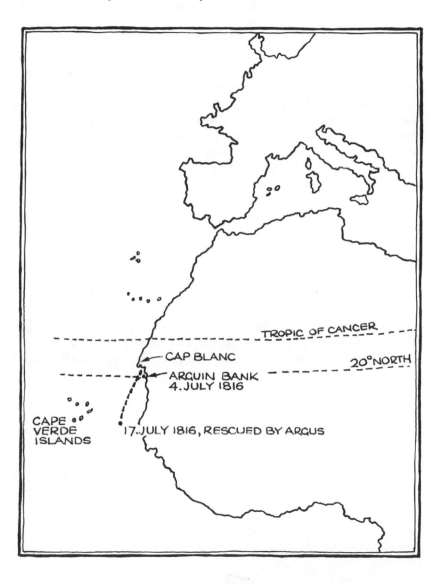

they opened and closed with the movement of the waves. Others were swept overboard and drowned. The emotional and psychological shocks of these first scenes of horror seemed to have helped bring about the wave of madness which from that time onwards swept over the raft. A cask of wine was opened, then another; and the survivors partook freely. Drunkenness awakened some of the soldiers' worst instincts, and they mutinied and threw an officer overboard. Night fell on a raft gone mad, and in the darkness there followed a pitched battle which left dozens of victims for the sharks to fight over.

When the third day dawned, calm was restored and the survivors counted themselves. Only sixty-seven were left, and all the water and provisions were gone. It is scarcely credible that a mere three days of relative fasting could have produced unbearable hunger, yet it was on this third day that 'one of the men started dismembering a corpse. A moment later a score or more were tearing at the prey like a pack of wolves'. As one of the survivors later related: 'Seeing that this revolting food had given new strength to those who ate it, someone proposed drying the flesh to make it less repugnant'.

Day followed day. Each morning the sun brought a truce and stilled passions; but rancour and new hatreds built up through the day and exploded every night. The number of survivors diminished, as much due to brawls as to privation. On the sixth day only fifteen were left. On the ninth day 'a white butterfly of a kind very common in France alighted on the raft. It brought back hope'. Four days later, on their thirteenth day adrift, thirteen dazed survivors were rescued by the *Argus*.

This tale may not contribute much to our study, but it teaches one lesson: panic was what this drama was really all about and, however it may be caused, panic is the worst of the evils that can afflict the ship-wrecked.

12

Commandant Houiste

(1826)

After a story which does little credit to the French Navy, we return to more informative accounts with the extraordinary tale of Houiste, mate of the *Nathalie*, a French ship which set sail from Granville with seventy-four men on board on 25 April 1826, bound for Newfoundland to fish for cod. On 29 May, at position 51° North and 56° West, the *Nathalie* struck an iceberg and sank. Only seventeen men managed to reach a lifeboat. Houiste relates:

I was sinking with the rest, but I quickly came up again and Providence showed me two pieces of wood near by. On this frail craft was the sailor Potier. I took my place beside him . . . we soon saw a flat piece of ice. We steered towards it and after prolonged and painful effort managed to climb on to it.

Paralysed by the long time they had just spent in the icy water, they soon felt, through their soaked clothing, the bite of wind and snow. All night they paced the ice to avoid freezing to death. When day broke, they saw in the distance four human silhouettes, castaways like themselves on a drifting fragment of the ice-floe – but beside the four black dots they saw a three-master setting about rescuing them. Houiste and his comrade did everthing they could from their patch of ice to attract attention but in vain, although the ship spent the whole day cruising the waters looking for possible survivors.

Darkness fell once again. Houiste continues:

The castaways passed their second night and the one after it in freezing rain, paralysed with cold and plagued by hunger. . . . By day hunger was the worst of our afflictions; by night it was the cold that stopped us taking a moment's rest.

On the morning of 1 June, after they had neither slept nor eaten for three days and their thirst had been soothed only by the ice they sucked, they saw a man clutching the debris of the *Nathalie* which still showed above the surface. They decided to go to his aid and bring him back to their ice island.

Nearby was a little piece of ice just about capable of carrying a man. I took the risk of transferring myself to it and, with Potier's knife, made a notch in which to place our oar. (*They had recovered this just before getting on to the ice.*) Thus the ice served me as a craft to cross over to the debris . . . I managed to get hold of a chicken coop. In it were four drowned chickens. My joy at the sight knew no bounds.

The man in the shrouds of the *Nathalie* made no reply to Houiste's cries, for he was frozen to death. Houiste returned to his little ice-floe, and he and Potier ate a hen completely raw – 'we tried in vain to pluck it'.

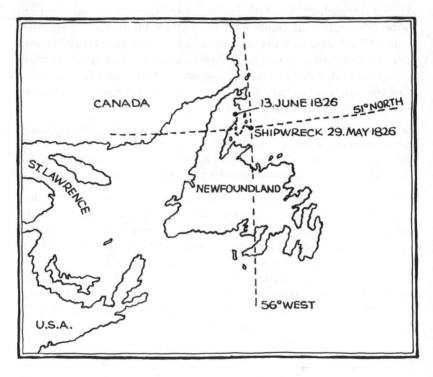

In his 'boat' Houiste moved about among the debris of the shipwreck and was also able to pick up some empty hogsheads and a barrel of cider mixed with seawater which made a very acceptable drink for them. Everything still afloat was worth its weight in gold to the two men. 'To get nails we took off the end hoops of every barrel we found.' During these expeditions from their floating island they discovered a gig. 'It was awash. When we got in it, we had water up to our waists. In the state it was in, a little more weight would have sent it to the bottom.' It was at this point they noticed a man who, like them, owed his life to a small piece of ice. After an hour and a half of sculling the gig, Houiste and Potier reached their new companion. The three of them managed to heave their boat on to the ice and plug the leaks with the scattered planking and the nails they had collected. For Houiste the discovery of the gig and the rescue of a man by the name of Joret were signs that they still had a chance of surviving if they worked hard enough at it. This chance was Newfoundland, and they decided to make for it.

Now three, they got aboard the botched-up gig, taking it in turns to scull with the single oar. After two days of slow progress among the ice-floes, which became more and more numerous, the pack ice closed and shut them in, immobilizing the boat. They had to spend four days waiting for the ice to break up again and set them free. 'One limb of chicken divided into three was our ration for a whole day.'

The sunny morning of 6 June showed them a spectacle that sent their hearts leaping – thirty or so fishing boats silhouetted on the horizon. Straight away, taking with them a plank to use as a bridge for crossing from one piece of ice to the next, the three men abandoned their boat and made their way towards the fishermen across the ice. 'We had covered about half the distance which separated us from the boats, when a high wind from the north-west blew up, breaking up, separating and scattering the ice-floes.' Demoralized, they abandoned themselves once again to a death which the cold would make an easy one. They were cut off on a new iceberg and began to let their extreme weakness overcome their will to survive.

It was in a state of torpor not far from death that, on 10 June, Houiste realized that the ice was beginning to join up again. He saw land ten miles or so away.[1] He shook his two companions and managed to persuade them to make one last effort. In the forty-eight hours that followed, urging each other on, they found the strength to get within half a mile of the coast. But between pack ice and the coast there was an icy stretch of open water. To plunge into it would have been certain death in their weak and undernourished state. They already had widespread frost-bite; their extremities had long been numb; their hunger was unbearable. They could do little but place themselves in the hands of God by getting on to a new piece of floating ice. The tide

---

1. The original says '10 leagues', which would be 30 miles, which does not seem credible. [Trans.]

took them towards the coast. Four times they succeeded in crossing from one piece of ice to another, and about 5.00 p.m. on 13 June they reached land. They collapsed on the snow-covered grass and fell into a sleep which the cold might well have made their last.

On 14 June the sun warmed the three men's shattered bodies and aroused them. Jorct was blind and Potier paralysed. Houiste alone was able to summon up the strength to get up and fill his cap with mussels. This put new life into men who had eaten nothing for seven days. On 17 June Joret recovered his sight and became the first to spot an English schooner making along the coast. They were picked up and rescued. Despite very serious frost-bite, all three recovered.

13
The Duroc
(1856)

At the time, the repercussions of the shipwreck of the *Duroc* were very considerable. The newspapers ran splash headlines on it and fed their readers so much detail that it is still possible to draw together the story of this incredible adventure.

On 13 August 1856, five days after leaving New Caledonia bound for Java, the *Duroc* had its bottom ripped out by a coral reef not far from an atoll that the master, Captain de la Vayssière de Lavergne, identified on his charts as the Mellish Reef, near Torres. The *Duroc* was lost, impaled on the coral and had to be abandoned. With the help of a small gig the crew transferred to the Mellish Reef itself, a basic kind of atoll with no vegetation but covered with seabirds' nests.

Before continuing this dramatic account, it is worth stressing the important role played by the captain's wife Madame de la Vayssière and her daughter Rosita:

Full of affection and devotion for their captain, whom they looked on as a father [the crew] did everything in their power to prove to him that their feelings for him went well beyond mere respect. They knew how to find the way to his heart – by doing their utmost to be kind to his wife and Rosita.

So, while the sailors warded off the sharks with gaffs, a kind of shuttle service was set up between the *Duroc* and the Mellish Reef to bring ashore, or rather on to the blinding whiteness of the coral sand, as many provisions, casks of water and objects of every kind which were to prove like manna for the thirty-one people lost in the middle of the Coral Sea.

In the very early days Captain de la Vayssière decided to build a large open boat capable of carrying them all to more hospitable shores. While tents were rigged as shelter from the heat of the sun, a real shipyard was set up in temperatures of 40°C (104°F) in the shade. Even the forge was unloaded from the *Duroc*. After a few days it became clear that this construction project was going to take a long time. The water and provisions saved from the wreck would not be sufficient and were therefore very carefully rationed. The water was even mixed with seawater to make it go further.

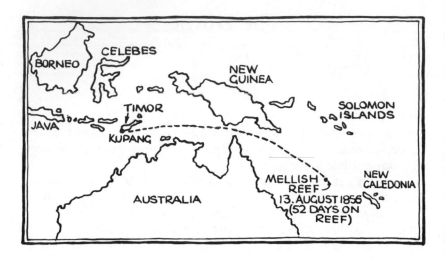

The newspaper *Le Moniteur* of 23 June 1857, which reports the life of the survivors in detail, tells how the sailor Givaudan, working at the forge, managed to make 6000 copper nails, some screws and bolts and even an anchor. Francis Robert, sailor second class, was a Hercules of a man. He had the massive appetite of those endowed with his size and strength. Because of the rationing he made up some recipes: 'When it became clear that the sharks made fishing impossible and that the seabirds, of the kind known as boobies, made everyone who ate them ill', he got someone to fry in oil from the boiler the only vegetables that grew on the island – mosses. These he seasoned with wood chippings.

It took fifty-two days to build the great boat which was christened the *Délivrance*. Without waiting a day longer or taking a moment's rest, the thirty-one survivors embarked, taking with them the few provisions and the small amount of water that remained.

The poet Méry, who became the historian of this shipwreck, described the first days of their voyage:

The mind which helps us to see the most distant events, boggles when we follow this nutshell lost in the midst of infinite waves, voyaging under the sun and the stars with its thirty-one wretched survivors, all exhausted by hunger, thirst and insomnia and expecting each day to be their last.

Storms gave way to flat calm. The provisions were exhausted or rotten. The purification plant they had managed to salvage could provide only rather brackish water which simply aggravated the thirst of those who put it to their parched membranes. Some tropical showers gave them a few days' more water. They passed through the Torres Strait. The *Délivrance* approached Timor, giving new hope to its dying crew. It was at this point that the boat sprang a leak; but this ultimate threat was received with something like indifference. Only the Herculean Francis Robert reacted. Day after day he wore out his strength by continuously manning the pump. Thanks to him, after a voyage of almost 2200 miles, the *Délivrance* reached the region of Kupang.

Whether it is due to the extremes the crew went through or to an omission in contemporary accounts, it is impossible to discover how many days their suffering lasted.

14

Second Engineer Tice

(1857)

The odyssey of the survivors of the *Duroc* was still alive in people's memories when it was supplanted by another drama of the sea. After sailing from Havana on 8 September 1857, the American liner *Central America* was caught in a cyclone on the 12th.

The ship soon sprang a leak in the engine-room, which was quickly flooded. Everyone, including the passengers, took their turn at the pumps. At noon on 12 September a small brig from Boston, the *Marine*, took on board a number of people which put her well beyond her safety limit. It was with pistols in their hands that the liner's officers supervised the transfer of women and children in heavy seas. Approximately 500 men, members of the crew and passengers, had to remain on board the *Central America* and resign themselves to their fate with nothing but life jackets to help them. At about 7.00 p.m. the *Central America* sank. Of those who swam around hour after hour looking for debris to hang on to, 442 were to be lost. A Norwegian ship came on the scene and rescued forty-nine. The others were so scattered over the surface of the waves as to be invisible to the rescuers. Unseen by the ship, although not far from it, Tice, the liner's Second Engineer, was clinging to a plank he had managed to grasp just as the *Central America* went down.

For seventy-two hours he watched people dying around him; every hour was punctuated by the last prayers of men overwhelmed by despair and deprived of their strength. Finally, he was alone in a sea calm enough for him to see an empty lifeboat. He was unable to say how he forced himself to let go of his plank to swim towards the boat or how he succeeded in reaching it and dragging himself on board before losing consciousness.

Two long days passed. Clearly, he could not have eaten or drunk since the shipwreck, but his loss of consciousness had restored his strength. This did not help him much, for he found no means of propulsion on board and remained at the mercy of the currents. On 17

September he spotted two other survivors, Alexander Grant, a member of the crew and Mr Dawson, a passenger. They had spent five days clinging to a plank. He managed to pick them up. Three more days passed by before the three survivors, half dead with thirst and exhaustion, were rescued by a brig which spotted their drifting boat.

15

Armstrong

(1867)

On 16 July 1867 the *John T. Ford*, a ketch-rigged fully decked boat with a length of 22 ft 6 in, set sail from Halifax. She had been specially built at Baltimore to cross the Atlantic and subsequently be shown at the Great Exhibition in Paris. She carried a crew of four – the captain Gould, his mate Shering, Armstrong and a youngster by the name of Murphy. It was a little late in the season to tackle the North Atlantic, which was apt to be difficult in August, but the *John T. Ford* made good progress up to 5 August when she suffered her first severe damage.

On that day the boat took a pasting in a storm and was knocked down by a freak wave. Luckily, her stability was good and she righted herself straight away. The four men were soaked and shivering. They decided to strip the boards holding the ballast in place to make a fire, so that they could warm themselves and have some hot food. This action was to cost three men their lives. On 19 August, at 10.30 p.m. on a dark night, the *John T. Ford* was nearing southern Ireland when she was swamped again by a giant wave. This time there was no cabin sole to hold the ballast in place; it shifted and some of it fell into the water through the only hatchway in the deck. The *John T. Ford* turned turtle and stayed keel-up.

What happened then can best be told in the words of Humphrey Barton, who tells this story in his spendid book *Atlantic Adventurers*:

They managed to hold on to the upturned boat all through that awful night, and the next morning, but occasionally they got washed off and had to struggle back again. Gradually they became more and more exhausted and the mate, the lad Murphy and Captain Gould, one after another were drowned.

Armstrong refused to be beaten, however. He hung on to that boat for 87 hours – four nights and three days!

He had upended an oar to which he had fastened some canvas and at 4 a.m. on 23rd August this was sighted by the ship *Aerolite* of Liverpool and he was rescued. The poor chap was very exhausted and almost unconscious.

16
Bernard Gilboy
(1882)

Bernard Gilboy is the first sailor to have made a non-stop single-handed crossing of the Pacific from east to west. He stayed with his boat throughout, but its size and the damage which it suffered and which transformed it into something more like a raft combine with Gilboy's sufferings from thirst and hunger to make this a real survival story – as the reader can judge for himself.

For this 7000-mile crossing Gilboy had a schooner-rigged boat, the *Pacific*, a little under 20 ft long with a beam of 6 ft 6 in, fully decked and divided in two by a vertical watertight bulkhead to form what Gilboy called his two 'rooms', each of which had a protected companionway. Four months' provisions were put on board in the far from ideal packages of those times. There were also 126 gallons of water in fourteen kegs.

The *Pacific* sailed from San Francisco at 1.00 p.m. on 18 August 1882. There is not a great deal to say about the first months of the voyage, except that Gilboy very soon realized that he had been extremely optimistic in his assessment of the time it would take and that he would have to ration his food and water. This was the point at which he realized too that he had failed to bring with him any fishing tackle other than a harpoon. With this, however, he managed to spear some fine fish from among the bonitos which were escorting the *Pacific*. He also caught some turtles by their fins, so his diet improved, and more important still, his rations went further. It is worth noting, however, that he did not keep the blood of these turtles but threw it back into the sea. One day it attracted an enormous hammerhead shark which was not to be put off even by revolver shots. In addition, he lost some fine sides of meat and large fillets of bonito which, he relates, would not stand the tropical heat. He did, in fact, do his best to preserve them with salt but he was short of this and, he tells us, had very great difficulty in collecting it by evaporating seawater. In spite of everything, his living conditions were still far from critical, and he felt that all

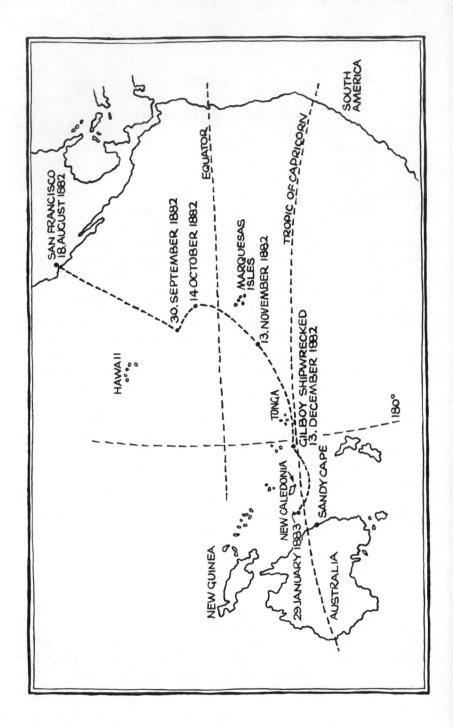

SAN FRANCISCO
18. AUGUST 1882

EQUATOR

SOUTH
AMERICA

30. SEPTEMBER 1882

14 OCTOBER 1882

MARQUESAS
ISLES

13. NOVEMBER 1882

TROPIC OF CAPRICORN

HAWAII

TONGA

GILBOY SHIPWRECKED
13. DECEMBER 1882

180°

NEW CALEDONIA

SANDY CAPE

NEW GUINEA

29 JANUARY 1883

AUSTRALIA

this waste would not matter too much – an attitude he was to have occasion to regret.

On 13 December, almost four months after leaving San Francisco, he had just crossed the 180° meridian and had 1430 miles to go to Australia. That day drama struck. A freak wave swept him overboard. When he surfaced, Gilboy found his *Pacific* down to leeward with her keel in the air. He managed to return to his boat, but the swim exhausted him. Hanging on with one hand, he undressed with the other, made a parcel of his clothes, tied this to the warp of the sea-anchor and then tried to right his boat; but the seas were no longer high enough to help him get her swinging. Mérien, in his book on single-handed sailors, tells of the manoeuvres performed by Gilboy in mid Pacific: 'He took the sea-anchor warp, led it from the weather side amidships and passed it over the keel. Then he took position by the lee side and heaved the moment a rather larger wave came.' This was a failure. He took up a better position and waited for a larger wave. In this way he managed to swing the keel over to 45°. Straight away he climbed on it, hauling himself up on the rope. This worked, and the masts were on the surface. With unbelievable strength, and without anything really firm to support himself on, Gilboy cut the shrouds, first on the lee side and then on the weather side, and then managed to unstep the mainmast from its tabernacle. He followed the same drill for the mizzen mast, and at last the *Pacific* righted herself. Next, Gilboy had to recover the masts and spars. He bundled them up and attached them to the boat, where they would serve as a sea-anchor. Without resting after these superhuman efforts, Gilboy went to work again to bail out his boat with a box, struggling hour after hour to beat the sea which used all its cunning to decant waves into the one hatch still open.

The dawn of 14 December 1882 rose on a boat with dry bilges but so damaged as to be little more than a wreck. During the night the mainmast and mainsail had disappeared, along with Gilboy's clothes which had his watch in them. The rudder was gone. Most of the victuals and the kegs of water were at the bottom of the sea. So, 1430 miles from Australia, Gilboy embarked on life as a survivor. He made a jury-rudder with an oar lashed to an outrigger. Luckily, he had re-covered the mizzen mast. This became the mainmast, carrying a jury rigged sail. Only when all this was done did Gilboy take a short rest.

The following day, 15 December, a swordfish stuck its sword through the side, struggled to free itself and started a leak. Hardly had Gilboy recovered from the efforts of righting his boat when the unfortunate man had to exhaust himself again on the pump until he could see the leak. Water was pouring in through a clean hole, but he managed to plug it.

Day followed day. The *Pacific* dragged painfully along. Gilboy imposed on himself a starvation diet and grew weaker and weaker. On 27 December he was awoken by a heavy blow. His boat, which had become his liferaft, was aground on a coral reef; but it was moving so slowly that there was no damage. The following night another judder roused him. This time the *Pacific* stayed put – she had passed through a barrier reef and grounded in the lagoon of Matthew Island. Unfortunately, this was a desert island without water, but it abounded in bird life. Gilboy managed to catch some birds and have a feast, for he still had about half a pint of kerosene for his stove and was therefore able to cook them.

By 7 January 1883 Gilboy had only 2 pounds of beef and 7 gallons of water left. By 13 January the beef was no more than a memory, and the only items on his menu were the occasional bird and a few flying fish. On 15 January he lost the steering oar but managed to rig another jury-rudder with some planking. Hunger gnawed away at him and became real torture as he watched the large number of fish escorting the *Pacific*. He did indeed try to make two hooks by bending back the points of a pair of dividers, but he had bad luck or lacked perseverance and caught nothing.

On, 21 January there was not even a flying fish to be picked up off the deck. Gilboy was reduced to spending most of the day chewing, without swallowing it, the flesh of barnacles and the like scraped from the hull below the waterline.

The morning of 22 January brought him two flying fish – 23 January just one more, and two again on the 24th. 25 January was a good day – four flying fish and a bird which Gilboy, without a drop of kerosene left, cooked over a pile of matches. By contrast he spent the next 48 hours in a complete fast, broken only on the 28th when a good 5 inch flying fish landed on the deck and was eaten straightaway.

On the morning of 29 January Gilboy was desperate. The wreck he was living on produced no fish for him, but it was working its way mile by mile towards his objective, and at that moment hope was reborn. A schooner, the *Alfred Vitteng*, drew near him and picked him up. This was 420 miles from Sandy Cape on his 164th day out of San Francisco and his 47th day of life under survival conditions. His adventure cost him 45 pounds in weight.

17

Howard Blackburn

(1883)

There is no shortage of biographies of Howard Blackburn. They have told an unbelieving world just how far the will of man can drive him to survive. *Le Mutilé de l'Atlantique*, as Mérien calls Blackburn in his book, was a young sailor of twenty-five, a fisherman on board the schooner *Grace L. Fears* under Captain John A. Griffin. They were fishing for cod on the Grand Bank of Newfoundland.

On 25 January 1883, as usual every morning, the dories with their crews of two were lowered and dispersed to increase the catch. The sea was calm, and a wan sun took the edge off the cold. In one of these dories Howard Blackburn and his friend Tom Welch were in luck: the fishing was good and the cod were piling up on the bottom of the boat.

In the afternoon the drama began in the form of a north-west wind which put them to leeward of the schooner, about three miles away from the safety she offered them. The wind freshened and brought on a blizzard. The two men were worried and immediately took to the oars, rowing hard towards the *Grace L. Fears*. But they soon felt that their efforts were in vain and that they were wearing themselves out to no good purpose. They decided to drop a grapnel anchor. Night falls early in these latitudes, but with it visibility improved and the schooner's lights were the only stars for them to steer by. They took to the oars again, but still their desperate efforts achieved nothing against the head wind. They dropped the anchor again but it dragged. The current swept them away faster and faster, while their boat grew heavy with ice in a sea that was threatening to swamp them. All night they bailed, broke the ice and threw their fine fish back into the sea, keeping just one 10 pound cod.

At dawn on 26 January the seas were still heavy, and wherever they looked no schooner was to be seen. To the west, a hundred miles or so off, lay Newfoundland. Like many fishermen before them who had suffered the same fate, they decided to make for it. The sea, however, had other ideas; it headed them. While Welch at the oars kept the dory on an even keel, Blackburn took off his gloves and rigged a sea-anchor. When this was put over, life was rather easier and Welch went to work with a bailer. In a single movement he added a new dimension to the drama; Blackburn's gloves, which were floating in the bottom of the boat, were swept into the sea. When Blackburn realized he was losing the feeling in his hands, he mustered up superhuman courage and made an entry in the log 'If my hands freeze I shall be unable to hold an oar and Welch will have to row for land on his own. Since my hands are lost, they may at least still be of some use to us.' Then he grasped the oars, tightening his fingers round their frozen handles, and waited for the cold to do its grim work. In twenty minutes the cold had frozen his hands into a shape which enabled him to pass them over the ends of the oars. With these two hook-like stumps, he clutched the bailer and resumed his task of bailing and breaking ice.

During the night that followed Welch became delirious, and by the morning of 27 January he was dead of cold and exhaustion. Blackburn, who had not drunk, eaten or slept for three days, was now alone in the company of a stiffened corpse. He bailed all that day and the following night, snatching only a few moments of rest without allowing himself to drop off and freeze to death. On the 28th the weather improved. Blackburn took in the sea-anchor, hooked his hands on to the oars again and rowed for land. The skin came off his hands, but they were anaesthetized by frost-bite and he felt no pain. His right foot, however, bare in his boot, was succumbing to frost-bite. The last rays of the sun on 28 January showed him a rocky islet covered with snow. He saw it again just as far off on the morning of the 29th, for he had been forced by a sharply freshening wind to spend the night on the sea-anchor.

A few hours later, towards noon on 29 January, he saw land. He redoubled his efforts, pulled with his frozen hands, and by mid-afternoon reached the mouth of a river and started to row up it. In the evening he landed by a deserted cabin where he spent the night. He lay down to rest, if one can call it rest – for he had to struggle minute by minute against sleep, knowing that if he fell asleep under these conditions he would not wake again. On 30 January he got back into his dory and continued to row up-river. He had not drunk or eaten for six days; the cod he had kept was a block of ice that he could not even bite into. Rather than rest and allow himself to be overcome by sleep, he went on pulling away at the oars for the whole of that night, helped by a full moon which lit up the river. On the morning of 31 January his ordeal was over. He reached the small fishing village of Little River. There he was warmed and given food and water. There was no doctor or medicine, but what a doctor would otherwise have done, nature did for him. Over two months he watched all his fingers and the top joints of his thumbs drop off, as well as all his toes and the front part of his right foot. After spending three months at Little River, he was repatriated via Burges[1] to Gloucester, Massachusetts, his home town. He reached home on 4 June 1883.

---

1. I cannot locate this. It may be a misprint for Bruges, but such a journey seems rather improbable. [Trans.]

18
The Atlantic crossing of Franz Romer
(1928)

In 1928, twenty-four years before Alain Bombard, Franz Romer, an ocean-going captain of the Hamburg America Line, became sufficiently interested in the problem of survival at sea to want to prove beyond all doubt the possibility of tackling the ocean in a collapsible craft. His choice fell upon a German designed and built Klepper collapsible canoe, a kind of kayak based on the Eskimo craft.

This kayak, named *Deutscher Sport*, was made of rubberized cloth stretched on a frame, fully decked so that only the crew's body was in the open air. Romer put a yawl rig with a sail area of about 50 sq ft on this and rigged the controls so that he could steer and sail the boat entirely with his feet. For safety he added some air-filled floats and a system of collapsible compressed CO_2 tanks with automatic inflation. Laden with 130 gallons of water, provisions and as much equipment as possible, the *Deutscher Sport* was at its buoyancy limit. Its draft was a long way from the classical figure of 10 in for a length of 21 ft 6 in and a beam of 3 ft.

One may indeed feel that Romer had set about organizing his survival well, but one needs only to think for a moment of this man forced to remain permanently seated with half his body enclosed in his kayak tackling the Atlantic crossing. One has to admit that the lot of many shipwrecked people was better than his; and it is for this reason that his voyage is included.

It was from Cape St Vincent in Portugal that he took to the water. To familiarize himself with his craft his intention was to cover the 580 miles from there to the Canaries before tackling what he considered to be the only proof of his theories – the Atlantic crossing. For anyone but him the eleven days of this first passage would have been remarkable enough, both for the short duration of the voyage and for the foretaste of what was to come: ceaseless vigilance over a sea whose every wave seemed to do its best to capsize him; the lack of sleep which made him depressed; a posture made unbearable by the fearful pain of the stiffness it caused; and a steering defect which allowed a wave to tear the cloth and enter the kayak. He had already demonstrated what he set out to prove. But for him, as for Bombard later, there was nothing for it; nothing counted except the Atlantic crossing.

So it was that on 2 June 1928, strengthened by his experience and well rested, he left Las Palmas. His ordeal was to last three months, exactly eighty-eight days, until he reached St Thomas Island in the Virgin Isles on 31 August. He was sent at once to hospital, incapable of standing.

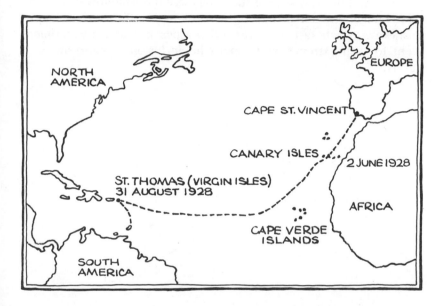

For Mérien, in his book on single-handed sailors, Romer's voyage is 'the most superhuman trial a man has ever undertaken voluntarily at sea'. For three months Romer was really pinioned in his seated position, with the lower half of his body virtually immobile. Sweltering as if in a Turkish bath, he had to restrain himself from pedalling away at the rudder bar. The upper half of his body was exposed to the spray and, even worse, roasted in the full summer sun of the tropics.

For three months he had to suffer the exasperating flapping of torn clothes which exposed his body, already gnawed at by the sun. For three months he lived in fear of sharks and cetaceans which, attracted by the kayak's long slim hull, came and rubbed themselves against it, threatening at any moment to capsize it or to pierce the cloth. All he could do about this was bang on an empty jam tin or, by night, frighten them off with his torch; and in this case he ran the risk of getting a flying fish full in the chest or face.

For three months he had to twist and turn to bail out his kayak without upsetting its delicate balance, and for three months, to avoid worse evils, he had to force himself to sleep literally with one eye open. He relates how he even gradually became conditioned to just dropping off for the few seconds separating the dangerous waves which so often threatened him.

In the end the only kind of suffering these three months spared him were hunger and thirst. Indeed, these are basic afflictions which most castaways have to face; but every other aspect of Romer's experiment went to such extremes as to merit his inclusion as an example of survival.

19
Roy Widdicombe and Robert Tapscott
(1940)

During the night of 21 August 1940 a roving submarine torpedoed the British merchant ship *Anglo-Saxon* 500 miles off the Azores. To avoid leaving evidence of the attack the submarine opened fire on the ship, which went down very rapidly, and on the lifeboats and liferafts full of survivors. Despite this, seven men, taking advantage of the darkness, climbed into an 18 ft lifeboat and lowered it on the side away from the submarine. Quietly, they slipped away from the scene of the massacre.

Dawn on 22 August broke on a deserted sea and on the opening scenes of a horror story to match that of the previous night. First Officer Denny, the *Anglo-Saxon*'s mate, was one of the lifeboat's occupants; he quietly took command and organized his men's first day as castaways. First, they had to deal with the casualties. The left foot of Pilcher, a radio operator, had been torn open by a shell-burst; they washed the wound in seawater and made Pilcher as comfortable as they could in the bow. In the same way the wounded right thigh of Richard Penny, a gunner, and the half-severed ankle of Leslie Morgan, an under-cook, were cleared of all dirt and bathed in large quantities of seawater. These two were placed alongside Pilcher in the bow. The wounds of the other four survivors were painful but not serious. Apart from First Officer Denny, they were Third Engineer Leslie Hawkes and two deckhands, Roy Widdicombe and Robert Tapscott. Gritting their teeth, they set about bailing and rigging a sail. They had agreed to make for the Antilles, about 3000 miles away.

Then they checked their stores. They had three 10-lb tins of mutton, eleven tins of condensed milk, around 33 lb of biscuits and 18 litres of fresh water. In addition there were a razor, an axe, 1 lb of tobacco, a pipe and Pilcher's radio log sheets, which were used mainly as cigarette papers. It was pretty short commons for seven men who knew they faced several weeks at sea. So on this first day they decided not to eat or drink anything. On 23 August they rationed themselves to half a ladle of water each morning and evening, with a little condensed milk

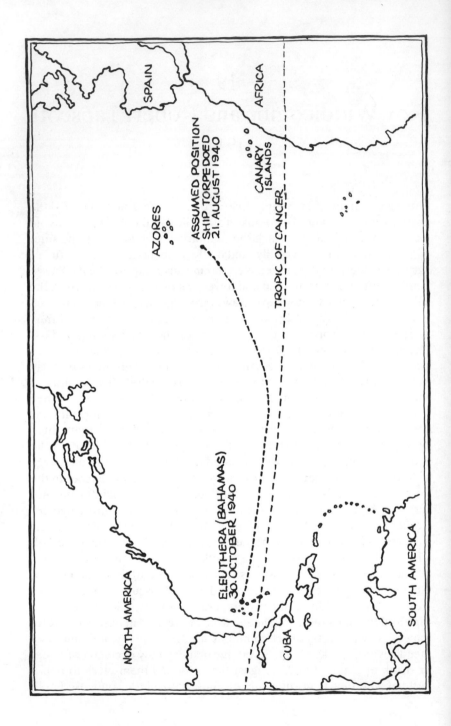

and half a biscuit per day. On this diet dehydration and under-nourishment steadily set in.

A few days later the situation grew much worse when the wind dropped, leaving the lifeboat steady on a sea like a millpond under the almost intolerable heat of the sun. The two most seriously wounded men, Pilcher and Morgan, went through hell. Through the burning stillness of the air there gradually spread a fetid smell, the odour of the gangrene which was invading their wounds. The four fit men sprinkled the casualties with seawater to cool them, while they themselves bathed. This refreshed them greatly and made them much more comfortable, but the survivors related how they took great care to keep their heads well above water so as not to yield to the temptation of drinking this liquid which seemed so refreshing. The condition of the casualties grew worse, that of Pilcher becoming critical:

It looked as if the only chance of saving him was to amputate the foot. The only instrument that could conceivably be used for this purpose was a rusty axe with a blunt edge. There was no antiseptic or anaesthetic. Pilcher was conscious again but was very weak. He bravely consented to the operation; but at the last minute it was the mate who lost his nerve despite his great self-control. 'Cheer up old man,' he said to Pilcher, 'we're sure to be picked up tomorrow and then we'll have a qualified doctor to do everything you need.' With a ghost of a smile Pilcher closed his eyes, asking that his water ration should be given to someone with greater need of it than him. At 8.00 o'clock the following morning he died in silence, discreetly as it were. The rest stared incredulously at him. So soon, just like that! Surely it couldn't be! And they sat there, nonplussed and overwhelmed by their impotence, crushed by the terrible reality of death. The mate gave some brief orders in a low voice. There was only one thing to do. Tapscott and the engineer heaved the body overboard and let it slip quietly into the sea. There was no shroud to wrap it in or weight to ballast it, so that it just drifted away on the waves. The men followed the corpse with their eyes until it was finally lost to sight.

On 4 September, the fourteenth day after their ship went down, the wind had got up and was pushing them along nicely. But that day the last ration of water was dished out. First Officer Denny, who up until then had been a tower of strength to his men, organizing games and competitions to keep their spirits up, was at the end of his tether. 'His skin, even where it was sunburnt, looked lifeless and ashen.' He was so weak, he collapsed at the tiller. Penny, the gunner, took over, despite his wounded thigh. But a few moments later a wave swept him overboard. Then there were five. On the sixteenth day Denny roused himself from his stupor when a big wave nearly capsized the boat and carried away the rudder. His swollen discoloured lips moved: 'I'm going overboard', he said. 'Who's coming with me?' 'Me', answered the engineer.

First Officer Denny turned to face his men. All of them, one after the other, refused with a shake of the head, but they were seized with terror at the thought of what they were about to witness. They stared fixedly at the two men who had condemned themselves to death – 'Just a second', said the engineer almost cheerfully, 'I'm going to have a drink and a bite to eat'. He filled a food tin with seawater and drank greedily; then he dipped a biscuit in the salt water and ate it. The mate took off his signet ring and handed it to Widdicombe: 'Give it to my mother if you come through', he said, 'and now head west'.

With a struggle the mate and the engineer straddled the gunwale and let themselves fall into the sea.

The three remaining survivors were left with no means of subsistence. They had no water and, without water, the biscuits were of little use. Most of the time Morgan's mind was wandering. Tapscott and Widdicombe were too weak to take the helm for more than an hour; but, none the less, they hung on strongly to life and conserved the little strength they had left.

One fine morning Morgan got up from where he had been lying in the bow and remarked in a calm, detached voice: 'I think I'll just pop down the road for a drink.' He then rapidly walked aft and threw himself overboard. His body came up again, swept away on the waves – but not a movement, not a cry. Tapscott and Widdicombe regarded each other in silence.

The nineteen-year-old Robert George Tapscott and Wilbert Roy Widdicombe, two years older, were on their own. They can recall nothing of the two or three days that followed. Their bodies continued the struggle against dehydration, but in this terminal stage it numbed their consciousness. It was during this period that Tapscott suddenly decided the game was not worth the candle. He stood up: 'I'm going over, are you coming?' With a slight movement of his head Widdicombe signified agreement. But once he had jumped he hung on to the lifeline. Then Tapscott jumped; he floated without effort. The coldness of the water gripped him, producing a reaction that restored his failing courage. Opening his eyes, he saw that he was only a short distance from the boat. Widdicombe was still hanging on to the lifeline. 'Come on then, let go the line,' called Tapscott again. But Widdicombe did not seem to hear and stayed where he was. Then Tapscott broke into a laborious crawl, astonished he could still swim.

When he got up to the boat, he asked again: 'Why won't you let go?' Widdicombe shook his head furiously. Tapscott was livid; he felt his companion was not playing the game. He too grabbed the lifeline. With them both hanging on to it the argument broke out all over again. Tapscott was determined to make an end of it but he did not want to go without Widdicombe. But immersion had eased Widdicombe's pain and made him feel much better. 'If you're strong enough to swim,' he remarked to his friend, 'you've enough strength to hang on a bit longer.'

Tapscott admitted that Widdicombe was right and needed no more convincing. With some difficulty they climbed back on board and slid under the boat's canopy. They felt as if they had taken out a new lease of life.

Then Tapscott had the idea of drinking the alcohol from the compass:

They poured the precious liquid into two empty tins; there was almost enough for a large glass each. They sat on the thwarts and drank as if they were having a drink at a nightclub. The alcohol tore at their parched throats and burnt their guts – but it was wet. After several swigs they forgot about their danger and their suffering. They clowned about and laughed and rolled around grunting. They soon rolled into the bottom of the boat and passed out.

Quite a few hours later a violent clap of thunder drove away the heavy sleep which, in the state they were in, the alcohol had induced in them. The long-awaited miracle had happened: it rained. It was on the twenty-second day of their voyage, 12 September, when they had not drunk a drop of water for eight days. The canopy was stretched between the thwarts and rinsed down. The salt encrusted on it was dissolved, and soon they were able to drink their fill, with seven gallons or so over to pour into their barrel. 'Their thirst quenched, they suddenly realized, for the first time in several days, that they were really hungry. They dipped a ship's biscuit in the water and ate it. Although still very weak, they came back to life.'

Six days later, on the morning of 18 September, their reserves of water were exhausted. 'They were less worried about this than before; they had learned to play a waiting game. More rain fell early on the 20th. They arranged the canopy to collect the water, drank a lot of it, filled their cask and ate six moistened biscuits each.' On 24 September, the thirty-fourth day after the shipwreck, things got tricky again when they drank the last drop of water, and the biscuit box had nothing more in it but crumbs. Periods of hope and despair followed one another, dependent on the rain, which fortunately was becoming more and more frequent. Just as the wind carried them to an area where the gentle rain prolonged their life, so too the sea became kindlier. Flying fish started to crash into their sail; these were eaten raw, bones and all. The men were delighted to find a hotchpotch of small crabs, shrimps and tiny shellfish. They collected plenty, but it took hours of work to get a meal out of them.

A forty-ninth notch cut in the gunwale of the lifeboat with their shipmate Pilcher's razor told them that the sun rising above the horizon was heralding 9 October. It was a date they would never forget. That day a ship passed only a mile or so away without seeing them in spite of their sail and all the signals they made with the oars. 'Tapscott and Widdicombe collapsed on the thwarts, shattered. Their hearts were beating fit to burst. They were panting for breath, choking with convulsive sobs.'

It was around the fifty-third day that a storm brought them plenty of fresh water and a new lesson in their battle for survival. For two days and two nights, weak as they were, they spent their time desperately bailing. As each wave came, the two of them threw themselves on the oar which had served as a rudder since Denny's death to stop the boat being swung beam on. 'After the storm, their harvest from the sea was poor. The survivors were seized with a desperate hunger. They pulled off the skin which was peeling from their body and ate it. They tore off the rubberized cover of the radio operator's wallet and chewed that. Then they started to get light-headed and found a vent for their shattered nerves in argument.'

The last two weeks of their ordeal produced nothing much in the way of memories, apart from the flying fish they found one morning and ate just as they sighted land. They learned later that the day was 30 October 1940, sixty-six days after the *Anglo-Saxon* had blown up. They touched down on a beach in Eleuthera, one of the Bahama Islands east of the southern tip of Florida. They posed the doctors who had to revive them quite a problem both physically and psychologically, but they came through and told their story, which Guy Pearce Jones has passed on to us. Widdicombe, however, was never to read it. On 18 February 1941 the ship taking him home was sunk. This time there were no survivors.

20
Harold Dixon, Gene Aldrich and Anthony Pastula
(1942)

Like the preceding account, this tale of endurance comes from the annals of the Second World War. It is set in the Pacific. Harold Dixon was the forty-one-year-old pilot of a US Navy torpedo bomber. His crew members were the operator Gene Aldrich, twenty-two, and gunner Anthony Pastula, twenty-four.

In January 1942 Dixon's aircraft was on a reconnaissance sortie. Suddenly he was caught in an electric storm which made him lose contact with his carrier. He soon ran out of fuel and was forced to ditch. The aircraft sank almost straight away, only leaving the three airmen time to inflate the liferaft (8 ft by 4 ft) and snatch their life-jackets, a pistol, a pocket knife and a pair of pliers.

The contribution of these three men to the heavy price the US Navy paid in the war against Japan started under the worst possible conditions. They had no food or water on their raft. Despite this their main preoccupation to begin with was not to fall into Japanese hands:

I spent that first day studying the behaviour of the raft. With its flat bottom it ran well before the wind. To check its drift in a south-westerly wind,[1] I jury-rigged a sea-anchor with my lifejacket by tying this to the end of a half-inch rope and securing this rather crudely right round the raft. This jury-rigged anchor produced enough drag to reduce our drift by at least one knot in a Force 4-5 wind. I knew our position, and from our speed and observation of the stars I had a rough idea where we were heading. I made a sketch-map on one of the lifejackets. Luckily, like all pilots, I had a small celluloid protractor which allowed me to plot our route.

Even before thirst and hunger made themselves felt, the men had to face one of the other classic problems of survival at sea – extreme discomfort preventing any real rest. Their raft was just not big enough for them all to lie down at once. So they had to set watches, each one

---

1. The French says 'to stop it going off course', but this must be a misprint. Their intention was clearly to minimize drift north-eastwards into Japanese waters. [Trans.]

waiting for the moment when he could stretch his cramped limbs. But even then, he suffered from the repeated impacts of the waves which hammered on the bottom of the raft and prevented sleep.

About the fifth day the lack of fresh water started to pose real problems. The wind had driven us at a good pace in a general southerly direction but had not brought us any rain. We sat grilling under the sun, watching the rain-squalls as they approached only to vanish without reaching us. Since some sharks were gambolling around the raft, we didn't dare risk a bathe to refresh ourselves. We had to be content with dipping our clothes in the sea from time to time and putting them on as they were.

Adversity brought back to their minds their childhood prayers. These worked, for the end of their fifth day without food or water brought the first rain, a real tropical deluge lasting only a few minutes. It was not enough to quench their thirst, particularly as they had nothing to collect the water in, but it did serve to revive them enough to carry on.

The seventh day was a red-letter day. In the morning Aldrich, leaning over the edge of the raft with his pocket knife, speared right through a large fish and heaved it on to the raft. It was divided up at once and eaten raw. In the afternoon a shower gave them a drink, and a few hours later they caught an albatross:

The bird came and sat on the stern of the raft. Gene very carefully bent down, picked up the pistol and fired right by my ear. We dismembered the victim and, after eating the liver and the heart, wrapped its skin along with the rest of the fish in some rags. Killing an albatross is supposed to bring bad luck, and during the night we had good reason to recall this old superstition. Towards midnight I noticed a strange silvery-blue glow on the bow. It was coming from the bundle with our provisions in it. When I unwrapped this I was absolutely astonished to see the craft and the water round it lit up by light from the bird's carcass. Its tail in particular was glowing like an electric light bulb. We put this phenomenon down to the action of the phosphorus in the albatross's food. But we had no wish whatever to luxuriate in this ghostly glow and threw the bird and the fish overboard.

In the days that followed the wind fell. Dixon made some paddles with the thick rubber soles of his flying boots. Hour after hour he and his companions took it in turns to paddle south-westwards where friendly islands were awaiting them. The days went by. Some brought rain and sudden storms dangerous for so frail a craft; others thirst and torrid heat on a sea like a millpond. In his account Dixon was no longer able to quote dates, just notable events which served as reference points. Thus:

I can still see Aldrich catching a baby shark about a yard long. He impaled it on his knife at the level of the gills and heaved it on board. Its skin was so hard that Tony had to hold its tail and Gene its head so that I could slit its belly. We started by eating the liver. Then we investigated the stomach where we found two pilchards about six inches long. One of these was awarded to Aldrich who had caught the shark, while Tony and I shared the second. I've never tasted anything more delicious. We ate the rest of the shark's entrails. Then, holding up its head and tail so that its body was bent in an arc, we collected its blood in the pocket formed in the middle. This liquid had a strong taste, but that didn't stop us drinking it. Finally we ate our fill of the flesh. Incidentally this barbaric feast acted on our bodies like a laxative. This was the only time our bowels functioned in the course of thirty-four days at sea. That same night, Aldrich dipped his hand in the water to check the direction of the current. Unfortunately a shark was watching and snapped at his fingers. Gene whipped his hand back so violently that the shark kind of skidded over the raft and fell back into the sea on the other side. Its vicious teeth had caught Aldrich's first finger, piercing the nail in two places, and the other fingers were cut to the bone. Later the wound under the nail became infected and I had to excise it to let the pus flow out.

As Aldrich's companions were the first to stress, they would never have survived without him. With infinite patience, equipped with just his knife and taking great care not to damage the rubber of the compartments, he kept constant watch for a chance to impale and catch the fish sheltering beneath the raft. Dixon for his part became something of a specialist in catching birds. After the albatross, his bag consisted mainly of terns: 'Their flesh struck us as tender and savoury.' From time to time coconuts drifting on the current gave a major boost to their provisions and aroused their hopes that the islands at which they were aiming rather haphazardly were not too far off. One day they passed through an area infested with tiger sharks[1] 'so aggressive that they threatened to overturn our raft at any moment. At one time we had to beat off one of the sharks by hammering it on the nose with our fists; we succeeded in killing another with a pistol shot before rust finally put our only firearm out of action.'

They were in a very weak state indeed when the thirty-third day faced them with a final ordeal in the shape of a hurricane:

Enormous breaking waves started to fling themselves at our craft. We had scarcely the strength or the will to bail out the water we were taking in. To give ourselves greater freedom of movement, we stripped off our clothes. The waves

---

1. The French states 'leopard sharks', but I think this must be a confusion with 'leopard seals', and the fishes' behaviour suggests they were tiger sharks. [Trans.]

rolled in higher and higher, roaring. Suddenly the raft capsized. Everything in it disappeared apart from just one boot sole. We found ourselves facing the seas, which became more and more furious, naked as the day we were born and with nothing to help us but our bare hands.

Then the sun came out again. Our bones stuck out through our skin which burnt and sweated in turn under the sun. We felt ready to give up the struggle. Nonetheless with a combined effort we managed to get back on course. We passed the night huddled against one another to keep warm, and the thought of death crept slowly and solemnly into our minds.

On the next day, 19 February 1942, they saw on the horizon the fringe of coconut palms that characterizes the low-lying Pacific islands. The whole day they churned away relentlessly with the one paddle they had left. But it was not until evening that a wave swept them over the reef, setting them down in the calm of a lagoon.

We could hardly keep our feet but we went ashore with a military step and in good order. If there were any Japanese around, we didn't want them to see us dragging our feet. But there weren't any Japanese. It was a friendly island. We spent the night in a hut and the next morning a native found us and informed the authorities.

21

Poon Lim

(1942)

On 23 November 1942 in position 0°30' North and 38°45' West the British cargo ship *Ben Lomond* was torpedoed. The abandon-ship drills had only just begun when the cargo exploded and the ship went straight down. This is just one of the many dramas of which wars are made, and soon no trace of it remained on the surface.

Nevertheless, there was one man still alive, clutching a piece of wood. Poon Lim, a Chinese sailor, had jumped at the moment the ship blew up, clutching his lifejacket in his hand. In the next two hours he had plenty of time to realize that he was all on his own in the middle of the ocean waiting for the sharks that would snap him up. He regained hope when he saw a raft, one of those rafts which cargo ships carry on their decks and which break away automatically in the event of shipwreck. He swam strongly towards it, climbed on board, stood up and then saw in the distance another identical raft with three men aboard. But this type of raft has no means of propulsion; it is completely at the mercy of wind and current. The two rafts could not meet up; in fact they drifted steadily further apart, and the other one disappeared eastwards. Now he knew for sure that he was alone as a castaway, Lim explored his raft. In the locker he found some provisions, a little fresh water, a small first-aid kit and some distress flares. These he was able to put to use very soon; on one of the next few nights he saw the half blacked-out lights of a ship and fired his flares, which worked perfectly. There must have been at least three men on watch in wartime, and it is impossible that they did not see the signals. But war is war with all its ruses, and the ship was justified in not altering course. In the days that followed he was to see several ships, but all his signals and all his acrobatics on the raft did not succeed in attracting attention.

He rationed himself very strictly from the beginning, for the provisions were slender enough. In the event water was no problem, for in the sea area where he was adrift frequent torrential rains provided him with large quantities of fresh water, which he collected by using his lifejacket as a funnel.

It was towards the fiftieth day of his slow, solitary course that, despite the frugality he had imposed on himself, he ate his last rations. So he started to work out how to fish. These rafts are surrounded by loops of rope to allow survivors for whom there is no room on the raft to hang on while remaining in the water. That would do for his line. After a long, hard struggle he managed to detach one loop. Separating its strands, stiffened as they were from salt and sun, he tied them end to end. As a hook he used a galvanized nail which he had removed from the raft with great difficulty and then bent with his teeth. For bait he had put aside a piece of his last biscuit, making it into a paste with saliva and letting it dry in the sun. This lash-up fishing tackle was good enough for him to catch his first fish. Restraining his hunger, he left it alone and kept it as bait for larger ones. This paid off, and from that point on he lived on raw fish. Later, the monotony of his menu was relieved by some seabirds which came and sat on his raft and sometimes even on his motionless shoulders.

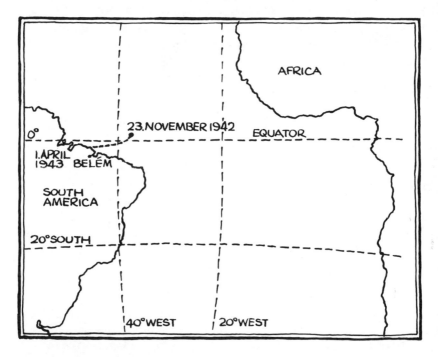

The weeks went by. The rudimentary knowledge of navigation he possessed made him realize that his almost imperceptible movement was taking him day by day nearer to the coast of South America. By now his clothing was in shreds and no longer gave him protection against the combined action of sun, salt and wind. Exposure to the burning sun turned his skin into a mass of blisters which the nights were not long enough to heal. Despite all this Poon Lim, with all the wisdom of his race, did not lose hope. Even around the 100th day, when he ran short of water, he waited stoically for rain. The elements left him parched for five whole days, but eventually the rain fell and revived him.

Around the 120th day an aeroplane which flew over made clear to him by its manoeuvres that it had spotted him. As this herald of hope flew off, Poon Lim thought he was safe. Searches must have been made but ended in failure. For it was not until ten days later, on the 130th day, 1 April 1943, that some fishermen picked him up ten miles off the coast of Brazil. There was nothing left of him but a supine body, lying on his raft, incapable of sitting up or walking. Some days earlier he had lost even the strength to fish. To the doctors' astonishment it took only fifteen days in the hospital at Belém to restore Poon Lim's body, reduced almost to a skeleton, to its former healthy state. Poon Lim's 130 days adrift give him the record for survival at sea. It is a figure which gives cause for reflection when one knows just what cards he held in his hand at the start.

22
The 'voluntary castaway'
Alain Bombard
(1952)

It is impossible to summarize the history of the 'voluntary castaway', the name under which Alain Bombard will most probably pass into posterity.[1] Even if all those who told of their adventures had left complete and detailed stories, these are never anything more than accounts made with hindsight – always very instructive on the topic under discussion but in the last resort nothing more than reports of events. Alain Bombard's experiment is quite another matter. He is a doctor, a research worker who devoted several years to coming to grips with a precisely defined problem. He took all the data apart, established from them a certain number of hypotheses and, to round off his work, carried out a 'field' experimental programme which left no doubt that his conclusions were right, at least in principle.

This adds up to an intellectual and practical step forward too great to allow the story of his Atlantic crossing to be summarized. Every line of every page is packed with information, and we shall return to it frequently in the second half of this book. For the moment it is enough to try and give a concise but accurate account of his experiment.

It was during the morning of 25 May 1952, ten miles or so off Monaco, that life as a survivor began for Alain Bombard and his companion Jack Palmer. The first hours were just as difficult for them as for real victims of shipwreck. Distress and anxiety swamped them and they spoke in low voices; but soon determination took over, and this was their first and one of their most far-reaching victories.

In the inflatable, which is now synonymous with the name of Bombard the world over, no water or provisions were to be used. Such as there were were sealed and left untouched, which must have been at times very tantalizing for them. From the first day Bombard started to drink the quantity of seawater he had calculated, about 800 millilitres per day taken little and often. Palmer, by contrast, preferred to wait a

1. *The Bombard Story*, Alain Bombard (trans. Brian Connell), André Deutsch, 1953.

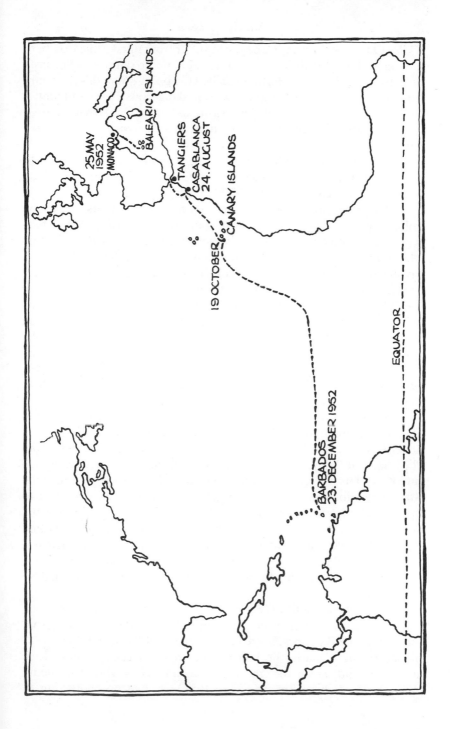

while. On the second day he began to suffer from thirst while Bombard had no problems at all. This encouraged Palmer to sample his first taste of seawater before dehydration reached the point where this consumption would have become futile and even dangerous. The cloth tent of their raft was not as yet fouled with salt, and in the nights that followed condensation left them about a pint of fresh water which they collected with a sponge.

On the ninth day they caught a fine grouper weighing about 10 pounds. This allowed them to try another method of obtaining fresh water by an incision into the fish's back where an unsalted liquid collected. They used their plankton net for several hours every day, collecting the equivalent of two soup-spoonfuls of a dish which was pleasant-tasting and rich in vitamins. Fishing is mediocre in the Mediterranean, and Bombard admitted that this sea is one of the least favourable for survival. This was one problem; storms, which the raft seemed to tackle with a kind of zest, were another. During these the men shut themselves in by covering the boat from end to end with its rubberized roof; the waves broke over them without worrying them too much. Yet another difficulty were the navigational dangers of the Mediterranean with its high density of shipping; at night they shone an electric torch on their sail so that they were seen. Despite all these problems and the difficult early stages of acclimatization inevitable in any trial on this scale, they reached the Balearic Isles.

As is well known, Alain Bombard left Tangiers on the next stage of the voyage single-handed. The teething troubles they had met with, severe as they had been, had encouraged Bombard in his plans; but they had put Palmer off. On his own now Bombard started by putting into Casablanca after having had great difficulty in passing through the Straits of Gibraltar where the strong tidal streams did their best to oppose his progress. He left Casablanca on 24 August to reach the Canaries in eleven days – an excellent time when one considers that most of his spare time was given over to learning celestial navigation, to exploring all the ways of keeping his raft on course without steering and, of course, to fishing for food and the 'fish juice' that satisfied his need of water.

It was really not until 19 October, the day Bombard left Las Palmas, that the great experiment began. Certainly, in the three stages from Monaco to the Balearics, from Tangiers to Casablanca and from Casablanca to the Canaries he had proved to every sailor that survival at sea would never be the same again. However, the media made little of these first trials, so Bombard had no choice but to sacrifice himself to a universal lack of understanding and stage a trial that would put his theories beyond doubt. He set off on 19 October under even more rigorous conditions, with even his box of fishing tackle sealed. One must bear in mind here that fishing was the only long-term means of obtaining food and water open to Bombard.

The first rain did not come until 11 November, twenty-four days after he had left Las Palmas. During these twenty-four days Bombard had drunk nothing but seawater to start with and then fish juice. He had had no choice but to find out how to fish without breaking into his box of tackle. Using an oar as an anvil, he bent the blade of a knife into a hook and lashed this to the end of the oar with an ordinary piece of string. With this improvised hook and a great deal of patience, he caught the first of a long series of dorados on 25 October.[2] For the first time in six days he was at last able to quench his thirst with fish juice and to eat. Moreover, he now had a reserve of bait and, above all, a splendid natural gaff in the shape of a little hooked bone located behind the gill cover of dorados (which shows that they must in fact have been *Coryphaena hippuris*). He was, in fact, following the example of prehistoric man in whose tombs specimens of this bone have been found along with everyday objects.

From this point on what had been the exception in the Mediterranean became the rule. There was an abundance of fish; they accompanied *l'Hérétique*, swimming closer and closer to it, and were almost easy to catch. As an extra snack, every morning brought Bombard between five and fifteen flying fish caught by the sail as they skimmed the surface. He used his shirt to squeeze the fish and extract the juice, and consequently he had no need to resort to his ration of seawater. In addition, to avoid slowing up his raft he collected plankton for only half an hour a day, the exact vitamin ration he considered necessary. With the first rain on 11 November he spent some time carefully rinsing the roof sheet which twenty-four days of spray had covered with a layer of salt. He was then able to collect about 3 gallons of beautiful clear water which he stored in the inflatable thwart he used as a pillow.

From this day forward squalls were frequent enough to leave him with a constant reserve of water. In fact they became so frequent that he had to sleep with the boat completely closed in and, every quarter of an hour, to empty out the heavy load of water which collected in the roof. He had no dehydration problem, but his sleep suffered seriously.

Reading all this one might almost think that he was on a pleasure

2. See footnote, page 10.

cruise. In reality, however well he had the experiment under control, Bombard had few days without problems – difficulties which cropped up over and over again, most of them originating not in the alimentary canal but in the survivor's mind. Briefly, once your stomach is full, it is imagining all the things that may go wrong that makes life difficult. This is a rule of very general application, even in everyday life ashore.

Bombard's main worry was his equipment. Anything that chafed on the rubberized cloth led to incredibly rapid wear; he was always having to stow the equipment so that it never made contact with the skin of *l'Hérétique*. Every morning Doctor Bombard sounded the inflatable's compartments, his ear glued to the rubber for the least sign of rubbing or the whistle of a leak. In addition, he had to deflate the craft slightly every morning so that the heat of the day did not burst it. Then in the evening came the reinflation session. He had only one sail, torn and sewn up over and over again. He felt sick at the very thought that the next tear might be beyond repair. Then there was the problem of humidity, which can clearly never have been far away. This reduced his skin to a kind of pathological madhouse which would have driven anyone except Bombard and men of his mettle crazy with the itching.

These were the medical problems, even more worrying for a doctor whose knowledge, as always, swamped him with pessimism when the problems were his own. In addition to these skin conditions, he had trouble with his eyes, ophthalmia and conjunctivitis caused by the reflection of the sun on the ocean surface. Then there were attacks of weakness that he did not seek to explain – understandable as they were in any other victim of shipwreck. And last but not least there was the violent attack of diarrhoea of 30 November followed by rectal bleeding and discharge. As well as all this there was the fear of the sharks which nudged his boat on every side with violent rubs that spelt a tear in the skin; and of a swordfish which for twelve hours threatened to impale *l'Hérétique*.

As we said at the start, it is very difficult to sum up sixty-five days at sea, the duration of Bombard's crossing from Las Palmas to Barbados, which he reached on 23 December; but they were sixty-five days which changed the history of shipwreck and the lives of those who survive it.

23
Antoine Vidot and Selby Corgat
(1953)

On 31 January 1953 an old woman lay dying in a house in Port Victoria, the capital of the Island of Mahé in the Seychelles. Her last wish was to see once again before she died her daughter who lived twenty-one miles away on the Island of Praslin. The respect for the last wishes of someone on their death-bed is stronger even than the fear of putting out into a heavy sea raised by the north-west monsoon. So it was that Théodore Corgat finally had his arm twisted into making the return passage; he was the owner of the *Marie-Jeanne*, an old tub of 33 ft or so driven by a car engine. The community spirit continued to do its work until finally, at about 11 a.m., six men put to sea without even warning the harbour-master. In addition to Théodore Corgat there were an old sea-dog by the name of Louis Laurence, the grandson of the dying woman, Joachim Servina, seventeen years old, his cousin Auguste Lavigne of eighteen, and a twenty-year-old engineer called Antoine Vidot. At the last moment Selby Corgat, the proprietor's fifteen-year-old son, managed to persuade his father to take him too.

The twenty-one mile passage was a tough one. 'Three times the boat was laid on her beam ends when the motor stopped', and it took them thirteen hours instead of the usual four to reach the Island of Praslin.

Because of heavy seas the start of the return passage was delayed until 9.00 a.m. on the morning of Sunday, 1 February. The *Marie-Jeanne* now had ten people on board. The crew of the outward passage had been joined by Auguste's seventeen-year-old brother Jules Lavigne, two women of sixty or so, Ange Finesse and Mrs Arrisol – and the twenty-five-year-old Noël Rondeau who wanted to take a crate of papayas and mangoes to one of his friends who lived on Mahé and for whom the *Marie-Jeanne*'s impromptu trip was an unexpected piece of luck.

So the scene was set and the cast on stage for the drama that was to follow:

The old car engine ran smoothly until they were about eight miles from their destination. Then it misfired several times and stopped completely. 'Out of petrol,' said Vidot. He filled the tank from the reserve can and the engine started again. But when he tried to change to third gear, he couldn't make it. Then he tried to get back into second and the gear lever broke. With a long face Vidot stuck his knife into the base of the lever, declutched and gave it a few jerks. He smiled all over his face when he managed to get into second and the

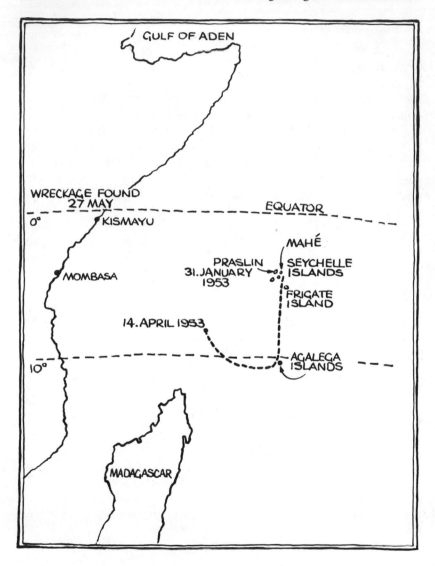

boat resumed its course for Mahé. Two miles out they ran out of fuel again. When they saw the expression on the men's faces, the two women burst into tears.

Now at the mercy of wind and current, the *Marie-Jeanne* started to drift rapidly. They dropped anchor and it held on the coral. They all prayed that someone would spot them and come to their help. Night fell – and with it came a fatal blow. The anchor chain broke. The *Marie-Jeanne* was adrift again.

As dawn broke the next morning they saw the tip of the island fading into the distance.

Laurence checked what victuals they had on board. This added up to about a pint of water each, a little cassava flour and Rondeau's mangoes and papayas. As the land sank below the horizon, Laurence set about cutting up the canopy to make sails. The direction of the wind ruled out a return to Mahé but Frigate Island was fifteen miles to the south and Laurence reckoned that with a bit of luck they might make that.

On the third day, Tuesday, 3 February, all hope of reaching Frigate Island vanished and the last drops of water were consumed:

Corgat took charge of rationing out the provisions and made sure that the young ones always got a tiny bit more. He conserved everything meticulously but, despite his efforts, after ten days there was not a bite left to eat. . . . They took turns on the helm. They also organized duty watches for bailing and sprinkling water on the cabin top to cool it. The men carried out these tasks with determination. They had just one aim – to survive. . . . By day the heat was so overwhelming that the planking of the hull shrank. By night they had to huddle together to keep warm. At dawn they sought out the drops of dew and licked them with their swollen tongues.

It was only on the thirteenth day, when everyone on board was drowsy and already suffering from a critical degree of dehydration, that the first rain fell. They drank the water cupped in their hands as it ran off the sails, and subsequently collected about twenty gallons.

Revived, they tried to catch some fish with a piece of bent wire, but the fish would not bite. They fixed a pointed piece of metal to an oar as a harpoon and tried again, but still they had no luck. On the fifteenth day a small flying fish hit the sail and fell flapping into the cabin. Selby Corgat caught it and the two women, excited by the event, sat up for the first time in days. Their weakness was terrible. Rondeau split up the flying fish, and the two women ate their share without a word. For the next eighteen days no one ate a bite.

Here I feel bound to interrupt this tale and make a point, in case I have not laid sufficient stress on it in the second part of this book. This group of survivors illustrates it very well. They had the ingenuity to make up a rudimentary fishing tackle, but they had no luck. They rather hastily concluded that fishing was impossible. They fasted for eighteen days without making any further attempts to fish, although the very slow speed of the *Marie-Jeanne* provided ideal conditions for the bottom of their craft to be colonized by a crowd of fish. Without digressing further, the lesson is that one of the key qualities of a survivor is not just the will to survive but real patience and the perseverance that goes with it.

So it was after eighteen days with nothing to eat, on the thirty-third day of their experience, that a bird caught by Laurence provided a mouthful for each of them. Then:

On the evening of the thirty-fifth day Vidot, who was at the helm, saw two gulls sitting on the bows. He dragged himself painfully forward; none of the others moved or even opened their eyes. There was a brief flutter of wings as the engineer, tortured by hunger, wrung the nearest bird's neck and swallowed its blood without even thinking of sharing it with the others. Then he lay in wait for the other gull to come back. It did, and he caught it. Again he drunk some blood, but this time he saw the look of reproach on Selby Corgat's face and the young man's stretched-out hands. 'Give me a little. Next time, Antoine, wake me up,' he said, 'I want a drink of blood too.' The flesh of these birds stopped the men actually starving to death.

The presence of the two gulls suggested to the survivors that they were approaching land, probably the Island of Agalega. In fact on the thirty-sixth day they saw an island. Laurence used his seamanship to the full and managed to head the *Marie-Jeanne* towards the land. Soon the survivors saw the coconut palms and houses that lined the shore. At that moment the wind dropped and the boat, once again at the mercy of the tides, started to drift in the wrong direction again.

There were two small oars on board but no rowlocks. Old and young alike took it in turns to paddle – weakly, desperately, struggling to bring the *Marie-Jeanne* nearer to the shore. They cried out under the strain. But although they managed to keep the old tub headed for Agalega, the tide set her astern. In the end the rowers dropped their oars and collapsed. The island vanished in the mist.

There cannot be words in any language to describe the despair of these ten survivors. A few hours previously they had feasted their eyes on the land that meant safety; now they were back in the open sea. What is more, this latest blow brought an immediate change in their attitude. Apart from Vidot and Selby Corgat, they lay down and dozed to forget their hunger.

On the thirty-seventh day, two boobies settled on the boom.

Vidot was the only one to try and catch them. He was so weak that he secured himself with a rope round his waist to make sure he did not drown if he fell overboard. He got his hands on the birds and this time he shared their blood with Selby Corgat. When they had eaten all the flesh, they sucked the bones.

One after another the days dragged by under the relentless sun. The survivors were in a state of collapse. They had still not repeated their one attempt to fish. Their attitude became more and more passive, except for some upsurges of revolt against death as they felt it creeping up on them.

On the fortieth day, 11 March, Mrs Finesse died:

She passed away so peacefully that it took a little time to realize she was gone. By way of obsequies, Jules Lavigne started to recite the Lord's Prayer, but when he reached the phrase, 'Give us this day our daily bread' the words stuck in his throat. Then they lifted the thwart on which Mrs Ange Finesse had been laid and tipped her body overboard.

On the forty-third day it was Mrs Arrisol's turn to go. Laurence started to show signs of madness, so that on the following day Vidot and Selby had to tie his wrists and lash him to a post in the cabin. This effort cost them their last ounce of strength. On the fiftieth day Joachim died, to be followed two days later by Rondeau and Jules.

After Jules' death, it got difficult for Selby, Auguste and Vidot to heave the bodies overboard. Poor Laurence in his madness was no use any more. Now came the crowning horror. The boat was being followed by sharks. Sometimes the hungry monsters battered themselves against the hull of the *Marie-Jeanne*.

(Here again, knowing how greedily hungry sharks will snap at anything, one wonders why no one thought of catching them and thus acquiring an ample supply of meat.)

We owe the account of this ghastly tragedy to James Brown, News Editor of the Johannesburg *Sunday Times*. By going over it with the two who ultimately survived he reconstructed a complete diary of the drama. But from this fifty-sixth day onwards the memories of Vidot and Selby Corgat were quite simply blank. What would have interested me in my attempt at a detached analysis of extreme human suffering would be to learn some details of the subterfuges they used to keep themselves alive for so long; but it was just a vegetable existence that did not provide any material for analysis.

On the sixty-second day Auguste Lavigne died. As he threw the body into the water Laurence, still mad but now released from his bonds, threw himself overboard and disappeared.

On the seventieth day, Théodore Corgat had a violent haemorrhage and went into a coma. After his death Vidot and Selby did not have enough strength left to drag the body from the engine room. Vidot tore off the cover of the seat on which Corgat was lying and fixed a boat-hook to it with the intention of lifting the corpse by the handle. The two young people got it halfway out when Selby fainted. They left the body where it was and covered Corgat's face with some sacking. Later, when the stench became unbearable, Vidot sprayed the corpse with the foam from the fire extinguisher.

During the two days that followed Vidot and Selby remained unconscious for most of the time. On the seventy-fourth day, 14 April 1953, a ship's siren roused them from their lethargy.

Vidot dragged himself out of the cabin at the very moment when the master of the Italian tanker *Montallegro* had just come to the conclusion that the boat was empty. Three attempts to pass a rope to the *Marie-Jeanne* failed because the two young people were too weak to secure it. In the end, the sailors hoisted them on board in a basket. The two lads collapsed on the deck, weeping and thanking God. Hardened sailors looked away with tears in their eyes.

Forty-three days later, on 27 May, an Arab found the *Marie-Jeanne* washed ashore thirty miles north of Kismayu in (as it was then) Italian Somaliland.

24
Wiktors Zvejnieks
(1954)

Thursday Island is located at the northern extremity of Australia, forming the southern side of the Torres Straits. It was from this island that on 6 January 1954, a fine Australian summer day, Wiktors

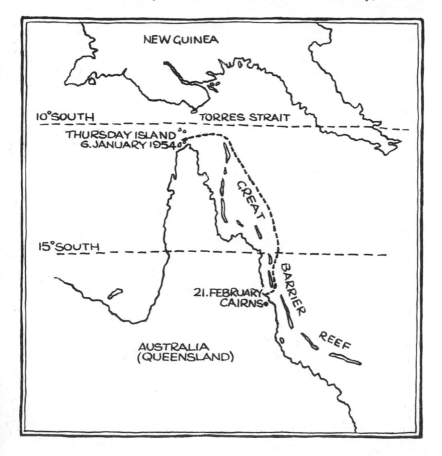

Survival At Sea

Zvejnieks, a twenty-nine-year-old Australian of Lettish origin decided to take his open 13 foot dinghy for a row in the sea. For a trip of only a few hours he had, of course, brought nothing with him, not even a picnic meal. When he was only a few miles from Thursday Island, the wind got up. In his rush to ship the oars to return to the island as quickly as possible, he lost them and was suddenly at the mercy of the winds. All around, the horizon showed him nothing but the Coral Sea.

On board the dinghy he had absolutely nothing – no provisions, no water, nor any kind of equipment that human ingenuity might adapt to aid survival, but Zvejnieks never lost the will to live. Leaning overboard, he gathered some floating seaweed and ate it. Now and then rain allowed him to quench his thirst.

Of his memories the only fact that emerges is that one day he succeeded in catching a little shark by the tail and ate the lot. That was all – seaweed, a little water, with no chance to build up reserves, and one shark for forty-six days adrift. During this time he had drifted without knowing it for 390 miles right along the Great Barrier Reef before grounding in a wretched state just north of Cairns. He was immediately rehydrated and owes his recovery to modern methods of resuscitation.

25
William Willis
(1954)

In 1947 Thor Heyerdahl with his raft *Kon-Tiki* crossed the Pacific from Callao in Peru to Raroïa in his efforts to prove that the Peruvian civilizations could have colonized Polynesia. Most probably it was his example that gave William Willis the idea of doing the same thing. Be that as it may, it was in 1954 that Willis, then aged sixty-one had a very similar raft built. It was made of seven large balsa trunks, from which it derived its name, *Seven Little Sisters*. In this raft he made a fine single-handed passage, taking 115 days to cover the 6700 miles between Callao in Peru and Pago Pago in the Samoan Islands.

Willis earns a mention here because he encountered the difficulties normally faced by castaways, at least as far as water is concerned. It was right out in mid-Pacific that Willis discovered to his horror that his water tanks were leaking. They had emptied themselves without his noticing it, and what was left was a meagre ration indeed. He was probably familiar with Bombard's conclusions and decided to drink some seawater every day. He took it in moderate quantities, along with one bowl of fresh water per day – little enough in those hot latitudes.[1] He had good reason to congratulate himself on this happy mixture; he had no problems or discomfort and reached Pago Pago in excellent condition.

1. Unfortunately, the original does not make clear how big the 'bowl' was or how much seawater Willis drank per day. The wording suggests that he took equal quantities of fresh water and seawater, but this is of course quite different from Bombard's 'little and often' recommendation. [Trans.]

26

Arne Nicolaysen

(1955)

The story of Arne Nicolaysen lasted for just twenty-nine hours – little enough in comparison with the others we have examined but a kind of record in its own right. For he spent these twenty-nine hours in the water, 'swimming, floating, swaying between hope and despair and thence to prayer, in the darkness of the night and the burning sunlight. Twenty-nine hours of seeing ships pass too far away to hail them or reach them'. I decided to include his story simply to illustrate the will to live which is the basis of all survival at sea.

Nicolaysen, twenty-five years old, was a deckhand on board the Norwegian ship *Höeg Silverspray*; on Christmas Eve 1955 she was steaming between Cuba and Florida. The Christmas dinner[1] was generous, but the presence of the officers stopped the crew drinking much. The feast dragged on and on, and Arne was finding it heavy going. About 11.00 p.m. he went back to his cabin, stretched out on his bunk and fell asleep dreaming of all the Christmases he had spent at home. 'When I regained consciousness,' he relates, 'I found I was in the water.' The only explanation that was ever offered was that he had fallen overboard while sleepwalking.

After a moment of very understandable panic, he realized that his situation presented a number of problems that would bear examination. There was no trace of the *Höeg Silverspray*; she must have been a long way off because he could not even hear the engines. The water was not too cold and, as long as he kept moving, he could stay in it a long time. But to keep moving meant swimming; and in the depths of the night he had no idea which direction to swim in. He reckoned his absence would not be discovered until late morning and that the best thing was to stay as nearly as possible in one place. To avoid being weighed down he decided to take his trousers off, but the thought of sharks sent a shiver down his spine.

1. The word used implies a late dinner to see Christmas in, rather like New Year's Eve in Great Britain. [Trans.]

Arne kept his trousers on for, however formidable they may be, sharks are surprisingly cowardly. The least noise, like the flapping of a trouser leg in the water, is quite likely to scare them and make them keep their distance. His shoes would serve the same purpose. He carefully slipped his heels out of them so that they were flapping on the end of his toes like a kind of underwater scarecrow.

We owe the account of this extraordinary adventure to Robert Littell who published it in *Reader's Digest* in 1956:

Rising quickly, the sub-tropical sun warmed the survivor and gave him a little encouragement by showing him in its light the silhouette of a ship. The young man estimated its speed, heading and distance from him and started to swim to the far-off invisible point where, logically, he should cross it. This attempt cost him a lot of time and precious strength before he finally realized that he would not make it. At least it was some consolation for him that he was on a shipping route.

In the hours that followed four or five other ships passed within sight of him. Some of them seemed so close that Arne shouted, whistled and took off his jersey and waved it in the air – a pathetic flag dripping with water. God alone knows how many ships he saw that day. Fifteen or twenty he thought – all of them blind, deaf and unattainable. Arne is one of those people who reacts with anger under circumstances where weaker mortals give way to despair. This explains why he is still alive today. Furious, he shook his fist at these uncaring boats and shouted at them: 'I'll report you to your Company for the negligence of your watch!'

But he started to get weaker and to feel more and more uncomfortable. He had severe sunburn and his face was stiff with salt. He was forced to keep on massaging his legs. 'If I get cramp,' he thought, 'I'm done for!'. . . The intense heat soon made him sleepy, and more than once he woke to find his mouth full of seawater. . . . When the sun went down, chagrin made him a little light-headed and he made several attempts to drown himself by letting himself sink and swallowing great gulps of seawater. 'But I felt straightaway a kind of explosion in my ears and brought it all up again.'

Late the following night Arne had a vision of two of his ship-mates 'walking on the water'. He asked them: 'Where is land?' 'You just have to swim towards the moon,' they replied. So Arne, by now swimming with difficulty, tried to follow the silvery track of the moon on the water, a kind of gleaming ethereal spider's thread which he hung on to and which probably saved his life. Suddenly he felt an impact on his chest. He had just seen the lights of a ship headed straight for him. He took a few hasty strokes to get across its course and as the ship slid by, he shouted over and over again: 'Help! Man overboard!' Then he heard a noise which must have made his heart burst with joy – the sound of the engines slowing down and stopping. There was some shouting and a lifebuoy flew through the air towards him. It was 4.00 o'clock on the Monday morning, and the captain of the tanker *British Surveyor* which fished him out couldn't believe that this survivor had been in the water since Christmas Eve.

27

Teehu Makimare and his companions

(1963)

On the morning of 15 August 1963 seven Polynesians set about loading a small cutter, the *Tearoha*, with twenty sacks of puruka, a kind of green vegetable, ten sacks of breadfruit, four pumpkins and some coconuts. They also put on board a small amount of food, all cooked, for their one intended meal and a carboy with about 2 gallons of water – more than enough for the 21 miles which separated them from Manihiki Atoll where they were to take this merchandise.

The small trading cutter was really overloaded, for it was only 16 feet overall with a 5 foot beam. The seven men had to pile on to the sacks. The oldest was Taia, forty-two; then came Enoka, Toka, Kira, Tupou and Tom, the youngest at twenty-four. The seventh man, Teehu Makimare, who is the hero of this story, was a thirty-two-year-old pearl fisherman, married, with a small son.

At 8.30 a.m., with Enoka at the helm, the other six paddled the *Tearoha* through the channel in the reef. They set sail, main and jib, and set course for Manihiki. About 2.00 p.m. the line of coconut palms of their native atoll appeared on the horizon but much too far to the east. The *Tearoha* had gone alarmingly off course to the west; the cutter, mainly designed for fishing in the lagoons, could not run before the wind on a sea which was now getting up steadily. Enoka brought the boat close-hauled and battled away for hours while the waves broke against the side and submerged the sacks. As darkness fell they were having to bail hard.

The *Tearoha* had been sighted from the island. A Tilly lamp hoisted up a mast burnt through the night as a leading light. But it was a leading light which was soon lost to the sight of the seven men in the cutter. This frail craft was being driven inexorably westwards.

On the morning of 16 August the situation reached the point of drama when the bowsprit was carried away and fell in the water taking the jib with it. They lowered the mainsail too and threw most of the cargo overboard. Throughout the day the seven Polynesians wore

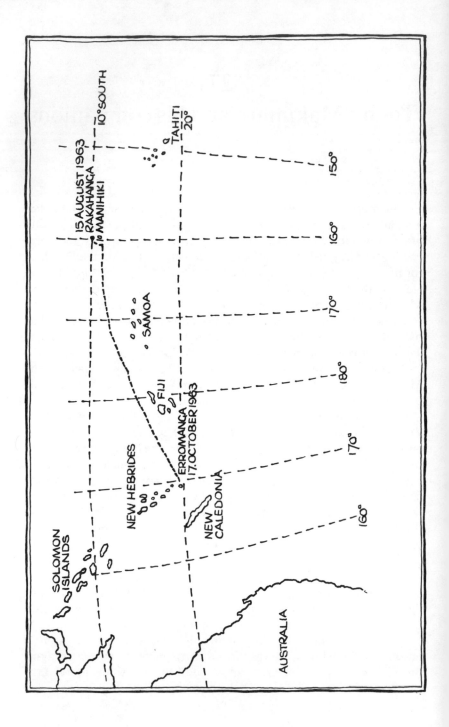

themselves out paddling to keep the boat head to wind, up to the moment when Teehu took the helm and turned the ship about. Manihiki was now astern of them and very soon vanished. It was with this turn of the helm that their life as castaways began.

For three days, despite the storm, the Resident of Manihiki ordered a search with the official cutter, while some police seaplanes, put on the alert on the morning of the 16th, constantly flew over the area where the wrecked cutter must be. On Sunday 18 August the Governor of Rorotonga had to bow before the inescapable conclusion that the seven men must have been drowned. Just as the Governor called off the search, the storm died down and everyone on board the *Tearoha* set about repairing the bowsprit, which was still dragging in the water along with the bobstay and the jib. A few hours later the cutter was able to set course again, this time towards Pukapuka, an island some 200 miles to the south-west of Manihiki.

The provisions they had brought for a one-day passage were long since exhausted. Water was rationed to two mouthfuls doled out three times a day using half a coconut shell as a measure, but despite this the carboy was almost empty. They had no choice but to start eating the puruka and the other vegetables raw. Then Teehu had an ingenious idea. This is how Barry Wynne, who recorded Teehu's story, tells us what he did about it:

Suddenly he remembered that stowed away in a locker were two bottles of kerosene he had been carrying to light his aunty's lamps on Manihiki. Also aboard the boat were several tins, which they had put to good use during the height of the storm as bailers. Surely, with tins, kerosene and a little ingenuity he might be able to construct a stove?

In an instant the *Tearoha* became the scene of bubbling excitement as Teehu, with the help of a strong fishing knife, attacked the side of an old half-gallon milk can.

Having studied the problem he realized that the source of heat must be protected from draught or wind and concentrated in such a way as to bring a twelve ounce tin of water to boil as quickly as possible. After all, they only had two pints of kerosene and, therefore, the stove must be as efficient as humanly possible. He cut a large flap at the side and to the bottom of the main can; through this hole he would be able to place a small half-pound meat tin which would contain the source of heat. He left that problem to the last.

Next, halfway up the milk tin he bored two tiny holes, one on each side, and threaded through them a piece of wire he had found lying in the bottom of the boat, securing either end. This enabled him to rest the medium sized tin inside the dried milk can a few inches above the source of heat.

With much hilarity suggestions were put forward for a makeshift wick, each of these being rejected for one reason or another until suddenly every one agreed on Tupou's trouser pocket, which with much ceremony, was cut adrift and placed in the tin! Teehu hacked a little hole in the lid which was still partly secured, forced a piece of linen through it and then added half a tin of precious kerosene. Pressing down the lid as effectively as he could he placed the small tin inside the stove.

They now prepared the puruka and breadfruit, cutting it into cubes and placing them inside the twelve ounce can. Covering the vegetables with sea water, Teehu gently rested it inside the makeshift stove and with one of Kita's precious matches lit the home-made wick.

It was on 21 August, the seventh day, that their fervent prayers were answered with the first rain. They lowered the mainsail, stretching it right across the cutter, and in ten minutes they managed to fill the carboy. To add to their delight a number of frigate birds were circling them, seeming to suggest that they were near Pukapuka.

The days went by. Although sharks escorted them, they took frequent dips, which were their only chance to relax their stiffened limbs. The level of rainwater in the carboy rapidly went down, and they added a little seawater. On 27 August a third vegetable casserole used up the last of the kerosene; in the days that followed they had to resign themselves to chewing slowly away at the raw vegetables which, to make matters worse, were beginning to grow mildew and become inedible. The discovery of some old fish hooks quickly aroused the instincts of these fishermen. To make a line they undid some of the bunches of knots that formed the protective net of the carboy. A strip of white shirt served as a lure, but it was a total failure; they plugged away for a whole morning without catching a thing. Each day wore away a little more at the morale and the physical state of the survivors. Teehu alone kept going. He was everywhere, comforting his friends through the long day while always keeping an eye fixed on the horizon. So it was that in the last days of August he noticed a mass of seeds floating on the surface of the sea. As he told Barry Wynne:

As he turned one over in the large palm of his hand, Teehu noticed that one end of the seed had already opened preparatory to sprouting forth a shoot. Looking at it more closely he suddenly became aware that secreted inside the opening were two tiny sea snails firmly attached, harboured and protected by the outer shell. He pulled them off, showed them to his friends and with the point of his knife extracted one of the tiny bodies from its shell, popping it into his mouth with a grimace. Leathery it might have been, but sweet was the taste and joyfully he realized that they had hit upon a minute but valuable source of fresh food.

On 7 September and again on the 9th he found a coconut; the milk and the flesh were carefully shared out. On 11 September during a period of flat calm, Tom, hanging over the bow, felt something thick dragging at his wrist. He pulled quickly at it and caught a bunch of fifteen octopuses all stuck together. They were devoured with delight. From time to time a brief shower roused the survivors from their torpor; but they collected less and less water, for their movements were slow, and by the time they had lowered the mainsail to collect the rain the showers were often over. So the men were in a bad way as they watched dawn rise on the thirty-third day of their survival. It was 15 September, one of the most dramatic days in the whole history of shipwreck:

There was an unearthly stillness, the sails hanging limp, as the *Tearoha* rolled in the gentle swell. . . . From utter silence they were suddenly engulfed in tumultous noise. . . . The main wind smashed against the canvas of their sails. For a second *Tearoha* trembled, as if offering one token gesture of defiance, before with a mighty flip and a roll she turned turtle in the boiling sea.

All this had taken only a few seconds, and Teehu found himself wedged in the hull. He managed to get clear, reaching the surface with the last of his breath. A quick look round told him that Kita was missing. He took a deep breath and dived again. Threading his way through an inextricable tangle of cordage, sails and objects of every kind, he saw Kita stuck under the foredeck. He pulled him clear and managed to get him to the surface. The sea was now very choppy, but Teehu kept his friend afloat for ten minutes before he regained consciousness. All the rest were resigned, apathetic, hanging on to the hull and snatching quick breaths between the waves.

Teehu did not know which way to turn. He handed Kita over to Taia so that he could swim towards the carboy which was floating away; he spoke to his shipmates, calming their panic and getting them better supported by the hull. Finally, he set about the superhuman task of righting the *Tearoha*, whose keel mocked him as it stuck in the air. To do this he had to dive again and again to find the halyards, clear the knots soaked in water, get the mainsail down and clear away the boom before he could tackle the jib. For several hours Teehu did what no pearl diver had ever done before. Dive after dive, his fingers probing a moving green-grey universe, he struggled to free the wet and swollen halyard from its cleat. He was overcome by nausea and came up half-suffocated. While getting his breath back, he took a look at his friends, told them how he was getting on and suddenly caught Kita, who was losing consciousness again, by the hair. Then he dived again for the hundredth time, cleared the halyard away completely, pushed the gaff upwards along the mast and, with an enormous effort despite the lack of firm support, cleared away the boom. Tupou and Toka, stirred from their stupor, now came to help him. They hauled at the boom and the sail, and with two paddles made a kind of canvas raft on which they put Kita and Tom, the two weakest.

The hours went by and the moment came to try and right the cutter. It was a failure. After clearing away the jib, a fresh effort finally got the *Tearoha* upright. Teehu climbed on board to start bailing, and while he was looking for something to use as a bailer, the ill-fated boat capsized for the second time.

All were overwhelmed by despair, except Teehu who made them say the Lord's Prayer and egged them on to try again. Once again the cutter was righted. This time Teehu climbed very carefully on board, swimming in the water which filled the boat until he reached the mast, while the others who could kept the boat head to wind. Teehu succeeded in freeing the wedge which held the mast in its step and with a final heave lifted the mast and threw it overboard. He bailed away for several hours with a big food tin and the lid of a suitcase, and at last he was able to help his friends to climb on board. As he was getting his breath back, he noticed that the canvas raft had disappeared. Night fell without its being sighted; Kita and Tom would never see Manihiki again. During the night Enoka died; the four survivors were by now so weak that they had to use two paddles they had salvaged to heave his body overboard.

On Monday 16 September Teehu was able to take stock of the extent of the disaster:

Apart from the two paddles, the tin and the suitcase lid, the boat was empty. They no longer had a mast and the sails had gone, bearing with them the bodies of Kita and Tom.

The compass case was still secure, but now no longer contained that elementary pointer of direction. They had absolutely no food of any description, nor indeed a water bottle. They did have a little more room to lie down and this was their sole consolation, although without the bottom boards their bodies became racked with pain for their bones had little enough flesh to protect them.

It was at this point that a second phase of their survival began – even more terrible than the first. It was to last until 17 October.

During those thirty-one days nothing was spared the four survivors. For the first six days they had nothing to quench their thirst but small mouthfuls of seawater. On 21 September they collected a little brackish water with the suitcase lid but could not collect enough to put into their tin as a reserve. So it was back to seawater, relieved only by the occasional brief shower. Every morning they licked the wood of the boat on which a fine dew had settled. By now the nights had become distinctly cold, but in the day the tropical sun had not lost its terrible heat. The kindly shade of the sail was lost when it carried off their friends. During this month all they ate between four of them were thirteen flying fish, the only offering the sea made in answer to their fervent prayers.

It was on the sixty-third day at sea, 16 October, that Teehu spotted an island dead ahead. He roused his friends, trying to help them to get up and look at the land; but they were indifferent, almost unconscious. Hour after hour Teehu watched the mountains growing larger; but he also realized very clearly that although the wind was favourable the current was starting to carry them out to sea. He stripped his companions and took off his own shirt. With all the clothes and the two paddles he rigged up a kind of scarecrow of a sail.

. . . Teehu struggled back toward the tiller in the stern. Pushing it hard to starboard he noticed with exultant joy that he was able to incline the bow several degrees to the south and for the first time in over five weeks, the *Tearoha* reluctantly came under some sort of control. Her movement through the water seemed to be infinitesimal but at least she was no longer drifting toward the wrong side of the island.

Gradually, Teehu made towards land. He found a channel and managed to get through it. On Tuesday 17 October, about 4.30 p.m., the *Tearoha* grounded a short distance from a beautiful beach of dazzling coral sand. Teehu alone was capable of standing. He dragged his companions to the bottom of the first coconut palms he saw, talking to them to stir them from their torpor. He collected some very ripe coconuts. With shaking teeth he tore at the thick hairy shell. His gums began to bleed but all he could think of was the liquid which would soon slip between the closed teeth of his friends.

On the following day they were discovered by some Kanakas, who gave them their first meal. They were at Erromanga, one of the islands in the archipelago of the New Hebrides. Their joy was marred when, three days after landing, their friend Taia died.

At Manihiki on 8 February 1965 Teehu received this letter from the Governor General's representative:

The Department of Island Territories in Wellington has just telegraphed us to say that His Royal Highness the Duke of Gloucester has decided that you should be awarded the Stanhope Gold Medal for 1964. This is a very high honour indeed as the Stanhope Gold Medal is awarded each year for the *bravest deed* of life-saving *of the year* reported to the Royal Humane Societies in the British Commonwealth.

28

Henri and Josée Bourdens

(1967)

In his book *Croisière cruelle* Henri Bourdens tells us more about his adventures on a desert island and thus about the problems of survival on land, in the jungle, than about the questions which concern us here. Nevertheless, to get out of a situation which he felt was getting worse he and his wife decided to try and reach inhabited territory by casting themselves on the mercy of the tides in a home-made raft. This was how they made an interesting study as castaways. They started, moreover, at a considerable disadvantage, for they were both already in an advanced state of exhaustion and undernourishment when they put back to sea.

In mid-January 1967 Henri and Josée Bourdens, sailing *Singa Betina*, a Malay boat known as a *bedor* which is a cross between a Mediterranean hull and a Chinese rig, were not far from the Celebes when damage caused them to turn for Darwin for repairs. However, this sea area was not included in their plans and they had no charts for it.

On 27 January they reached the Island of Bathurst. In looking for the channel which separates this island from its other half, Melville, they entered a lagoon and ran aground. The following night the tide was so high that it put the *Singa Betina* high and dry on the shore. Expecting another high spring tide which would help them refloat their boat, the Bourdens settled down on the island in conditions which can fairly be described as very comfortable, for they could make use of all the conveniences offered by their boat. The only things that made life difficult were the clouds of mosquitoes and sandflies. However, a storm came and finally put paid to any hope of leaving Bathurst in their boat.

It was then, over several weeks, that they learnt more and more distressing lessons about survival on a desert island. To describe all the problems of this other aspect of survival would be outside the scope of this book. In many ways it is just as harsh. Certainly it was harsh enough to make the Bourdens decide after two months to abandon terra firma, the goal of shipwrecked mariners, and to trust themselves once more to the sea – but this time on a simple raft made from the wreckage of the *Singa Betina*. The mainmast, mizzen mast and bowsprit were cut in two, lashed together with the standing rigging and strengthened by four thick beams laid and lashed crosswise. Two strong bamboos lashed together and topped with a single long mangrove trunk served as a mast. The *Singa Betina's* storm jib became the raft's lugsail, whilst stability was improved by some plastic jerricans forward and some kegs aft.

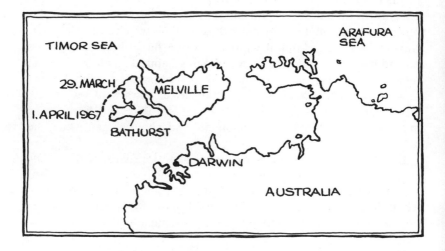

With a jerrican of water and a small stock of sea-snails, which had been their sole diet for some time, they set off on 29 March. For the Bourdens the dangers of grounding, which form the final scene in most stories of shipwreck, were the initial problems they faced in survival at sea. They made good use of the current and passed over the reef. On 30 March they discovered to their horror that the raft was settling in the water; the dry wood used in its construction was sodden with water. That day, in addition to some sea-snails, they ate little raw crabs, about half an inch long, which were swimming along their craft or clinging to the timbers.

On 31 March the raft once again settled, so that their feet were now under water. They drank some water, but they no longer had the strength to collect the crabs which were still with them. They faced death with resignation and acceptance, knowing that their raft would very soon sink and that they had no hope of returning to the Island of Bathurst.

On 1 April Henri Bourdens was almost comatose. The last hours of daylight were slowly fading when the miracle happened. An hour before sunset they saw a sail. They fired a smoke flare and were spotted and rescued.

29

The Robertson family

(1972)

The *Lucette*, a 43 ft fore-and-aft schooner of 19 tons had just sailed from the Galapagos Islands. On board were Dougal and Lynn Robertson, their children Douglas, aged eighteen, and the twelve-year-old twins Neil and Sandy, and Robin Williams, a Welshman of twenty-two.

About 200 miles off Cape Espinosa, at 9.45 a.m. on 15 June 1972, a pack of killer whales attacked the schooner and shattered her planking. In four minutes the *Lucette* went down. In these four minutes six individuals were translated from the happy life of the amateur yachtsman to the arduous existence of survivors in a raft and a dinghy – with nothing but the water, provisions and few bits of equipment that they had been able to snatch up in those four short minutes.

In his book *Survive the Savage Sea*[1] Dougal Robertson tells the story of the thirty-eight days that followed these terrible moments. Its pages are so packed with information and lessons that it is not easy to summarize this book. Perhaps the best method of extracting the facts of the story is to consider the major problems the Robertsons had to cope with.

The first and by no means the least was their raft. Six of them were packed into an inflatable raft of 9 ft 6 in, only just over half the size of Bombard's. Their bodies were tangled together; every movement by one member of the family required advance warning and a whole series of moves by the others. From the first night onwards their weary bodies were constantly bruised and battered by the blows on the bottom of the raft made by the fish that had immediately taken shelter beneath it. They never managed to get used to this. Right from the beginning too the pressure in the inflatable compartments was low, and the air pump performed very badly. They had to use lung power to maintain an acceptable pressure and take it in turns to try and repair

1. *Survive the Savage Sea*, Dougal Robertson, Elek, 1973.

the leaks. Around the eighth day they had reached a point where the person on watch spent all his time bailing out or blowing up the raft. On the fourteenth day the leaks from the raft were becoming more and more difficult to plug, and the watchkeeper's job was becoming really hectic. It was at this point that the idea of transferring everyone to the dinghy began to take shape. This was done on the seventeenth day after careful preparation of the drill that would be needed to avoid capsizing. From this point on this drill of keeping the boat balanced when they were fishing, when someone moved or when a big sea struck became a continuous part of their life until they were rescued.

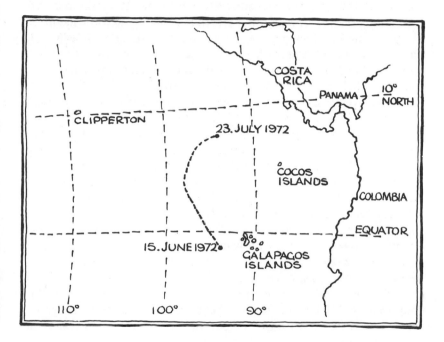

The second of the major problems they had to surmount was clearly thirst. The sum total of their liquid assets on 15 June was the 10 litres (rather over 2 gallons) of water in the raft's survival pack plus ten oranges and six lemons snatched up as the yacht went down. The weather statistics for the sea area they were in made rain highly unlikely for six months. So they decided straight away to ration water to 1 litre per day between the six of them and to use the ten days this would give them to head north towards areas where rain could be expected.

Despite all this they had a rain squall on the third day. The water they collected was yellow and even saltier than seawater. They could not use a single drop of it, but this first experience provided the basis for a comprehensive drill to deal with future rain. It was only on the seventh day that this procedure could be put into practice when a long shower gave them a chance to perfect their technique of rinsing, collection and storage. This shower allowed them to renew all their reserves; but not knowing how long they would have to wait for more rain, they maintained rationing and suffered continuously from thirst. On the fifteenth day further rain restored a situation that was becoming critical; their reserves were down to 5 or 6 pints. It was this paradox of suffering several days of thirst and then drinking their fill and more when it rained that gave Lynn, a trained nurse, the idea of using salt water as an enema. She made up the equipment from a bag to form a funnel and a piece of rubber tubing from the air pump which had never condescended to function. Enemas were administered to all.

On the twenty-second and twenty-third days fresh water became a curse in the shape of a series of absolute cloudbursts. These beat down on the Robertsons, making them colder and colder and forcing them to bail continuously. At the same time the sea got up, and one can only wonder by what miracle this tiny dinghy overloaded with six people did not capsize. The lack of receptacles to store fresh water in meant that they alternated between plenty and shortage, but on the twenty-eighth day they hit on a brilliant solution. They had kept the raft with them and were using it as a kind of bow float for the dinghy. By half-filling one of the compartments with water and then blowing it up hard by mouth they managed to combine adequate buoyancy with a good reserve of water. In spite of this, the thirty-second day saw them down to half a gallon of water, with another crisis looming. It was at this point that the blood of turtles and the 'juice' squeezed from fish in the way recommended by Bombard kept them going until their rescue on the thirty-eighth day.

The third serious problem for the Robertsons was hunger. In the survival pack they found rations for ten people for two days in the shape of vitamin-enriched bread and sugar. In addition, they had managed to collect as they abandoned ship a sack of onions, a tin of biscuits and a half-pound jar of glucose sweets. This made their cupboard rather bare. It was not until the morning of the third day that they found an 8-inch flying fish lying in the dinghy. It had struck the dinghy's sail during the night, but at this point they were all still in the raft. This fish meant a good deal more than a few ounces of protein; it was the spark which triggered off a whole series of actions aimed at fishing. They took a fish-hook from the small packet of fishing tackle in the raft's equipment and used the head of this first fish as bait; but they lost both bait and hook. This was critical for they had only three hooks left. The kit also contained a spoon and a reel and line, so Dougal Robertson tried the spoon. That was swallowed by a shark. These two experiences were enough to teach the survivors to think everything out very carefully before committing themselves. They made a new spoon from the lid of the biscuit tin, fitted a hook to it and added a piece of cloth as a lure. The other thing they needed was plenty of patience; it was almost a question of educating the fish which were cruising underneath the boat. Then on the sixth day the first of a long series of dorados,[1] weighing about 35 pounds, was landed in the dinghy. Some of it was eaten straightaway, and the remaining fillets were put out to dry.

From this point on their technique improved steadily. They succeeded in catching more and more fish but never enough to provide an adequate diet for six. Every morning they woke up hungry. Dougal Robertson carefully analysed the reasons for the setbacks he had experienced. He made first one harpoon and then another, and these improved his daily bag. We shall see later the various things he might have done, but for the moment it is enough to note that his fishing would never have been enough to keep his family alive. Fortunately for them the combination of position and season meant that there were plenty of turtles about.

It was on the seventh day that their first turtle announced its presence with a dull thump on the bottom of the raft, quite different from the more or less continuous blows of the dorados. It was grabbed by one of its back fins and tipped into the dinghy. It must have weighed about 90 pounds. This was a great stroke of luck, although at this first attempt, in their zest for the banquet that awaited them, they forgot to collect the blood and discarded the liver, thinking it poisonous. They were too busy probing the depths of their knowledge of anatomy to think of everything. The turtle was dismembered; it was a female full of eggs. Then followed a feast, and after that the work of drying the fillets. These had to be kept for less plentiful days, and at the same time the sky had to be watched to put them under cover if a storm was coming up. They caught their second turtle on the fourteenth day. This time they quenched their thirst with the blood and then conserved

1. See page 157.

some of it in a congealed state – a delicious kind of 'pudding' with plasma which they used to season other dishes. There were plenty more turtles to come. As practice made perfect it took less and less time to kill, dismember and prepare them, while all the riches they contained were noted and put to better and better use. For instance, there was the oil for oiling instruments, making ointments and giving enemas; some was even set aside for calming the waters in storms.

In the thirty-eight days of their experience they caught ten good-sized turtles. Looking back, it seems fair to say that they owe their lives to these reptiles, all the more because seabirds played no part in their diet. On the nineteenth day a blue-footed booby had sat on Dougal's shoulder, but they did not catch it for they thought – wrongly as we shall see – that its flesh would be 'tough, salty and verminous'.

On the other hand, one point worth stressing is the way the Robertsons made provision for less fortunate days to come. In this way they could count on dried fish and meat on days when heavy weather made fishing impossible. This is a point I shall return to, for it is evident that few survivors have managed to achieve these techniques of conservation.

A great deal more could be said about all the ways in which the Robertsons' experience has added to our knowledge of the subject of survival, and I shall be drawing on this in Part Two. However, before concluding this brief account of their experience, one other key point needs highlighting – that of medical and psychological problems. Lynn Robertson was a nurse. Her physiological knowledge combined with her maternal instinct to work miracles. Quite apart from the restrictions she imposed, often without her husband's knowledge, for the benefit of her twelve-year-old twins, she managed to control the disastrous effects of the seasickness which afflicted them in the first few days. The vomiting and the resulting effects on the electrolytic action of the digestive juices could have proved fatal for them. From the second day onwards, after a night in which they all suffered from cramp that left them in little doubt about the smallness of the raft, she undertook prolonged daily massage of her children's legs. Every day she insisted on a programme of exercises despite the extra calories this cost. As already mentioned, she set up the routine of enemas, first with salt water and then with oil. Dougal Robertson remained constipated for twenty-six days and Neil, one of the twins, broke the record by not having a motion until the thirtieth day. Last but not least, Lynn Robertson provided a major stabilizing influence throughout. The problems of temperament and the psychological shocks were numerous; but she always managed to alleviate them and turn them to good effect with her deep understanding of human nature.

On 23 July, the thirty-eighth day after their shipwreck, the *Toka Maru II*, a Japanese tunny boat, crossed their path as darkness was starting to fall. A first flare lit up the dusk and Dougal hung on to it until his fingers were burnt. A second failed to go off. He grabbed his torch, but it was not needed. The tunny boat had altered course and was coming to pick them up.

I myself have no doubt that the Robertsons would have reached the coast of Nicaragua for which they were making. At the moment of their rescue they were 290 miles away from it, having already covered 750 miles; but that is the end of their story. If one thinks of the way in which they were packed into a basic dinghy, of the presence of two young children, of the very short time they had to abandon ship and of all the other factors, theirs is, I think, one of the most splendid stories of survival – even if it falls far short of many others in duration and distance covered.

30

Lucien Schiltz and Catherine Plessz

(1972)

Back in 1952 Bombard had made clear that the Mediterranean was not favourable to survival. Twenty years later two young people were to confirm this. The story of their shipwreck is told in the words of an expert and experienced sailor, Jacques Vignes.

On 11 September 1972 there sailed from the little port of Beaulieu a steel-hulled cutter, the *Njord*, bound for a long cruise in the tropics. She was about 26 feet long with an unladen displacement of almost 7 tons. On board were Lucien Schiltz, twenty-five years old, and nineteen-year-old Catherine Plessz, whom fate had brought together to live through a truly remarkable adventure.

In their first days out the Mediterranean was so rough that, despite a sea-anchor led from the stern, the cutter laid over. The *Njord* did indeed right herself, but this incident created the distressed atmosphere of the drama that was to come. It was only 5.30 p.m., but in September, in such a storm, it was already dark and the lights on board failed. At this point a freak wave broke over the cutter sweeping overboard both Lucien, who was on the helm, and Catherine, who was holding the mainsheet. They were both in the water. With a desperate effort, at the same time battling against and taking advantage of the violent movements of the boat, they both managed to get back on board. The helm did not answer any more. Without a rudder and under bare poles the *Njord* was adrift. In the darkness the saloon was flooded, and the chaos below was indescribable.

What happened then is really rather difficult to analyse. An exceptional set of circumstances led the two of them to abandon this boat which, although badly knocked about, showed no signs of being in immediate danger. The crucial events of the next few minutes are told by Jacques Vignes:

In their minds, numbed by fatigue and stress an obsession began to grow: the life raft. 'I was sure it wouldn't inflate when we tried to use it,' Lucien later explained.

A moment later, he could not stand it any longer. The life raft was there in its bag, lashed to the cabin top aft of the mast. He was going to test it. He just did not think further. Why bother, since it would not inflate anyway? Slumped in the cockpit, dead tired, Catherine made no move to interfere.

Lucien climbed to the cabin top, seized the toggle, and pulled. The raft unfolded immediately, caught the wind at the same instant, and nearly blew overboard. Grabbing it, Lucien managed to get the raft under control, and wrenched it away from the shrouds, where it might have ripped. He dragged the raft back to the cockpit, but there was no room. The large round basin measured nearly six feet across, it was topped by an inflated arch-like tube supporting a nylon tent. The only solution was to put the raft in the water, solidly moored to *Njord*.

Soon after that, by mental processes that would surely be a feast for any psychologist, the only solution that seemed left to Lucien and Catherine was to take refuge in the liferaft which represented safety – still, as we see it, in a pattern of psychological aberration which explains the inevitability of everything they did.

It was 7.50 p.m. on 14 September 1972. Lucien and Catherine had now sought safety in their liferaft after throwing into it some tinned food, some distress flares, two 20-litre jerricans of water, a compass and the leather sack with their money and their papers. Then the line linking them to the *Njord* parted.

In the darkness the black hulk of the cutter was soon gone. In the eight hours that followed they capsized three times, losing almost all their provisions. Every time it was an exhausting business righting the raft. When day broke, they were able to re-inflate the compartments, but only to capsize once again. This time they were thrown 50 ft from the raft. Joining forces, they managed to regain the raft, but only to crawl on to its bottom without either the will or the strength to right it. Slowly, they recovered and regained their breath. The will to survive reasserted itself. With the help of a big wave the liferaft was once again floating the right way up, but without its tent; all that was left was the swan neck.[1]

Throughout the day of 15 September the wind continued at force eight with heavy seas. Every wave left behind it another gallon or so of water in the raft; it gradually got heavier, and every two or three hours it capsized. Having thought themselves already at the end of their tether in the morning, they almost tirelessly righted their raft. Their technique steadily improved and it became easier. It was daylight too, and the wave which would help them right the craft was easier to see.

. . . they began to realize that, while sitting on the inflatable ring, they could balance the raft to reduce the risk of capsizing. All they had to do was shift their weight in the right direction at the right time. The principle was simple. The raft rotated slowly, at the rate of about one revolution every ten minutes. Thus under ideal conditions, one sat facing the oncoming waves, and the other sat with his back to them. The person who was downwind, who saw the waves approach, had to warn the other and lean forward a little to counterbalance the weight of his own body, while the other person prepared to lean back for the same purpose. . . . The raft filled up, wave after wave. When the water reached their knees, the moment was at hand. When they capsized, they held on in such a way that they landed on the upturned bottom of the raft without really falling into the sea. They righted the raft on the first try – they had found

---

1. An inflatable tent support shaped as its name suggests. [Trans.]

the rhythm – then climbed aboard one after the other, helping each other in order to avoid unnecessary effort. Lightened, the raft regained speed. Once more wind and sea swept them along their desperate course.

The morning of the 16th brought a slight respite:

The wind had definitely moderated to about force five or six but the seas were still crossed and unpredictable. The raft was almost half full, and that greatly increased the risk of capsize. The first thing to be done was to empty it. But how should we do it? Capsizing on purpose was unthinkable. Then we had an idea. I took off my oilskin pants, we tied a knot in each leg and we used them as a container. It worked fairly well as long as we didn't fill it too full. Otherwise it was too heavy and we didn't have the strength left to lift it. At the same time, whenever we felt the raft being swept along by a wave that seemed dangerous, we dropped everything and rushed to the rubber gunwales to balance it. We used the pump to finish the job but, handy as it was for reinflating the raft, it was so hard to bail with that Catherine could hardly work it.

For these forty-eight hours the unceasing struggle to avoid being drowned, the battle against cold and sleep made them forget thirst and hunger. They did not eat, but every three hours they drank a few mouthfuls of the 5 gallons of water in the only jerrican that was left after the first capsize. Careful analysis of their story makes clear that, although they had to ration water when it was short, they did not really suffer from thirst. Rain was frequent, and they quickly learned to collect it when conditions were good. On the other hand, apart from a few mouthfuls from a can of corned beef they had nothing to eat. For the twelve days they spent adrift a complete fast increased their weakness and the torpor that soon set in after the exceptional efforts of the first few days, from which they would not be able to recover.

On the fifth day a bathe certainly did them a great deal of good, as they were able to stretch their cramped limbs. They saw some fish underneath the raft, but they had no fishing tackle and practically nothing to rig it from. As a matter of fact, they did not even try; their weakness seems to have destroyed their ability to think. However, their imagination remained active enough to give them both ideas of cannibalism; each one weighed up how much there was left to eat of the other. It seems probable that in the final days their relations, on a more or less unconscious level, deteriorated.

Alain Bombard had good reason to stress that the Mediterranean is not favourable to survival; but he also explained that all its disadvantages were offset by one positive factor – the density of shipping which would lead one to expect speedy rescue. Unfortunately, this becomes questionable when we realize that Lucien and Catherine met a dozen or so ships in this dramatic conflict of the two survivors' hopes and the unconscious indifference of those sitting safely aboard their ships. About 2.00 a.m. on 15 September, a few hours after they abandoned ship, a ship passed them less than a mile away. Lucien fired a single flare with too much angle on it. The boat turned. Then Lucien lit one of his three hand-held flares. He waved it vigorously, burning himself badly. The ship knew that something was amiss near by; she scanned desperately with her searchlight. The second and third hand-held flares were lit, but without success – at dawn the ship which could have saved them followed some inexplicable imperative and resumed course.

As already mentioned, a dozen or so boats passed near them, some within earshot, some just a short distance away, splashing them with wash. It has to be said at this point, before we set about drawing any conclusions about survival at sea, that one can never rely on this new generation of sailors whose only horizon is what a sleepy radar operator sees on his screen.

It was not until 26 September, the twelfth day, that this comment was disproved. Crushed, prostrate and desperate at having missed all the Balearic Isles, just as they had decided that survival was too difficult and they would make a quick end to it by drinking all the rest of their water at once for a last sensation of well-being, they were spotted at fifty yards, despite 8-foot troughs, and rescued by a cargo ship, the *Abel Tasman*.

31

Maurice and Maralyn Bailey

(1973)

Of the accounts of survival at sea known to me the Baileys' experience comes second only to Bombard's voluntary scientific experiment and in the same class as the Robertsons' adventure. All the previous tales have something to offer in the way of information, but they are seldom as comprehensive and enlightening as that of this couple who, with the exception of Poon Lim, would seem to hold the endurance record for survival at sea. In cases where I have found an account too difficult to summarize, as with those of Bombard and the Robertson family, I have handled it by breaking it down into a number of key fields. This is clearly the way to tackle the Baileys' story too.

On 4 March 1973 the *Auralyn*, Maurice and Maralyn Bailey's yacht, was about 300 miles off San Cristobal in the Galapagos Islands when its hull was pierced by a sperm whale maddened by the wound inflicted on it some hours earlier by a whaler. The result was a hole of 12 in by 18 ins on the waterline. They tried to seal off the hole using the spare jib and some blankets, but when this failed they had no alternative but to abandon the sinking yacht. Forty or fifty minutes elapsed before they decided to launch their Avon liferaft and their small inflatable dinghy, and it was only in the last few minutes that they set about collecting the essentials for survival.

At this point I feel bound to add a comment, hesitant as I am to criticize a man and woman whose human feelings rose above the animal instinct for survival. In their book[1] there is a poignant photograph of the *Auralyn* as she went down in a calm sea. Maurice Bailey gives us a first-hand view through the eyes of a victim of shipwreck. This is a splendid photograph, but at the same time it disturbs me. Knowing what they were to experience in the next 117 days, I can envisage all the things that might have been done in the time needed to take a photograph before the boat sank. Their exploit was a marvel-

---

1. *117 Days Adrift*, Maurice and Maralyn Bailey, Nautical Publishing Company, 1974

lous one, but anything they could have picked up at that point would
have made it less arduous. I think every reader, sailor or no, should

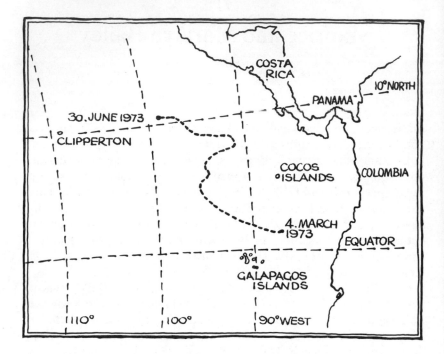

study this photograph; hidden within it is everything that makes the
difference between survival and failure to survive. For the Baileys it
was a case of all's well that ends well, so there is no more to be said.
However, I would advise anyone who faces these few minutes before a
sinking ship goes down to forget about photography and collect
everything they can like fishing tackle, a gaff, an underwater gun,
some extra provisions or another jerrican of water. All these things will
prove invaluable.[2]

But to return to 4 March: a few minutes later the *Auralyn* vanished
below the surface. The two survivors searched all round the debris that

2. I feel the author uses hindsight rather harshly here. It must surely have been right
(and in accordance with the principles he himself stresses elsewhere) to concentrate on
trying to save the yacht; and the procedure the Baileys used (the generally recommended one) requires two people. One does not know exactly what Maurice Bailey's
motives in taking the photograph were, but any evidence of this kind can be extremely
valuable – though secondary in importance, of course, to the saving of life. [Trans.]

was still floating. Then they took stock. By way of craft they had an Avon liferaft 4 ft 6 in in diameter – which the manufacturers quite seriously recommend as the model for four – and an inflatable dinghy of the same make, highly stable and seemingly indestructible. This type of dinghy is 9 ft long, divided into two by an inflatable thwart; it has two fixed rowlocks and a pair of oars. Even with the most stringent rationing, they had an absolute maximum of twenty days' water and provisions. Now let us consider the different aspects of their story.

As far as water was concerned, the Baileys started by imposing on themselves a ration way below essential needs. They took this mouthful by mouthful but always wondered whether it would not be better to swallow their daily ration all at once, since dividing it up made them feel they never quenched their thirst. In fact, this was only a subjective impression of little physiological importance. Very early on they faced the problem of their reserve of fresh water being contaminated with seawater. I shall return to this point later. With the first rainfall they ran up against all the same snags as their predecessors, finishing up with water that tasted of salty rubber and was absolutely undrinkable. But they reacted to the situation by drawing some highly sophisticated conclusions; as a result, they never encountered any real dehydration problem.

It is on the subject of fishing that the Baileys' experience is unbeatable. Although they had no fishing tackle, they were able to hold out three times as long as the Robertsons and almost twice as long as Bombard. Their first hooks were safety-pins cut short and doubled back. Patience in the face of every setback and a fisherman's instinct known, I would think, only to the initiated, enabled them to catch fish after fish – so much so that, as it continues their book almost becomes a kind of fishing manual. There are descriptions of all the methods used, from the simplest to the most complicated; of the behaviour of marine life; of the tastes of each species; of the pieces to be kept as bait; and so on. They even made their dinghy into a kind of aquarium to keep a reserve of live fish and small turtles.

Turtles are very common in the region of the Pacific where the Baileys were adrift; in their story I have totted up a total bag of twenty-two sizeable turtles. When their catches followed one another too quickly, they had the brilliant idea of securing the turtles with a line round one of their fins and letting them swim round the raft. They even tried to make the turtles tow them. Seabirds called in on them too – blue-faced Pacific boobies, brown boobies and petrels. These were duly caught and eaten.

This quick examination of the Baileys' victualling arrangements would be deceptive if it gave the impression that their life was idyllic. It represented a diet made up entirely of protein. This kept them alive for an exceptionally long time but caused severe physical deterioration. Apart from major skin problems amounting to chronic ulcers, they suffered amongst other complaints considerable loss of weight, stiffness of the joints, muscular atrophy and attacks of dysentery. Nevertheless, within their weakened bodies and behind their emaciated faces there lay, as with most of the survivors whose stories are told here, an almost indomitable will. Of course, they suffered a few periods of depression and anxiety, but these were always fleeting and always surmounted.

The eighth ship they saw, on 30 June, was a Korean fishing boat, the *Weolmi 306*, about half a mile off. This was the one that rescued them.

It would be wrong to close the Baileys' story without quoting the few lines in which they tell of the last few minutes of their life as survivors.

I called to Maralyn, 'Stop waving, save your strength.' She ignored me and continued to wave as the ship showed its stern to us. It was the first we had seen for 43 days.

'Please come back,' Maralyn shouted. 'Please . . . . ' I was oblivious now of the ship's movement as I knelt in the dinghy. Maralyn was still imploring it to return. Let it go on, I thought, this is our world now on the sea, amongst the birds and the turtles and the fish.

Maralyn had suddenly stopped her entreaties but continued to wave her jacket quietly. I looked up and stared for some time at the ship. I looked long and hard at it in disbelief. Was it returning or was it a trick of my eyes? Maralyn looked across at me, her eyes moist and gleaming. 'It's coming back,' she said.

Yes indeed – 'let it go on . . . this is our world now on the sea, amongst the birds and the turtles and the fish.' To my mind this thought that crossed Maurice Bailey's mind holds the most important lesson that a survivor has to learn.

Part Two

Introduction

In embarking on the second part of this book I must stress my awareness of all the dimensions of the great paradox of talking about survival at sea when one is sitting comfortably at one's desk, without having ever oneself lived through the numerous problems the book seeks to resolve. It is true that I have sailed round the world and been through some terrible storms. I shall never forget the long hours I spent under the threat of a typhoon, but I was all the time in the safety of a big boat with ultra-modern means of communication; and these by and large offset the sensation of becoming a castaway. It is true that I have experienced thirst, even to the point of not being able to drink when the water I was longing for was offered me. I have known the sickening sensation which makes one reject the water that means life, until rehydration of the skin with a good long shower relaxes the spasm of one's gullet and allows one to swallow the first swig of liquid. But all that only lasted a few hours. I have known hunger too; for as a young Parisian I lived under the German occupation of World War II – but never to the point of gnawing at whatever turned up or of suffering hallucinations. I have been cold and I have been hot – but this means nothing in comparison with the sufferings disclosed by the tales that make up the first part of this book.

In fact I do not feel worthy to sit in judgement over and to criticize all those whose adventures we have studied. Often, as I settle down in the depths of an armchair, book or papers in hand, my hackles rise at the way certain survivors failed to collect rainwater as they should have done, or did not even try to catch the fish swimming alongside them, or wasted the blood of a turtle or threw its liver into the sea, or refused to taste the flesh of a booby. Hindsight from other stories emphasizes these mistakes.

We have to accept straightaway that any one of these errors may be fatal. It was to expose them to the light of day that I decided to publish a file of old papers that had lain barren for years in a drawer.

I felt it would be clear and logical to design this second part of the book in the form of a chapter for each of the major problems a survivor may suffer. In an excellent article that appeared in the magazine *Bateaux* of April 1970 Dr H. Tanguy notes four major and two minor problems that the survivor at sea faces. Drowning, cold, panic and thirst are the four main ones; hunger and exhaustion are, he feels, the two lesser ones. Clearly, any classification of this kind, logical as it may be in terms of the story of one shipwreck, is completely academic in the circumstances of another. This is the price one pays for hasty classification. What is clear, however, after reading these stories, is that it is not a question of major or minor problems, but of resolving them.

Certainly, some problems are easier to solve than others. For instance, thirst is easy to solve in latitudes and seasons where it frequently rains, and so on these occasions it becomes a secondary problem. Fishing is easy if you have tackle and there are plenty of fish in the water, and so hunger becomes simply a matter of discipline. In the tropics the cold which was responsible for the suffering and maiming of Blackburn is something to be welcomed with open arms. Without giving too many examples we can see that each of the major problems may become the principal one, dependent on season, latitude or the equipment available when the ship is wrecked. We must be careful, then, about putting an order of priority on these factors and treat each of them as the one that may and often does prove vital.

TRANSLATOR'S NOTE. It may be helpful to the reader to explain at this stage that, while for obvious reasons most of the stories in Part I relate to large warships or merchant ships of their day, the advice in the second part is mainly aimed at yachtsmen and power-boat owners.

In fairness to the author, I should perhaps explain that the footnotes in this part are mine. Like the introductory note, they represent an attempt to acquaint the reader with the arguments on both sides of the 'seawater and protein v abstention and carbohydrate' controversy. In this part the publishers, at my request, have made great efforts to reproduce the original text of English works quoted, and to follow existing translations, with which the reader may be familiar, of French and other works.

32
The battle against thirst

Ocean and desert have one feature in common; for those trying to survive in them they are the kingdom of thirst. This is one of the most difficult problems to solve, for the time it takes for thirst to sap insidiously away at the human organism is short enough. Man is much more sensitive to dehydration than to hunger, and the whole train of troubles thirst brings in its wake soon becomes irreversible. What is more, its effects on morale and psychological state are more damaging than those of hunger. So thirst is practically always a main point of concern for survivors.

We can consider the problem under three main heads: (1) methods of obtaining fresh water and substitutes in the shape of other hypotonic liquids (see page 127); (2) methods of conserving fresh water when supplies can be obtained only at long intervals; and (3) methods of absorption, which will clearly be quite different depending on the ease of getting water in the zone or season in which the survivor finds himself.

1. Obtaining fresh water

Reserve of water on a liferaft

In theory most rafts carry a reserve of fresh water in metal cans. This ensures that by strict rationing the victim of shipwreck has several days to organize his survival. If, however, the raft is occupied by a larger number of people than it was designed for – as is very often the case in practice – this reserve of water will suffice only for a period of transition and adaptation from normal hydration to a quite different diet of water intake. The fact is that the amounts of water provided on inflatable rafts are pathetically small. This point is well illustrated by the French Order in Council published in the *Journal Officiel* of 24 January 1967. For Class I and II rafts respectively this stipulates 1500 ml (rather under 3 pints) and 600 ml (about 1 pint) of water per head.

Reserve of water transferred to the liferaft when abandoning ship

From what has just been said it follows that, no matter what the pressures of time, everyone at the moment of shipwreck must make it a matter of priority to recover as much fresh water as they can. For this purpose it is absolutely essential that vessels of all kinds take two precautions. First, the entire reserves of water must not be in the tanks but always spread over several locations; above all, some plastic jerricans of fresh water must be provided. Second, these jerricans must be only partly filled, with enough air left in them to ensure positive buoyancy. The Robertson family, which had to abandon ship more quickly than anyone else on record is an example of these two complementary basic principles. Lynn remembered to clear away some jerricans of water and throw them in the sea, but they sank because they were too full.

No jerrican of water should be taken on board a yacht or any other boat without assurance of its positive buoyancy; in other words, at least one must be tested every time they are filled.

For survivors these jerricans clearly become precious receptacles. It goes without saying that any other liquid and particularly some bottles of alcohol[1] are worthy of a place on board a liferaft, if the shipwrecked crew have time to snatch a few things from the bar before having to embark on the survival craft. Apart from their value as disinfectants in the multiple skin problems to which survivors are exposed, these spirits serve as a morale booster, a tranquillizer and a significant source of energy.

Condensation

Condensation is a rare source of water. In fact, it is only mentioned by a few survivors, among them Bombard, and by him only during his passage down the western Mediterranean. It can arise only in a climate and season in which the differences of day and night temperature are large enough to cause condensation to form during the second part of the night, like the dew on our lawns in autumn. When these climatic conditions are satisfied and the weather is calm, a layer of small drops of fresh water is to be found each morning on all surfaces exposed to the air. This can be sponged up (Bombard had a sponge, which could be a useful thing in many other ways too); or it can be absorbed,

---

1. Authoritative British opinion holds that alcohol is dehydrating and a depressant and should *never* be consumed under survival conditions.

although this takes longer, by any kind of cloth as long as this is not impregnated with salt. In the early days of his experiment Bombard was able to collect in this way ½ litre (1 pint) of water each morning. This was also the case with Vidot and Corgat and Teehu Makimare and his companions in the Indian Ocean but they were reduced to licking this fine dew. If the surfaces on which this condensation forms are impregnated with salt, condensation is clearly out as a source of fresh water. But it does offer a chance of washing sails and other cloths and getting rid of the salt, and this saves a bit of time when it rains – by no means a negligible advantage.

Rain

Rain clearly becomes the main source of fresh water once the duration of survival conditions or the number of survivors – or usually, in fact, a combination of the two – has exhausted the reserves we have just been discussing. Many accounts also tell us that among the first thoughts after shipwreck are estimates of the time which might reasonably elapse before the first rain in the season and latitude in question. A number of survivors who were in a position to steer their raft have gone further by making immediately for latitudes which offer the maximum chance of finding rain at the particular time of year.

This first rain has almost always proved a saving grace; most tales recount how anxiously it was awaited. Almost as numerous, by contrast, are the stories where the survivors have forgotten or disregarded the chores that have to be done to take full advantage of rain. One has to realize that it is not just a question of opening one's jaws wide – that only provides a square inch or two of collecting surface! The first requirement is to arrange the largest possible collecting surface. This is almost always the roof of the raft if there is one; otherwise oilskins perhaps or lifejackets – or even, in a story we have not included because the information is so sparse, an upside-down umbrella. In fact, anything that is watertight enough to hold water for a limited time will do. In the worst conditions, in an open raft or dinghy with nothing that will serve as a collector, the bottom of the raft has to fill this role.

Whatever the collecting surface, the first problem is getting the salt off it. Most survivors of shipwreck usually seem to steer clear of the trap of allowing salt to get into everything. Most have pulled a face as they wetted their mouths with the long-awaited water with an unspeakable colour, a taste of rubber and, worst of all, saltier than the sea. They have learnt the simple rule of clearing the salt off any surface on which rain water is collected. In most cases it is a question of waiting impatiently until the rain itself has washed the surface; but it is a battle against time to collect as much water as possible before the rain stops. Waiting for the rain to wash the surface wastes large quantities of rainwater, and no one knows how long the shower will continue to dispense its drops of mercy.

I think therefore that the best technique is as follows: as soon as potential rain clouds build up on the horizon, all collecting surfaces should be sprinkled with seawater or, even better, completely washed in seawater to dissolve and clear away most of the high concentration of salt deposited on them. The sodium chloride content of seawater is far from saturation point, so seawater will still dissolve a lot of salt. It would even be safe to continue washing surfaces with seawater until the first drops of rain started to fall. Then, the moment the rain squall starts, the rubber can quickly be cleansed of its film of salt. These precautions are the only way to win the race against time. The big problem then becomes storage, but this will be dealt with at length later (see page 132). Even slightly brackish water must be collected, for it can be very useful. If the rain lasts long enough and the quantities collected are large enough, all receptacles can be refilled in turn with purer and purer water.

Let us suppose now that everything which will serve to hold water is full to the brim and securely stowed on the raft – for one knows very well that rain, unfortunately, does not always fall in an ideal sea state. Let us suppose too that our thirsts have been largely quenched. At this point rainwater has another part to play. It is, in fact, a very important one and should be begun as soon as rain starts falling. This is to take a good shower. Right through the work of washing, rinsing, gathering and storing the rainwater, the survivors should put shyness on one side, strip and take advantage of the gentle action of fresh water on their bodies. They should rub themselves vigorously all over, using a cloth as a kind of loofah. Lesions and ulcers aggravated by the salt will respond to a more gentle treatment of washing in rainwater and dabbing lightly. Obviously, the kind of action outlined here really only applies in temperate latitudes and for relatively short periods. The evidence suggests that, because of survival conditions, many victims of shipwreck have problems with their bronchial tubes or worse with their whole respiratory system. It is therefore important to regulate the extent of this shower, so that people do not shiver with cold after having suffered the torments of very high temperatures.[2]

Brackish water

We have just seen that in the event of a shower that does not last long enough for all available receptacles to be filled some brackish water obtained from the final rinsings of the collecting surfaces should be stored. We shall see later how this can be used.

Obtaining other hypotonic liquids

The term 'hypotonic liquids' really means any liquid whose composition is largely similar to that of fresh water because of the absence of large quantities of dissolved salts. The main ones of interest here are 'fish juice', and the blood of sea turtles.[3]

Once again it was Alain Bombard who explained how a hypotonic liquid could be collected from any fish caught. (This assumes that the survivor has taken to fishing – a topic we shall be discussing later.) Water constitutes 60-80 per cent of the weight of fish, depending on the species. The problem is extracting it. There are two possible methods. The first, with a fish of good size, is to make a longitudinal incision in the back passing about an inch from the roots of the dorsal fins and deep enough to reach the main muscular tissue. When the fish is held on its side, the groove so formed fills with a liquid which can be drunk straight off either by pouring it carefully into one's mouth with the head of the fish turned slightly upwards rather like a waterbottle or – the safer and less wasteful method – by first pouring it into a receptacle. A second incision parallel to the first on the other side of the dorsal fins can be used; and further ones can be made an inch or so apart over the whole surface of the upper half of the fish. To save time several incisions can be made at once with the fish held over the receptacle. On the lower (ventral) surface the knife penetrates into the abdominal cavity; no juice can be recovered from there.

The second method consists of squeezing the juice out without

2. British opinion favours 'the more the merrier' in tropical rain, provided those concerned are stripped. The danger lies in having wet clothes on when the temperature drops at night.

3. This point is so important that it merits fuller explanation. In simple terms the 'tonicity' of a liquid depends on the amount of dissolved salts it contains. All human and other animal body fluids are in general of the same 'tonicity'; they are said to be 'isotonic' with normal human body fluid. Pure fresh water is '*hypo*tonic', i.e. has fewer salts than body fluids. Seawater (for instance) is '*hyper*tonic'; it contains more salts. 'Fish juice' probably consists mainly of fish lymph and would in any case be isotonic. Thus it is unlikely to decrease dehydration in man unless taken in great quantities. Even then the effort involved in catching and squeezing enough fish might offset any benefit.

waiting for it to exude into an incision in the muscle. Bombard took a lemon squeezer with him for this, but in fact any kind of cloth will do. The fish is first cleaned, its entrails and offal being set aside for other uses. Then its muscular tissues are first cut into strips and then diced, rather in the way the people of Tahiti prepare their raw fish. These cubes are put in a piece of cloth, a handkerchief for instance, which is then twisted so as to compress all the flesh and squeeze the juice out of it. Certainly, this method does not provide the 60-80 per cent of water the fish's flesh contains, but it does produce a substantial amount, 250 450 millilitres per kilogram of fish, depending on the species (1 gill-½ pint per pound). We shall see later how this partially dehydrated flesh can be used.

Fish, particularly large ones, contain two other varieties of hypotonic liquid in addition to what might be called the 'muscle juice'. These are the cerebro-spinal fluid and the humours of the eyes, which the Baileys say they particularly liked. The amounts in question are indeed very small in comparison with the amount of muscle juice, but it is worth bearing in mind that every drop of water and every change of taste it brings may tip the scales in the right direction and thus cannot be neglected. The cerebro-spinal fluid is contained in the spinal sac which protects the spinal column of fish. After drawing off the juice, the spinal canal can be opened near the tail by passing the blade of a knife between two vertebrae with the fish held head downwards. All you have to do then is to turn the fish head upwards to collect this particularly clear and pure liquid. With a large fish each vertebra can then be crushed between the teeth like a nut and the liquid sucked out of the spongy tissue of the bone. As for the eyes, they need only to be taken out, and then sucked and munched. The Baileys also tell us that they are rich in Vitamin C.

The second source of hypotonic liquid is the blood of sea turtles. We have seen in the accounts of shipwrecks in Part I the large proportion of survivors who owe their life to this blood. William Okeley and his four shipmates gained the strength to reach the Balearics thanks to the turtle they caught on the fifth day of their escape from Algiers. In those days turtles must have been more common in the Mediterranean than they are now, for recent survivors in the Mediterranean – Bombard in 1952 and then Lucien and Catherine in 1972 – never saw one. Nevertheless, Spanish fishermen confirm that they still exist. The best chances of meeting one nowadays are clearly in tropical waters. We shall discuss in Chapter 33 how to catch, kill and dismember turtles. However, it is worth stressing now that the blood simply must be kept and not poured into the sea as it was by Gilboy and many others after him. One might also bear in mind that the blood Gilboy poured on the water from his first turtle attracted a huge hammerhead shark.

The blood can be drunk as it is. If there is any over after the survivors have quenched their thirst, it should be left in a container to coagulate forming a clump of red corpuscles surrounded by a faintly straw-coloured liquid, the plasma. These two parts of the turtle's blood can, as we shall see, be used in many ways in the preparation of various dishes.

Urine

The consumption of urine is frequently mentioned in accounts of survival in the desert, but I have come across only one victim of shipwreck, Captain Bontekoé in 1619, who admits to use of this method. It is true that as soon as the total liquid intake is reduced the daily quantity of urine falls. A condition known to doctors as oliguria or urine deficit appears. Jacques Vignes, whose book *La rage de survivre* includes the story of Lucien and Catherine, reports that the amount of urine passed by these two still remained substantial the fourth day after they abandoned ship, although all they had had to drink (as the reader can easily work out for himself from data given in the book) was 6 litres of water between them. This corresponds to 750 millilitres per head per day (about 1¼ pints). One must appreciate that this statement may be a little coloured by the fact that the time of their shipwreck was one of exceptionally low temperatures for the Mediterranean. The two survivors were soaked and shivering all the time. The cold gave rise to a condition known as pollakiuria in which small quantities of urine are passed very frequently but the total quantity excreted remains far below normal.

One must assume, therefore, that the survivor on a very low daily water ration would reach a condition of urine deficit in thirty-six to forty-eight hours. However, although more and more concentrated in compensation for its reduced quantity, his urine is none the less a hypotonic liquid and so has to be considered as a possible source of daily intake – a kind of recycling of waste. The 15-20 g of urea per litre of urine, even when concentrated as in this situation, can be metabolized by the organism without major problems provided that the intake of urine is only occasional. On the other hand, urine must never be stored because the formation of nitrites makes it toxic.[4]

4. Modern British thinking opposes intake of urine, since urine is always *hyper*tonic and even more so in a dehydrated subject (see also page 4).

Use of snow and ice

We have already seen that a certain proportion of survival stories concern high latitudes, and in these harsh conditions these two crystalline forms of water can be used to quench thirst. Everyone knows that it takes enormous quantities of snow to obtain a little fresh water. Quenching one's thirst by letting snow melt in the mouth is the worst and slowest method, though often the only feasible one. If a large receptacle is available, it must be filled to the brim with snow, and some means must be found of melting this. This produces a more significant quantity of water in one operation.

The problem of ice is rather different. There are two types of ice. One is fresh-water ice formed from snow under the combined action of weather, temperature, wind and the pressure of superimposed layers of snow. These forces drive out the air and make the flakes pack. The second is sea ice, which is frozen seawater and is saline. The first is clearly an excellent source of fresh water, but the second is very valuable too. In sea ice the salt loses its solubility and collects in pockets in the form of a highly concentrated saline liquor. As a result, the ice itself is hardly salty at all. Furthermore, as sea ice approaches its melting point, the brine concentrate gradually escapes and the overall salt content is very rapidly reduced. Once this has happened, sea ice can equally well be used as a source of fresh water.[5]

Vegetable products from the sea

In 1954 Wiktors Zvejnieks survived forty-six days on almost nothing but floating seaweed. Apart from the extreme case of the Saragossa Sea, there are sea areas where masses of seaweed are found and more still where substantial quantities are carried on the currents.

Wherever it comes from, seaweed is a godsend for the survivor.[6] By chewing it, he can extract a certain number of calories and a hypotonic

5. Three points here deserve further explanation. First, the body of icebergs normally consists of glacial (fresh water) ice. Second, old sea ice, which is potable, can be distinguished by its clear to bluish appearance; fresh sea ice, which has a high salt content, looks grey. In any event, it is desirable to chip away some of the surface layers which will consist of newly frozen spray or seawater.

6. Here again the net benefit is questionable. The seawater and/or dried salt on the surface is likely to offset any gain from contained hypotonic juice. The calories gained are unlikely to be of importance except in very long-term exposure or survival conditions. It might, however, be possible to slit or peel some of the fleshier types of seaweed with a knife and squeeze or suck out the hypotonic juice.

liquid. Similarly, it is worth remembering that the currents in tropical regions quite often carry coconuts. Harold Dixon and his fellow airmen on their raft in the Pacific maintained their strength and kept hope alive in this way. Unfortunately, coconuts found adrift are very often almost 'dry'. The coconut milk has gradually disappeared, while the pulp has become rancid, almost exposing the copra. Although at this stage it has a revolting smell of soap, this pulp is still a very rich food with a significant water content.

In addition, the survivor who is lucky enough to pick up a coconut always runs into trouble with the thick layer of hairs that protects the nut itself. One needs a good knife and a good deal of patience to remove the hair and get to the shell. Then there is the problem of finding something firm to rest the shell on to break it. If shaking the coconut produces the characteristic noise of liquid inside it, the shell must not be broken as this would scatter the milk in all directions. Two of the three 'eyes' to be found at one of the ends should be pierced so that the liquid can be sucked out.

Making your own fresh water

A survivor suffering from thirst in the midst of all that salt water must bitterly regret not having thought of providing himself with some way of desalinating seawater. There are two processes.

The first uses the principle of ion exchange. The equipment consists of a bag made of special permeable rubber into which the seawater is placed. When the bag is shaken, a synthetic ion exchanger made up of zeolite mixed with silver and barium transforms the sodium chloride and magnesium salts of the seawater into magnesium oxide and silver chloride, both of which are insoluble. These stay in the bag while the water, now 'fresh', passes through it. The operation can be repeated several times before the ion exchange substance loses its effectiveness.

The second method is the solar still, a miniature replica of the desalination works which use the greenhouse effect. Water placed within a glass frame warms up much more quickly in the sun than the glass, so that water vapour condenses on the glass. This glass needs only to be tilted for the drops of water to run down it; they are easily collected at the bottom in a small channel. The yield of this method is improved by blackening the bottom of the containers; by adding colouring material to the water; by insulating the frame; and by reducing radiation losses by using materials of low emissivity. The solar energy can be concentrated by a focusing reflector.

For survival at sea the apparatus takes the form of a conical plastic bag, inflatable by mouth, with a black bottom. The condensed fresh water collects round the sides and runs down the outer wall. The model I am familiar with, the Airborne Solar Still used by the Royal Navy and the Royal Air Force produces 1.5 litres of water per day under conditions prevailing on the Equator in the month of March and 0.5 litres per day at latitude 51° North in February.

It is difficult to comprehend why none of the victims of shipwreck of the last few decades has had the benefit of a still of this kind. Its price is very reasonable; and it cannot be called bulky, for when vacuum-packed its size is only 9 in by 12.5 in by 1 in. The only possible explanation is that all sailors are convinced that shipwreck is something that happens to other people.

The question arises whether the survivor who has no solar still can make one with the few materials he is likely to have or might collect for the purpose. This seems unlikely. I have thought up a number of rigs starting with receptacles and plastic bags of the kind that are now to be found everywhere and might well be on board an inflatable raft. I have to admit that all these attempts ended in failure. It should be laid down in the regulations that one or more solar stills should be included in the equipment of Class I and II liferafts.[7]

2.   Methods of storing and conserving fresh water

Survivors at sea must always think of the future. While struggling to survive from one day to the next, they must also organize themselves to survive until they reach the safety of a ship or the shore. Since, with very rare exceptions, they can obtain fresh water only intermittently, the creation of a reserve of it must be one of their main concerns.

The great majority of the accounts which make up the first part of this book show how survival at sea is a matter of moral and physical ups and downs, the frequency of which is directly related to the facilities for storing water. So this is an important aspect which needs exploring in detail.

The survivor will indeed have the jerricans he has salvaged. He also has a certain number of cans, receptacles of every kind and other materials; but many of these cannot be properly sealed. Such containers will serve to store water during prolonged rain but they are not

7. Yes, but the successful use of solar stills in a liferaft at sea requires training and practice. Perhaps clubs which are Royal Yachting Association training centres could acquire a training model.

a great deal of use because the sea and the motion it imparts to the raft will quickly empty them or foul them with seawater.

There is therefore a twofold problem – having or making receptacles which are as watertight as possible, and preventing them being contaminated by seawater or by algal growths. The best way of storing water is, without doubt, in the conventional plastic jerricans which will have been put on board at the last moment, with their large air bubbles ensuring positive buoyancy. The survivor's main concern is to stow these firmly in the raft. Sadly, there are all too many examples of survivors, having acted with foresight and taken as many jerricans as possible, losing most of them in a capsize or simply through a violent movement of the raft or one of its occupants.[8] Once securely stowed, the jerricans can be filled to the brim the first time it rains. It is well worth checking that they are watertight, and, if necessary, screwing down the cap over a piece of cloth to improve the seal.[9]

Sometimes, however, there will be no jerricans, or not enough, so it is worth suggesting a number of other possibilities. The first is to convert all available plastic bags into water bottles. Several dozen bags should be included in the equipment of the liferaft for this purpose. They can be closed with a knot made in the plastic itself or a bit of string, in exactly the same way as a child ties up a toy balloon. If there are no plastic bags, Bombard's idea of storing water in his inflatable pillow (in fact, the thwart of his liferaft) is a sound one; or again Dougal Robertson's technique of using a compartment of his defunct liferaft as a storage tank. In this instance he was using the compartment as a float at the bow of the dinghy he still had left. His first idea was to put a certain amount of water in it and blow it up hard to compensate for the reduction of buoyancy. Then, when the compartment was punctured and started leaking, he made from it several cylinders tied off at each end with pieces of string. Each of these cylinders provided him with a large water tank.

I should like to suggest a further expedient in case all these possibilities are ruled out. This assumes that the fishing problem has been solved and is based on borrowing an idea from the butcher and using the intestinal loops of big fish and turtles. The intestine of a large turtle

8. Stowing jerricans on board is, of course, the correct procedure for lifeboats, rigid liferafts and the larger inflatables. With four or six-man inflatables it may often be preferable to leave the jerricans in their buoyant state and tow them, at least initially (see also Chapter 40).

9. If cloth as opposed to plastic is used, it must be completely enclosed by the cap to avoid wicking action.

forms a cylinder several yards long. This can be cut at its two ends and emptied by squeezing out the pieces it contains, which will then serve as bait for more fishing. Great care must be taken not to tear it. It can then be turned inside out like the finger of a glove, forming a long tube with the mucous surface on the outside and the normal outer (peritoneal) surface on the inside. One end is closed off with a knot tied in the intestine itself or, better still, with a piece of string; the result is an elastic-walled container capable of storing several litres of water. It would pay to scrape the mucous surface, now on the outside, to avoid the villi going bad. This can be used as a treat for tripe-lovers![10]

The intestine of big fish, and also their swim-bladder, can be used in the same way but will clearly have a smaller capacity. When water is stored in improvised containers of this kind, it must be checked daily. It would be terrible to ration oneself strictly while some of the reserves of water were getting polluted and becoming undrinkable, so that they have to be thrown overboard or used for some other purpose. Spray and the water from waves which break over the raft in heavy seas get everywhere and may make the water brackish.

Even with plastic jerricans exposure to the sun may bring about the growth of microscopic algae which multiply rapidly, giving the water a greenish tinge. If this happens, the water can be filtered through the finest available cloth, recovered and drunk first.[11] Likewise, when there is heavy rain, one should have no qualms about emptying a jerrican full of old water and refilling it with cleaner water.

3. The battle against thirst and methods of fresh-water intake

Thirst is a sensation produced within the human organism when the level of hydration of its cells begins to drop. Normally, this hydration is the result of an equilibrium established between intake and loss. The intakes are, of course, the liquids taken through the mouth either as drinks or contained in food. The losses are the water in urine, faeces (particularly in cases of diarrhoea), evaporation from the skin and perspiration, water vapour in the breath, and so on. Broadly speaking, then, dehydration starts when the losses outweigh the liquid intake. Thirst is the warning sign of this imbalance, and to counter it the

10. But see notes elsewhere on consumption of protein by subjects in a dehydrated condition.
11. These algae tend to form in any plastic water container, even in the dark. They can be inhibited by adding a small quantity (about one-tenth of the purifying dose) of chlorinating tablets or potassium permanganate, either of which is likely to be found in a first-aid and or survival kit.

survivor must follow two lines of action. This is particularly so in high ambient temperatures, since the losses clearly increase with temperature.

A few figures will serve very well as an introduction to advice on what can be done to limit these losses. At a mean day air temperature of 43°C (109.4°F) the possible duration of survival with complete rest and with no intake of liquid fluctuates around the twenty-four-hour mark. We should note straight away that these temperature conditions are unlikely to be found at sea for, fortunately, the nights lower the mean temperature under consideration here. The same is true for approximately forty-eight hours of survival at a mean day air temperature of 37°C (98.6°F). On the other hand, the following sets of figures are important:

Mean air temperature 32°C (89.6°F), survival time 3 days
Mean air temperature 26°C (78.8°F), survival time 4 days
Mean air temperature 21°C (69.8°F), survival time 8 days
Mean air temperature 15°C (59°F), survival time 17 days[12]

This explains some of the accounts in the first part of this book which may have stretched the reader's credibility. These tell of survivors who went for ten or fifteen days and sometimes longer without drinking. Looking back on these stories we can see that their authors' experiences took place in latitudes where the mean day air temperature was well below 15°C.

The careful reader, however, will have realized that other accounts tell of record periods of going without water in the tropics – John Mackay, for instance, lived for twenty-one days in the rigging of the *Juno* in the Bay of Bengal with nothing but some heavy rain on the ninth day. The fact is that Mackay, like his fellow survivors and many later ones, understood what could be done against water losses.

Prevention of loss of fluid from the organism

The countering of water losses is based on bathing, sprinkling the body with seawater and wrapping it in damp cloths. In the tropics the temperature of the seawater is always way below the ambient temperature of the air, at least during the hours of sunshine. In these conditions the comparative coolness of the seawater must be used to reduce losses

12. This last figure seems high.

through the skin.[13] Dips should be taken very frequently and last for several minutes, long enough for the blood to benefit from the coolness and have its temperature reduced by a tenth of a degree or so. This is, in effect, one of the principles used in treatment by artificial hibernation, when ice packs are placed on the carotid arteries in the neck, the axillary arteries under the armpits, the femoral arteries in the groin, or the popliteal arteries at the back of the knees. Bathing also gives an opportunity for exercises in a state of reduced weight. These are extremely valuable in dealing with the stiffened joints and muscular atrophy suffered by those who remain virtually immobile in the cramped interiors of their rafts. Every survivor who has used this method has experienced a moment of intense euphoria during these bathes. The majority, however, have deprived themselves of this because of a twofold fear – of not being able to summon up the strength necessary to get back on board the raft, or of sharks. (Not to mention those, among them Bombard, who have seen their raft drift away more quickly than they expected and have been able to return to it only because they were strong swimmers!)

A little thought will resolve the first of these fears when there are two or more survivors. They can bathe in turn and help one another back on board. In any event it is wise for the person in the water to be attached to the raft by a light line, a rope, shirts knotted together or whatever is available, so that they can be recovered by their shipmate(s) if a gust of wind makes the raft drift fast. For a sole survivor who is still in good general condition there are considerable benefits in taking frequent bathes every day while remaining secured to the raft.

The second fear is a more serious one, for sharks are common in latitudes where frequent bathing is recommended; but it should not be exaggerated. Everyone knows that a shark comes and takes a close look to find out what is causing the shadow on the surface of the waves, which is how it sees the raft. Everyone knows that a shark is attracted by refuse thrown into the water or by the uncoordinated convulsions of a fish which has just been hooked. But there are no examples of sharks following a slowly drifting raft continuously, that is, for more than a few hours. This means that bathes can be taken near the raft, provided that none of the conditions which attract sharks is present. It is also worth stressing that among the many priority articles which should be

13. This is arguable. Quite apart from the risks of shark attack or separation from the raft, which the author mentions, any benefit in water retention is likely to be more than offset by water loss from exercise unless extreme precautions are taken to minimize effort.

included in a liferaft or the container attached to it are a mask and snorkel. These allow survivors to bathe in greater safety, for the arrival of a shark is not always signalled by the appearance of a dorsal fin.

If, however, the sea is rough, the rate of drift is high, or sharks are about, a substitute for bathing is to sprinkle oneself frequently with seawater. This, however, has the disadvantage of splashing the whole raft, making it damp all the time and, worse still, increasing the amount of salt with which it is coated.

It is therefore better to resort to the widely used and recommended technique of wetting cloths and wrapping oneself up in them as completely as possible. They should be wetted as often as is necessary to keep them damp enough to prevent all evaporation through the skin and, if there is a breeze, to remove a little heat.[14] However, it is inadvisable to bathe dressed or to wet the clothes one normally wears. These will in any case be heavily enough impregnated with salt to cause a host of skin problems without their being deliberately turned into a kind of salted outer skin.

Ways of taking in water

Whatever efforts may be made to minimize water losses, there is little doubt that the problem of liquid intake will quickly become the focus of a survivor's attention. In an attempt to simplify the explanation of the solutions to this problem, it may be helpful to think in terms of three eventualities.

In the first of these *the survivor is in an area and/or season with plentiful rain*. Rain falls almost every day and may even be more or less continuous. Here there is no problem. Even without large reserves – although it is always wise to establish these – the survivor does not suffer from thirst. In these conditions rain becomes an absolute pest. Everything gets soaked, and the raft has to be bailed frequently to maintain a safe degree of buoyancy. Rains like this are often accompanied by a dangerous sea, which in turn means that fishing is impossible. In these circumstances hunger may become the most pressing problem.

In the second eventuality *the survivor is in exactly the opposite situation*. He is in a region and/or season which offers him little chance of encountering any rain. The problem of liquid intake now becomes

14. This is the principle of the chagul used in hot dry climates to keep water cool. Water evaporates from the outer surface of the cloth, and its latent heat of evaporation takes up heat from the container surrounded by the cloth.

highly complex. To keep the discussion reasonably simple on the one hand and representative of the conditions most frequently experienced on the other it is best to consider two further possibilities.

i) Let us first examine the case of the survivor with a very large reserve of water at his disposal. The amount of water will, of course, immediately be worked out in terms of days of survival, and this calculation will depend on a host of other factors. The result will indicate the best line of action. It is impossible to go into all these factors in detail here; we shall be exploring them in later chapters. However, one has to establish a kind of equation. On one side of this is the calculated number of days of water, corrected to allow for possibilities of obtaining liquids from fish and turtles. On the other side comes the number of days likely to elapse before rescue, taking account of the position of the shipwreck, direction of winds and currents, any means of steering or propulsion offered by the raft, distance from the nearest land, distance from areas of frequent rain, distance from the most heavily used sea routes, and so on. One can never solve this idealized equation, but one can make some kind of approximation to a solution. On the answer obtained will rest the choice between a more or less passive attitude towards currents and a more active approach making use of wind to get to a certain area.

ii) The second case is that of the survivor whose reserves of water are limited to what he finds – to his horror – on his raft. At best he might have an extra gallon or two salvaged from the wreck. In these conditions his prospects of life are limited to a few days. It is then that he has to ask himself: *Must I or must I not drink seawater?*

We know that for centuries the drinking of seawater was absolutely forbidden. The history of shipwreck contained too many examples of victims who were already dehydrated and could no longer resist the craving to drink, and who paid rapidly and hideously with their lives for doing so. We also know that we owe it to Dr Bombard for having dispelled this prejudice and, using himself as a guinea-pig, for having proved that the intake of seawater was possible under certain closely defined conditions.

There is no need to go into the physiological factors which support his theory; his passage through the western Mediterranean followed by his Atlantic crossing is the most convincing proof. Three points should be considered, however. First, the key principle is not to wait until you are thirsty before starting to drink seawater. Second, the intake of seawater must be matched to the body's maximum needs of sodium chloride. For water with an NaCl content of 0.35 per cent by weight this amounts to about 800 ml per day. It must be taken in small doses, in eight or ten drinks of two or three mouthfuls each. Third, that this drinking of seawater must not go on for more than six to seven days – which, of course, gives the survivors time to organize themselves for fishing and thus obtain a source of hypotonic liquid. What is more, an interruption in the seawater diet allows its overall duration to be doubled.

To illustrate this one cannot do better than to quote from Alain Bombard's account of his Mediterranean passage:

From 25th to 28th May we drank sea-water: for four days in my case, and three in Jack's. During this period, our urine was perfectly normal and we had no sensation of thirst, but it should be remembered that it is essential not to wait for dehydration before drinking sea-water. We always found that a good remedy for any feeling of thirst, especially when our faces were in the sun, was to cover them with a towel or piece of cloth soaked in sea-water. Two days on sea perch then provided us with food and drink, but care had to be taken not to compensate too quickly for our fast. Six more days of sea-water followed, bringing us to the safety limit, and then two more days of fish, without any internal complications. In other words, out of fourteen days we drank fish juice for four and sea-water for ten. By interrupting the consumption of sea-water we were able to double what I considered the safety limit.

. . . I noticed none of the effects normally associated with the consumption of sea-water and neither Jack nor I vomited or had diarrhoea. On the contrary, we were subject to persistent constipation, without pain, coating of the tongue or mucous membranes or bad breath, and this lasted twelve days. However, we both suffered continuously from wind.

Bombard's theories are far from being universally accepted. In his book *Survive the Savage Sea* Dougal Robertson reproduces the Merchant Shipping Notice of November 1965, which I feel bound to quote here in full.[15]

Seafarers are reminded that if cast away they should NEVER UNDER ANY CIRCUMSTANCES DRINK SEA WATER which has not been through a distillation plant, or de-salinated by chemical means.

A belief has arisen recently that it is possible to replace or supplement fresh

15. Board of Trade Merchant Shipping Notice No. M.500, 'Drinking of Sea Water by Castaways', November 1965, reprinted March 1968. Reissued unamended, except for deletion of word 'recently' as Merchant Shipping Notice No. M.729, Department of Trade, August 1975.

water rations by drinking sea water in small amounts. This belief is wrong and DANGEROUS.

Drinking untreated sea water does a thirsty man no good at all. It will lead to increased dehydration and thirst and may kill him.

Even if there is no fresh water at all it should be remembered that men have lived for many days with nothing to drink, and therefore the temptation to drink untreated sea water must be strongly resisted.

With the greatest respect to the Maritime Division of British Department of Trade and Industry it has to be said that whoever wrote that circular has no understanding of the problem of survival at sea. Also, one would expect a survivor to be given constructive advice rather than a string of 'don'ts'. It is quite clear that if a survivor can obtain his fresh water by distillation or chemical processes he has no reason to drink seawater; but if he cannot do that and does not have even a drop of fresh water, he will do well, even before he becomes dehydrated, to fall back on Bombard's theories and not to misinterpret them. In my opinion that is what Dougal Robertson also did when, after quoting this Notice to Mariners, he launched into a plea against drinking seawater. His argument rests essentially on his not accepting that seawater can be drunk as a *preventive* measure against dehydration. I think the word in italics here is the right one. In my view his whole discussion of this vital problem is founded on a lack of understanding of the very strict rules which apply to drinking seawater. Dougal Robertson goes on to reject, without actually mentioning Bombard's name, Bombard's experiment, claiming that Bombard was motivated by scientific interest which kept his morale high. I feel this is a fallacious argument; I am sure that Bombard was just as keen to save his skin as Robertson. At the moral level Robertson too had something to sustain him – the saving of his family, including two small children. Surely this must be a motive just as strong as scientific interest.

To take these harsh comments to their conclusion we might recall that the Royal Life Saving Society, of which HRH The Duke of Gloucester is President, conferred its highest award, the Stanhope Gold Medal, on Teehu Makimare. In doing so it honoured a man who had deliberately disobeyed the instructions of the British Department of Trade by continuing to drink seawater for a month.

In the event of a survivor's finding himself in a region and/or season where he cannot count on rain and he has no water or only two or three days' supply, I believe that, in these conditions, he should begin by following Bombard's advice – two or three mouthfuls of seawater every three hours – *in the hours immediately following shipwreck*. If he has a gallon or two of fresh water, he can do one of two things. He can drink his fresh water up without trying to make it last too long and thus reaching a state of excessive dehydration by the time he has to start drinking seawater. Alternatively, he can follow Willis's example and drink fresh water one day and seawater the other. Or again he can do what Heyerdahl did in 1947 and add 30-40 per cent of seawater to his fresh water. Each of these three courses will give the survivor time to get his fishing organized. This is important because statistics show that fishing becomes effective and worthwhile only after several days. We shall see why later.

Depending on the latitude and the associated mean day air temperature, one of these three techniques in conjunction with the methods of countering dehydration will ensure survival for a period of one to several weeks. If at the end of this time the survivor has not been picked up or reached land and, because of weakness or for other reasons, cannot obtain fish, turtles, seaweed or plankton, he can drink his own urine. However, at this point the ocean is gaining the upper hand and the odds against survival are heavy.

Despair, however, is the number one enemy of the survivor, and he must not allow himself to reach this extreme. This book seeks to show that fishing is possible even without conventional aids. As explained in the early part of this chapter, fish represent a new source of water. There is also the method of liquid intake put to admirable use by Lynn Robertson – colonic irrigation with salt water. We know that the mucous membrane of the colon is an area which readily absorbs water, its normal function being to extract enough water from the waste material to allow the faeces to be excreted with a very low water content. Colonic irrigation can be used to hydrate the organism, to counter the constipation which is a constant problem for survivors at sea, and to avoid excessive intake of sodium chloride. To give an idea of the liquid intake involved it is worth noting that colonic irrigation is used in premedication for surgery on the colon. Every four hours 9-10 litres of a solution containing 6g per litre of $NaCl$, 0.75g of KCl and 3g of bicarbonates are perfused directly into the duodenum by means of a stomach tube. Quite apart from the surgical significance of this technique, it has been found that a gain in weight of 4 lb plus or minus 40 per cent results. This indicates the extent to which water is reabsorbed.[16] Lynn Robertson administered the salt water using the tube of the air pump connected to a plastic bag which served as a funnel.

16. See page 5.

The third eventuality, which we have not so far mentioned, is that of the survivor who has little or no idea of the weather conditions in the area where he is shipwrecked. It is very difficult for him to plan ahead and decide on a course of action. I feel that in these circumstances he should act as described above, start rationing his fresh water and drink a little seawater unless and until heavy rain tells him that luck is still on his side. After a few days he will be able to assess the climatic conditions and work out his survival diet.

33

The battle against hunger

Hunger is one of the less severe threats for the survivor at sea. The frequent hunger strikes by which our society is apt to conduct its disputes are there to remind us that, provided he takes it easy and drinks, man can go for many weeks without eating. The survivor of shipwreck, however, should not rely on such comparisons; he must do everything he can as soon as he can to get food. As we saw in the last chapter, quite apart from the calories it brings, food will meet all or at least part of his need for water.

I am going to explore the battle against hunger under seven main headings, each dealing with a different food source: (1) survival rations forming part of the raft's equipment and provisions taken on board when abandoning ship. Apart from these there are: (2) fish; (3) turtles; (4) seabirds; (5) plankton; (6) shellfish; and (7) seaweed.

1. Survival rations and provisions salvaged from the wreck

Survival rations and provisions salvaged from the wreck are always varied. They can range from almost nothing, like those of the three American pilots who ran out of fuel over the Pacific, to a degree of abundance such as enjoyed by the survivors of the *Duroc*, or the Bourdens, at least while they were ashore. Generally speaking, Class I rafts carry a food ration of 2250 calories per head for the laid-down capacity of the raft. Class II rafts carry none. Certainly, one can hardly expect a liferaft to be a larder, but it would surely be desirable for the pundits responsible for official decisions such as these to try and envisage for themselves one day what these 2250 calories mean to a survivor in mid-ocean!

Fortunately, those abandoning ship often succeed in transferring a very mixed collection of food – cans of every kind, sacks of vegetables or fruit, sugar, sweets, and so on; but there is little time or space, and their cupboard will be on the bare side. Again, it often happens in the

more or less chaotic activity of a shipwreck that many of the provisions
fall into the sea and sink because no one thought in time of having a
large bag or some kind of floating container which could be secured to
the raft. Whatever they may consist of, these provisions cover the first
few days of adaptation, and their diversity may provide very welcome
seasoning or flavouring for food from other sources.

2. Fish

All modern accounts of survivors in an inflatable raft stress, sometimes
right from the start, the shaking they feel through the bottom of the
raft caused by fish which rapidly take shelter in its shadow underneath,
and later all the animal and vegetable growths which develop on the
bottom. Older stories in which the craft was a ship's lifeboat or gig have
the same to say about escorting fish, but no mention is made of the
drawbacks of buffeting and rubbing that arise with inflatables.

Some fish are bolder than others about placing themselves in the
raft's protective shadow; some are more numerous than others, depending on the waters; and some make their presence felt quickly,
while others do not. Nevertheless, they are always there; the only
problem is to catch them. It will help to subdivide this section into two,
first fishing techniques and then the use and preparation of the fish
caught.

Methods of fishing

Fishing tackle is included in the equipment of Class I rafts only, and
even this strikes me as far from adequate. Apart from this, most
survivors find themselves without conventional tackle and have to
probe the depths of their ingenuity to devise something. Rudimentary
as this improvised tackle may be, it is often much more effective when
fishing ceases to be a sport and becomes a matter of life or death.

We might take two recent examples, which are highly comparable
because they took place in the same sea area. The Robertson family
had fishing tackle consisting of two large and two small hooks, a reel, a
spoon and trace, and a line of 25 lb breaking-strain. After reading their
story, one finds that they did not have much success at fishing. The reel
served no purpose, and the hooks were soon lost; it was the harpoons
and gaffs that Dougal Robertson made that produced some good
catches. The Baileys, however, quite simply forgot to take their tackle
with them, so they were reduced right from the start to improvising and
trying different techniques. In the end their bag was an impressive one.

The point I want to make with these two examples is that, generally speaking, fishing as practised by a survivor has very little to do with the leisure activity or sport as we normally know it. It is a tricky business calling for infinite patience, a highly acute sense of observation, a little skill and a good deal of ingenuity. It is by examining examples in which all these qualities have been combined that we shall pick up the threads of what fishing for survival is about.

Line. The conventional method calls for a line, a hook and a bait. The line can almost always be found from among the bric-a-brac taken on board – bits of string, cordage, flex, ropes of any kind. They all have their uses in lashing everything down on board the raft, and one needs to choose one of them to make the fishing line. In extreme cases where there is absolutely nothing, we might follow Poon Lim's example and patiently separate the salt-stiffened strands of a rope, subdivide them as many times as the strength required allows and tie them end to end. One might even unravel a wool or cotton garment and patiently pull out and plait the thread to make a length of line.

For the hook one needs to find a piece of metal thin enough to be shaped into the form required. Poon Lim had a galvanized nail which he managed to bend with his teeth. The Baileys used safety-pins, cut off short and bent back; Bombard, whose tackle was under seals, made his first hook with a dorado bone (see page 79). Again, a hook can be made from the lid of a food can with a serrated knife. In fact, any object, metal or otherwise, which is workable enough to be roughly cut to size and bent, and at the same time rigid enough to take the weight of the first fish, is a potential hook. The survivor must assess the strength of his first hook and set about his fishing very carefully, watching through the surface to see what is biting and only going for fish suitable for the hook. We shall return to this point later, but first a word about bait.

One needs to think in terms of different kinds of bait; the possibilities are infinite, for the curiosity, if not the appetite, of the fish escorting the raft can be insatiable. However, they can be choosy. It is worth stressing that sometimes they are driven only by curiosity, and the fisherman's patience goes unrewarded by a bite. If this happens, he must change the bait and turn curiosity into appetite. Poon Lim used as his first bait pellets of biscuit made into a paste with saliva and dried in the sun. Robertson used a bit of cloth hooked on to a spoon made from a food can. Others have used ham or corned beef. Jacques Vignes recommends that the raft's survival kit should always contain a can of mussels, certainly one of the best kinds of bait. I would add to this use of the numerous shellfish which adhere to the raft. There is no need to get into the water; just by leaning over the inflated ring and drawing one's hand round the edge of the raft's bottom, one can collect barnacles. When shelled, these make excellent bait. Most survivors will use as bait the remains of fish caught by another method, but before exploring this further it might be well to recall Alain Bombard's mishap. He was trying to troll with the line tied round his ankle, so that he could get on with something else and have instant warning of the least change in tension of the line. A big fish took the bait and nearly caused him a serious injury. Trolling may be all very well for an expert if there are not too many sharks about, but it is not as advantageous as pursuing the fish which are directly beneath the raft or in its immediate vicinity. It is best to fish with a vertical line. This is how the Baileys with their converted safety-pins caught most of their dorados, how Poon Lim with his bent nail became the record-holder for duration of survival at sea, and how Alain Bombard with his hook of bone was able both to drink and to eat.

We might conclude this section on fishing by quoting Maralyn Bailey:

At the beginning of June when, because of Maurice's illness, I had taken over the fishing I had to be extremely careful with the hook as it was the only small one we had left. Maurice always let the fish swallow the hook before he caught them and would use six or eight pieces of bait to catch one fish. This was too slow for me and my expertise had improved so much that, as soon as the fish got close to the bait, I gave the line a jerk. Rather than discourage the fish, this had the opposite effect. Once I had jerked it away from them they swam fast towards it and held on tightly to the bait. I would haul them quickly over the side and fling them in the dinghy. My fishing had little style about it but it was fun. Occasionally I got carried away and, jerking the line on board, the fish would whizz through the air attached to the line and land back in the sea on the other side of the dinghy. To me they seemed to enjoy this and there was no lack of contestants for the 'high-wire' act.

Compared with the classical simplicity of the line, other methods of fishing may seem rather inferior, but they turn out to be just as effective and often more so. Their common features are that they depend on eyesight and on the constantly replenished stock of fish which live in close proximity to the raft.

Harpoon. The harpoon may be the head of an underwater gun. Bombard had one for the Mediterranean section of his historic passage. In my opinion, even for a novice at this game, just like the mask and snorkel, which were the first real step in man's penetration of the underwater world, an underwater gun should be included in survival kits. Obviously, it can be used by a man in the water, but it can also be used from the raft. To begin with the survivor must only shoot fish vertically below him so as to avoid being misled by refraction. Gradually, he will learn to calculate the aim-off needed to allow for refraction and hit fish at an angle. The penetrative power of an arrow with its point just below the surface is such that there is little chance of losing a harpooned fish – by no means the case with harpoons made up from materials found on board.

Robertson used the handle of a paddle to make his first harpoon; he carved out the characteristic barbs and strengthened the point with two nails. When this broke, he made another, this time from a 'strong and well-grained' cypress thwart. It was very similar to the first except that its barbs were staggered. This broke just like the first, presumably because Robertson aimed at dorados of 20 lb or more.

The answer seems to be that in the absence of a metal harpoon it is better to resort to a gaff as a more suitable means of catching big fish.

Gaff. A good gaff seems to put the survivor in a very strong position to profit from his escort of fish. Together with the short line used alongside the raft, the gaff has certainly proved the most successful way of fishing. It is worth recalling some of its guises. Bombard literally forged himself a hook by using an oar as an anvil to bend back the blade of a knife, which he then fixed to an oar handle. Gilboy doubled over the ends of a pair of dividers. It was Robertson who, after his problems with harpoons, devised the most sophisticated gaff, re-using the handles of his harpoons. The hook was a large fish-hook he had left, firmly fixed to the handle with copper wire and, for safety's sake, also linked to the handle by a double safety line, with one end attached to the handle and the other held in the hand.

With gaffs like this carefully slid into the water and passed under the chosen fish, one can firmly hook catches of 20 lb or more. The only problem is not to damage the rubber of the inflatable compartments by clumsy movements and not to let the fish jump back in the water. To prevent this, the moment the fish is on the bottom of the raft it must be paralysed by forcing thumb and middle finger into its eyes and cutting off its tail fin as soon as possible. It is this fin which makes the fish capable of jumping over the inflated ring.

It is surprising that some survivors who in other respects have shown

Bombard's knife blade – bent round an oar used as an anvil and lashed to a wooden handle to make a gaff.

Poon Lim's nail – doubled over with his teeth to make a hook.

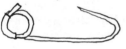

Harpoon head of underwater gun – used by Bombard in the Mediterranean.

The Bailey safety-pin – cut and bent back to make a hook.

Maralyn Bailey's 'ultimate technique' – the hand dipped in the water alongside the raft allows the greedy little fish to bite your fingers. Then you just flick them on board.

A seabird's wing, dripping with blood, serves as line, hook and bait all in one.

Fishing devices made by some of the more wily survivors

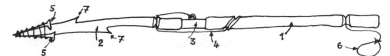

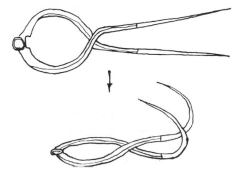

Dougal Robertson's harpoon
1. Shaft of paddle used as handle
2. Harpoon proper cut from a cypress thwart
3. Copper pin joining 1 and 2
4. Safety line joining 1 and 2
5. Nails seized on to head of harpoon
6. Wrist lanyard
7. Barbs cut in the cypress wood

Gilboy's dividers – with the points bent back to make a double hook.

The Bailey fish trap. This is a plastic jerrican-type container about 8 by 8 by 7 inches with the side opposite the normal filling hole cut away. A line with bait on it is dipped into the jerrican through the normal opening. Baited in this way, the jerrican is dipped into the water held by the handle. When a fish, attracted by the bait, swims into it, all you have to do is to lift the 'trap' and tip it into the raft.

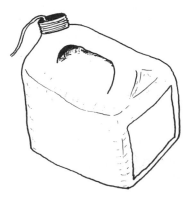

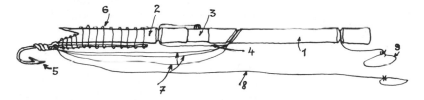

Dougal Robertson's 'Mark 2' gaff
1. Paddle shaft used as handle (previously used for harpoon)
2. Piece of wood carved from thwart
3. Copper pin joining 1 and 2
4. Safety line joining 1, 2 and 3
5. Fish hook used as gaff hook
6. Copper wire securing 5 to 2
7. Nylon line securing 5 to 1
8. Emergency nylon line fixed to 5
9. Wrist lanyard

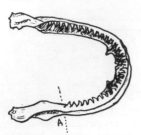

Shark's jawbone. I have suggested using the upper jawbone of a small shark as the hook of a gaff. One of the ends can be lashed to a wooden handle, the whole making a kind of sickle. It would then pay to break off the other end at A.

exceptional gifts of resourcefulness have not hit upon the gaff as a means of fishing. Some of them, it is true, had nothing to make it with; but knowing the equipment available to them, I believe that many others could have made themselves a hook and fixed it to some kind of handle. For those lacking the wherewithal I can suggest an original kind of hook. Many survivors have managed to catch a small shark by the tail. Instead of throwing the head back overboard in case the jaws tear the rubber, I suggest dissecting the jaws and separating the two jaw-bones. This gives one two arcs of a circle armed with sharp pointed teeth, which can be firmly fixed to a wooden handle. The result is a kind of sickle which could serve as a gaff provided that one hooked the fish and threw it into the raft in a single movement. In the absence of a handle the jaw-bone could even be held in the hand, with a little soft tissue left on it to avoid injuring the palm and fingers.

Finally, it is worth remembering that with just his knife Aldrich, one of the American airmen who ran out of fuel in mid-Pacific, used to impale fish and flick them into the raft. His two companions were full of admiration for his dexterity and felt sure they could not have done the same.

Bare hands with or without bait. Fishing by hand with bait relies on the greed of some species of fish and on the fact that, once having bitten, they do not readily let go. This was how Maralyn Bailey, after catching and dismembering a booby, came to put the wing, dripping with blood, into the water. Some fish bit straight away, and with a flick of the wrist she shot them into the raft. She had a fine day's fishing that day and managed to save her precious 'fisherman's safety-pins'. The same method was later used with a turtle's shoulder-blade, some strips of flesh or the bloody skin of sharks, and so on. An equally effective form of bait is a piece of cloth which has just been used to wipe up blood and scraps after dismembering a fish or a turtle. It is really always worth bearing in mind that almost all carnivorous fish are extremely responsive to the smell of blood – not just sharks as everyone is apt to believe. Alternatively, the piece of cloth can be steeped in faeces, which also attracts fish. It is true that constipation lasting for weeks is the lot of many survivors, but to combat this enemas with oil (turtle oil) or brackish water are extremely valuable. So, when the intestine condescends to function again, a source of bait is provided which should not be overlooked.

Fishing with the bare hand is reserved for sharks. I have already mentioned that sharks often come and examine the raft, circling round it and swimming under it to rub themselves. When they are large, everything possible must be done to get away from them. If, on the other hand, they are not over 5 feet in length, it is worth trying to catch them, for they provide a substantial quantity of food. The method almost always used is to seize the shark as it swims alongside, just at the point where the tapered rear end of the body spreads out into a large tail fin (the caudal peduncle). Be prepared for a good shaking, but remember that most of the shark's strength lies in this tail fin. The rough skin promotes a good grip and the shark can be dragged over the gunwale. The moment the mouth appears, stick a bit of wood or a piece of cloth rolled into a ball or the end of an oar in it. The shark will bite hard on this, and its terrible jaws will become less dangerous to the raft and its occupants. To kill a shark the best method is to strike it as hard as possible on the point of its nose with something like a large club. This is a particularly vulnerable zone, and the shark will stop throwing itself about. Then the knife can be used to cut off the gills and stab the eyes. If the stunning blow on the nose was not hard enough and the shark is still moving about, use of the knife is much more difficult. The biggest problem is not to damage the raft.

The Bailey fish trap. This trap is yet another example of Maralyn Bailey's positive genius for catching large quantities of small fish. She explains her invention herself:

As hook after hook snapped or was taken by larger fish, we had to seek another means of catching them. When gutting fish we dropped entrails and other unwanted pieces into a bucket to avoid fouling the dinghy floor. The bucket would then be emptied over the side and rinsed many times. The trigger fish would tumble over themselves to get at these titbits and on several occasions Maurice scooped a fish out with the bucket.

This gave me an idea. I took the one-gallon container which had held the kerosene. It was made of blue plastic, measured 8'' by 8'' by 7'' wide, and had a carrying handle on the top, the spout being beyond one end of this. I got Maurice to cut a square hole in the side opposite the spout. I now removed the

Some of the species of sharks you need to recognize

If you do not know the species, it is best to treat the shark with suspicion, but young ones up to about five feet can be caught.

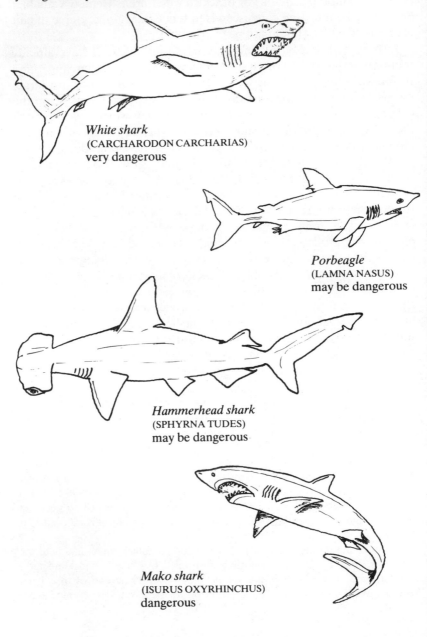

White shark
(CARCHARODON CARCHARIAS)
very dangerous

Porbeagle
(LAMNA NASUS)
may be dangerous

Hammerhead shark
(SPHYRNA TUDES)
may be dangerous

Mako shark
(ISURUS OXYRHINCHUS)
dangerous

Whale-shark
(RHINCODON TYPUS)
inoffensive

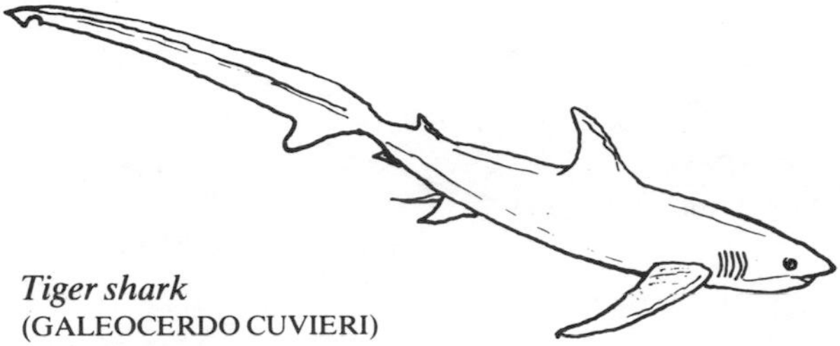

Tiger shark
(GALEOCERDO CUVIERI)
very dangerous

Fox shark
(ALOPIAS VULPINUS)
may be dangerous

Basking shark
(CETORHINUS MAXIMUS)
inoffensive

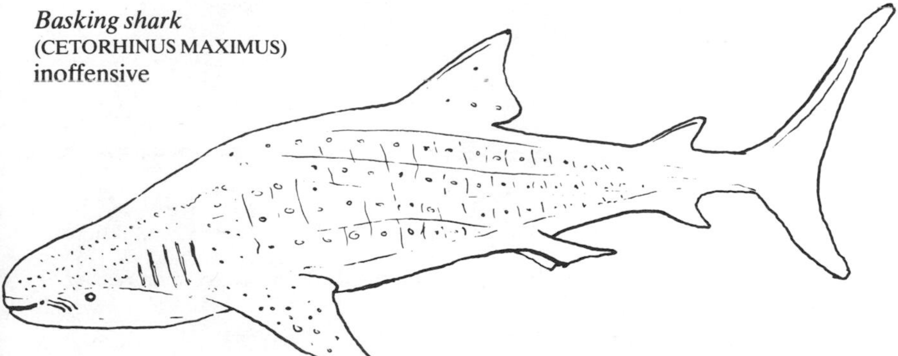

Other important species of shark

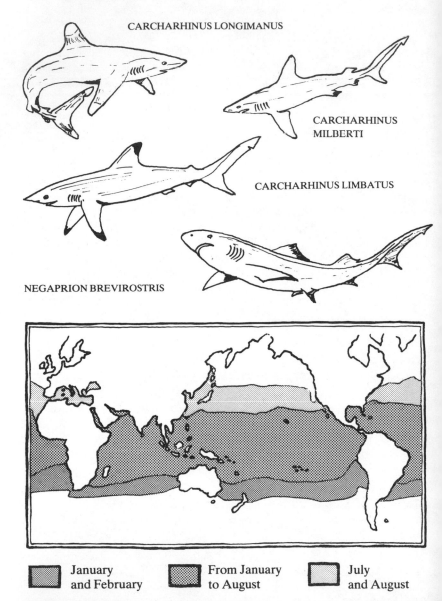

CARCHARHINUS LONGIMANUS

CARCHARHINUS
MILBERTI

CARCHARHINUS LIMBATUS

NEGAPRION BREVIROSTRIS

January and February	From January to August	July and August

Sea areas where attacks by sharks are statistically the most frequent, related to seasons

(Illustrations taken from *Les Requins* by J.-Y. and Ph. Cousteau.)

cap from the spout and threaded a baited line into the container. Using the handle I lowered it over the side until the aperture was below the surface of the sea.

At first the fish viewed it with suspicion, charging up to the entrance then veering off. But they were voracious by nature and seemed determined to outdo each other. Soon two or three fish had gathered at the opening gazing longingly at the lump of bait. Suddenly one of them dashed forward into the container and grabbed the bait and dragged it a little way towards the entrance before backing out. I resisted the temptation to scoop it out and explained to Maurice that we had to get them well trained first. Maurice marvelled at my patience. I fed them lump after lump until a large crowd of fish hung around and willingly played my fish trap game. Eventually, I decided to catch a few and it was so easy to wait for the right fish to swim in and to lift the trap out of the water and deposit the fish at Maurice's feet. The fish didn't appear to notice that some of their playmates had disappeared but continued to oblige with renewed vigour.

Maurice was delighted at the trap's efficiency when I caught our breakfast of approximately twenty fish using very little bait and with no danger of losing our hook. Unfortunately this method of fishing only attracted the trigger fish; the golden jacks and silver fish being much more timid and wary.

Also worth mentioning is a very special method, that of 'harvesting' flying fish. During the last days of his experience Bernard Gilboy was able to survive only on account of the flying fish which landed on his boat in the night. The examples are too many to mention: Romer was hit full in the face by a flying fish, and almost all survivors at sea have become familiar with this manna dispensed with a degree of generosity that depends on the dimensions of the craft and whether or not there is a sail to act as a trap. In the Atlantic Bombard caught between five and fifteen every morning; his sail seems to have been one of the biggest of all those mentioned in the accounts summarized in Part 1. This shows the advantage of making a sail, with shirts like the St Helena deserters if necessary, not only to gain speed but also to catch these fish in full flight. If there is a torch available with its batteries still working, the trap can be improved still further. Flying fish seem to be attracted by the light like many other species, so lighting up the sail increases the catch considerably.

To try to include everything, while knowing full well that human imagination has found or will find many other ways of catching fish, I should like to mention a very old method of fishing which Thor Heyerdahl rediscovered during the Kon-Tiki expedition. When one catches a shark or a turtle, some sucking fish are frequently brought on

board with it. These fish always try to cling by their dorsal sucker to a
sizeable floating object – in Heyerdahl's case to his balsa-wood raft.
Rather like the Japanese fishermen who tame cormorants and put a
strap round their necks, one can exploit this special instinct of sucking
fish. After detaching one of these fish from its support, a piece of string
or nylon line should be tied around its caudal peduncle immediately
and the fish should then be returned to the water. While you are busy
killing and dismembering the large fish which was its host, it is very
likely to attach itself to the bottom of the raft while waiting for a new,
less passive, host. If a large fish or a turtle passes near by, this sucking
fish 'on the leash' will most likely attach itself to it. Then all you have to
do is to tug on the 'lead' to recover the sucking fish, which will continue
doing this almost indefinitely, and the new host it has chosen for itself.
As in any method of fishing you have to pay attention. In this case it is
enough to watch the 'leash'; when it stretches, this means that the
sucking fish has found a companion. So powerful is the sucker of this
most original piece of fishing tackle that, with a certain amount of
dexterity, one can pull its new host on board by the sucker.

Use and preparation of fish

Very few survivors at sea have a stove. In any case its fuel is soon
exhausted and, even if he has had his first fish grilled or boiled with
some ingredients salvaged from the wreck, its happy owner very soon
finds himself in the common condition of survivors at sea – having to
eat fish raw. The flesh of some is delicious, of others repugnant. We
have Maralyn Bailey to thank for drawing up a veritable gourmet's
menu of all the species of fish she discovered during her 117 days of
survival. Before drawing on her experience I should like to quote
Bombard when, after three days of fasting, he caught a grouper and
started to eat it raw:

The pink flesh almost made me vomit, and Jack obviously felt the same,
although I had already tried the effect in the laboratory. It was up to me to show
an example. Of course it is delicious, I said to myself, and swallowed the first
mouthful. It was by no means so bad and the taboo was broken. Forgetting our
careful upbringing, we tore at the flesh with our teeth, each mouthful seeming
more appetizing. The rest of the fish was placed on top of the tent to dry in the
sun, after we had extracted the juice with my fruit press. At the next meal it
almost tasted cooked.

Each civilization has placed a taboo on certain forms of food. Would you eat
locusts or white grubs? No. But a Moslem cannot eat pork. Once, in Britain, I

even ate whale, but unfortunately I knew it was whale and thought very little of it. Plenty of people will eat horse or cat, if they are told it is beef or rabbit. It is all a question of habit, and I am sure our grandmothers would never have ventured to eat a steak tartare. But I ate so much that day that I was very nearly seasick.

Now let us return to the observations made by the Baileys. The fish most frequently caught on line or gaff are what most of the survivors in these accounts call 'dolphins'. In fact they are dorados (*Coryphaena hippuris*), tropical or subtropical fish which may reach lengths of 4 feet or more and are easily recognizable by their club-like head. Their flesh is excellent and they provide a good deal of water. In fact, dorados can be regarded as the fish which have saved the most lives at sea. Where there are dorados, there are bound to be plenty of flying fish too. Flying fish are the preferred prey of dorados, and it is generally to escape them that these small fish take flight above the surface. Moreover, it is by no means unusual to find one or more flying fish in the alimentary canal of a dorado. In many accounts these flying fish, already to some extent affected by the digestive juices, have been used as bait. This is a great mistake, since they give the survivor the chance of eating 'pre-digested' flesh – and one which, according to Dixon, tastes particularly good.

Flying fish are delicious grilled. Raw, they do not come up to the standard of the dorado or some other species. If there are plenty of them, they can be used as bait – or their heads can be used as bait and the fillets kept and dried.

Triggerfish (genus *Balistes*) are flat fish, 6-7 inches long whose heads take up almost half their bodies. The two front spines of the dorsal fin are retractable and need to be treated with respect. The Baileys managed to catch 100 or so of these fish in a day, for they are very greedy. Maralyn Bailey has this to say:

The catching was the easiest part, the gutting and cutting up was time consuming and exhausting. The softened flesh of our fingers had been chafed to the bone by the continual use of the scissors.

Unfortunately, their eagerness to grab the bait had other detracting features. We would wash our hands over the side and have them seized by the trigger fish, their small mouths biting into our flesh. Sometimes they broke the skin before we could withdraw our hands. At one time we even considered the plan that if we lost all our hooks or required fresh bait we could always use our fingers as bait.

Maralyn Bailey recommends dicing the fillets and leaving them to

Fish most often caught in the experience of the Robertsons and the Baileys
Drawings after Peter A.-G. Milne (Baileys) and Pam Littlewood (Robertsons)

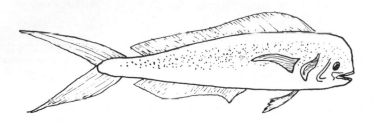

Dorado (CORYPHAENA HIPPURIS), *also referred to as 'dolphin'.* Recognizable
by its dished forehead which gives its head a club-like appearance, this fish
often hunts flying fish and likes to shelter in the shade of a raft. May reach 70
pounds. Bombard dissected out a hook-shaped bone behind the gill cover.
Many survivors owe their lives to this fish.

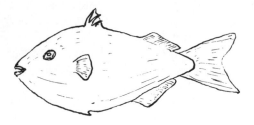

Triggerfish (GENUS BALISTES)
Recognizable by its three dorsal spines, which provide a capture mechanism. In
addition to numerous reef species, there are some edible ocean species (even in
the Mediterranean – BALISTES CAPRISCUS). This fish provided the Baileys'
staple diet. They like to shelter under the raft. They sometimes exceed 8 inches
in length.

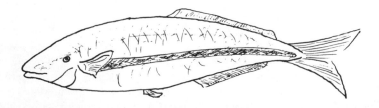

Fish described by the Baileys as being of the Chaenichthyidae family –
recognizable by the longitudinal pale blue stripe on each side of its silver body.

Fish described by the Baileys as a horse mackerel (GENUS TRACHURUS, *also known as skad*). This fish is golden in colour all over, with a protruding 'crest' either side, and 8-10 ins long.

Flying fish or exocet
There are about 40 species of these fish, which 'take wing' to escape their predators and frequently fall into rafts. They may be up to 18 inches long; they are also found in the Mediterranean.

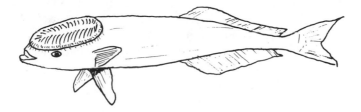

Sucking-fish (ECHENEIS REMORA)
Recognizable by its dorsal sucker. This fish is found in all tropical and temperate waters, attached to a mobile host (large fish, shark, turtle or even raft). May be used to catch large fish. The largest of the eight known species may reach rather over 3 feet in length.

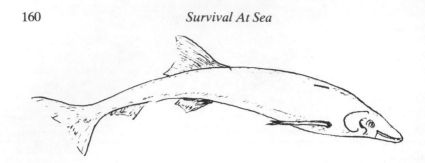

Fish described by the Baileys as a CHIROCENTRUS
Recognizable by their bright yellow dorsal fin, these fish like sheltering below the raft and may reach two feet in length.

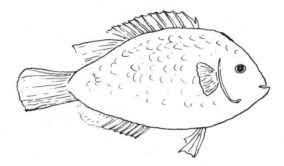

Fish described by the Baileys as belonging to the family Siganidae
This is probably incorrect, for this family contains only one genus, SIGANUS, known in English as the 'rabbit-fish', which only inhabits reefs. This fish has a brown and white marbled appearance, and the Baileys found it particularly delicious.

soak in fresh water, if the water situation permits. This produces raw fish Tahiti style, the only difference being that fresh water is used instead of the juice of green lemons. Lemon juice acts by acidity, while fresh water, the most hypotonic of all liquids, must act by a complex phenomenon of cellular disruption. At any rate, it makes the fish taste much better and thus stimulates the appetite.

Statistically, sharks – small ones, of course, that can be caught by hand – seem to come very near the top of the list of fish that can be caught. Opinions are divided on the taste of their flesh. Those suffering from extreme hunger appreciate it greatly, as do certain underprivileged island peoples who eat it regularly. On the other hand, those who have plenty of other kinds of fish available have tended to keep shark meat for bait, eating only the very rich liver and the soft roe, in the same way as the Paumotu who inhabit the Tuamotu Archipelago and have plenty of other succulent fish to eat. In fact, shark meat seems to improve when one can drink plenty with it, for it tastes very bitter.

Many other species of fish normally swim along with the raft. Even in a sea as ill-fitted for survival and fishing as the Mediterranean Bombard managed to chalk up quite a respectable bag – in contrast to Lucien and Catherine who never tried to fish, although, while they were bathing, they realized that there were a number of fish sheltering under their raft.

Many accounts, even the Baileys' excellently documented one, mention kinds of fish which, according to current zoological thinking, do not correspond with those likely to be found a long way offshore in the shadow of a raft. The vernacular names of many species have different meanings in different languages and in any case vary from sea to sea, so they cannot be bound by laws of scientific classification. It may be best to end this very brief review of the fish most often caught by survivors here and concern ourselves with three broader questions: whether all fish can be eaten; how a fish diet can be varied; and how fish can be preserved.

Which fish can be eaten

In his log entry for 29 November 1952 Bombard wrote:

Caught a trigger fish today with my knife on the end of my oar; hesitate to eat it as one book calls it edible and another poisonous. Prefer not to take the risk. You would think that those who have studied the problems of castaways would agree about something.

That is the problem, but it is really very simple. As far as triggerfish are concerned, there are some well-known forms, observed in coral reefs, which are toxic, and others, which inhabit the open sea, which are not. The case of the triggerfish can be extended to all species of fish – in the open sea one can assume, as an alternative to forcing oneself to go on hunger strike, that there are no poisonous fish. All observed and published cases of poisoning are the result of fish caught inshore around coral islands or in their lagoons.

To this rather sketchy answer it would perhaps be as well to add a few words in the realization that undue attention to the scientific data below would be disastrous for morale. The poison in a fish may be in its blood; this is found in certain conger and moray eels and torpedo rays, all of them fish which a survivor at sea has little chance of encountering. Again, the toxin may be secreted by the gonads; this is lethal in infinitesimal doses but is confined to globefish which can be caught only over a coral reef.[1] When taken out of the water, these fish blow themselves up in a highly characteristic manner and have simply to be thrown back again – although the Japanese make a very fine dish with them. Finally, the flesh itself may be poisonous; this condition is found in numerous species of coral fish and only a few other species – for instance, mullets and surmullets. This is the only pathology that concerns us, and it is worth repeating that it can be ignored in the open sea. If, however, by some exceptional mischance the survivor who has just eaten fish finds himself to be in a condition similar to alcoholic intoxication with visual hallucinations, he has no need to panic. He is suffering from a benign condition known as ichtyosarcotoxaemia which will not have any lasting effects.

It is also conceivable, although no account mentions it, that owing to a bacterial contamination of which they are carriers and which leads to an excess of histamine, tunny or mackerel could trigger off a generalized urticaria (allergic swelling and irritation) with congestion of the face and the upper respiratory tract. This is alarming but not serious.

Finally under this heading one might mention the pathological condition caused by fish known as ciguatera. This is a neuro-digestive syndrome of which the first symptoms appear about three hours after eating the fish – nausea, followed by vomiting, with tingling (paraesthaesia) of the lips and mouth. The response to this warning is to continue vomiting until the stomach is completely emptied. The best method is to drink two or three glasses of seawater, lean overboard and place the first and second fingers in the back of the throat to trigger off a nausea reflex that, when repeated, induces vomiting. This technique repeated two or three times washes the stomach out almost completely. This phase may be followed by abdominal pains, diarrhoea, pains in the joints, extreme muscular weakness, vision problems and violent headaches; but as a rule the prognosis is excellent. With ciguatera the toxin is contained in the liver of certain fish, among them sharks. This is a condition which, once again, in practice appears only after eating the liver of fish, normally edible, which have spent some time in a coral habitat.

To conclude, one should always be aware of the poisonous nature of certain fish so as to recognize the real cause of a sharp but passing indisposition. The basic fact remains that in the open sea the survivor

1. '*Tetrodotoxin*: A poisonous compound $C_{11}H_{17}N_3O_2$ that has been isolated from a Japanese globefish and a newt and blocks nerve conduction by suppressing permeability of the nerve fiber to sodium ions' (Webster).

can make use of everything he catches except perhaps jellyfish which, although abundant and tempting, are always dangerous.

Variation of a fish diet

Once again we must turn to the Baileys, who had plenty of time in the 117 days they were adrift to dream up some recipes. The first requirement is receptacles. If there are none of these to start with, the survivor can use the fish he catches to make them, by converting gut, swim-bladders, and so on into bags for storing certain precious morsels from the fish caught. It really is very important to try and vary the menus, as the Baileys did; one of the most insidious problems is lack of appetite, anorexia brought about by monotony of diet and the aversions that may result from this. Without realizing it the survivor eats less and less even when there is plenty of fish; then one day he breaks down and is faced with the whole problem of regaining lost ground.

The Baileys used to put the livers in one bowl and the eggs or soft roes in another, while a third was reserved for the eyes of all fish caught. When the weather was good enough for fishing, it was thus possible, at least once a day, to have a treat by breaking the monotony of raw fish flesh at every meal. Here it is worth pointing out that, once a fast is broken, it is important to respect the organism's daily rhythms by eating three or four times a day at the customary times. We shall see how, when the victuals include turtle, menus can be varied to provide a better balanced diet.

Preservation of fish

There is a certain degree of similarity between the problems of getting fresh water and those that form the subject of this section. Supplies of fish, and likewise of other sources of food, mainly seabirds and turtles, are subject to fluctuations of weather conditions. Fishing calls for a calm sea and waters which allow clear visibility; when the sea gets up a bit, it becomes impossible. It might even be fair to say that getting fresh water and fishing do not go together. The former is generally asso-ciated with winds and high seas, to say nothing of storms which drive the raft's normal escort of fish down to the still depths. Like fresh water, food must be stored in times of plenty.

For short-term preservation the fish fillets, whether or not they have already had the juice squeezed out of them, can be laid in the shade between two cloths, pieces of sailcloth for instance, and sprinkled from time to time with seawater. Evaporation cools them down slightly and deposits salt, with which the cloth becomes impregnated. In this way fillets can be kept fresh for a few days, depending on climatic conditions.

For longer-term preservation the only possibility is drying. Here the fillets are hung up, exposed to the sun. This method has the advantage of allowing them to turn so that both sides face the sun. If nothing can be found on which to hang them, the fillets should be placed in the sun on a cloth. In this event they must be turned frequently, every quarter- or half-hour; and they must be placed far enough apart to be turned on to a dry area of cloth, which allows the moist cloth on which they were resting to dry. When the sun goes down, the fillets are stacked until the next morning. This is the time when humidity may cause mildew; if there is plenty of cloth, a piece should be placed between each fillet.

Depending on the thickness of the fillets and the amount of sunshine, drying may take between a few hours and several days. Once they are dry, the fillets should be packed tightly together with as little air between them as possible. The stock must be checked regularly to avoid the unpleasant surprise of finding a mildewed bundle of fish when heavy seas prevent fishing. In some instances fish may have to be re-dried for a short while every other day or even daily.

3. Turtles

In theory current ideas on the geographical distribution of marine reptiles, mainly turtles, should mean that a survivor could find and maintain himself on them anywhere either side of the Equator between roughly the fortieth parallel north and the fortieth parallel south. Analysis of survivors' accounts suggests that this is very far from the case. Nowadays it is survivors only in certain areas of the Pacific or the Indian Ocean who really have much chance of adding this choice dish to their larder.

There are two families of turtles. The Chelonidae or hard-shell turtles are sub-divided into four species:

i)   The green turtle (e.g. *Chelonia mydas* or *virgata*) is the best known. The length of its shell may approach 40 inches in the male and exceed 30 inches in the female, while the weight varies from tens of pounds to 5 or 6 hundredweight. This species makes long migrations and is particularly fond of travelling on the surface of the sea. Its reproductive period varies a great deal according to geographical position, so it may be found in larger or smaller numbers at any time of year.

ii)   The hawksbill turtle (*Eretmochelys imbricata*) has a characteristic shell whose length does not exceed 35 inches in the adult. In the Pacific it reproduces between November and February; in the Atlantic between April and August. During these seasons it is very rarely found in the open sea.

iii)   The loggerhead turtle (*Caretta caretta*) is very rarely found in the open sea, preferring bays and estuaries. It may attain lengths well over 4 ft and weights of 1000 pounds or more.

iv)   The Olive Ridley turtle (*Lepidochelys olivacea*) is the smallest species, with most shells not exceeding 25 inches long even in the oldest animals. In the Caribbean Sea they reproduce from December to February, while the population in the east Pacific nests between August and November.

The sole representative of the second family, the Dermochelididae or soft-shell turtles, is the giant leather-back turtle (*Dermochelys coriacea*) which may exceed 6 feet 6 inches in length and half a ton in weight. Obviously, a survivor is in no position to take on monsters like this.

Just as we did for fish, let us examine in turn: methods of fishing; killing and dismembering the turtle; and, finally, making the best use of it.

Fishing for turtles

Like sharks, turtles are caught with the bare hands. There are two problems. One is to get near the turtle, or rather to bring the raft up to it without its diving. If this happens, it is very difficult to predict where the animal will reappear. The second problem is knowing how to get a firm hold on it and stop it disappearing altogether. This presupposes that a survivor will not go for the larger forms we have just been discussing or at least, if he has nothing to lose by doing so, will not be disappointed if he gets the worst of a very unequal contest. We need to look at these problems in more detail.

When a survivor sees on the surface a dark mass that looks like a turtle, the first thing he should do is watch it for a few moments. The mass may be immobile; this means the turtle is sleeping on the surface. In this event one has to paddle up close to it gently and silently. On the other hand, the mass may be moving, swimming. In this case it is best to wait until the turtle's curiosity leads it towards the raft. In fact, it seems highly probable that turtles take the raft for another of their

Distribution of the green turtle (drawing taken from the encyclopedia *La Faune*)

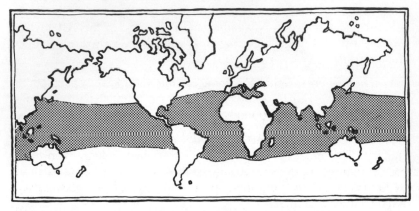

The species of turtle can be recognized by the appearance of the shell. All represent an immense reserve of food for the survivor at sea. Only relatively young ones can reasonably be caught under survival conditions.

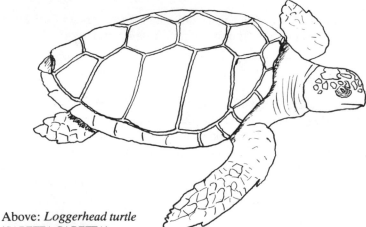

Above: *Loggerhead turtle* (CARETTA CARETTA) Length of shell up to rather over 4 feet, weight up to 800-900 pounds, lays 120-130 eggs about 1½ inches in diameter, plastron (bottom of shell) yellowish.

Right: *Leather-back turtle* (DERMOCHELYS CORIACEA) The sole species of the soft-shelled turtle family. Up to 6 feet or more in length and half a ton in weight. Lays up to 300 eggs of 5 inches diameter, plastron pale with black markings.

Left: *Hawksbill turtle*
(ERETMOCHELYS
IMBRICATA)
Length of shell up to
three feet, lays 450-550
eggs of 1-1½ inches dia-
meter, plastron yellow,
flecked with black.

Above: *Green turtle* (CHELONIA MYDAS)
Length of shell up to 40 inches, weight
550-650 pounds, lays 250-500 eggs rather
under 2 inches diameter, plastron
whitish except at the end and where it
joins the body, where it is dark-
coloured.

kind. Once disillusioned, they like swimming underneath it to make the best of its shade, to rid themselves of their parasites by rubbing on the bottom of the raft and to eat the little shellfish attached to it. The turtle can be caught when it swims alongside – best of all when it comes to the surface to breathe after several minutes underneath the raft. At this moment it is rather tired and relatively weak in its defences, so its struggle will be shorter and less vigorous. This was how the Baileys and the Robertsons succeeded in catching their largest turtles.

Finally, there is another possibility which I have personally experienced some miles off Panama. This is to surprise two turtles in the act of copulating on the surface. In such conditions they can be approached quickly and the male which is clutching the female's shell can be seized before they have time to separate and dive.

Once the turtle is alongside, it has to be caught and tipped into the raft. This is no easy business, especially when the raft is crowded as it was in the case of the Robertson family. The raft must be balanced while the strongest member of the party leans over the side. The best technique is to catch a fin where it is thick, as close as possible to the point where it emerges from under the shell, and to hold on to its thickened front edge. With the other hand grasp the shell half-way along its far side. In this position, with your body stretched out over the side and thus deprived of much of its strength, you have to tip the turtle so that its shell is resting first on the outer side of the inflated ring and then on top of it. Once you have done this, the worst is over, and you can let the turtle slide on to the bottom of the raft, keeping clear of blows from the claws on the four fins and nips from the beak which fortunately, has no teeth. With this method turtles of 80 or 90 pounds should not escape.

Other techniques are apt to damage the rubber – in particular sliding the turtle on the bottom of its shell, which brings the claws on the fins directly into contact with the raft's compartments. Obviously, the whole exercise is much easier with two people, but it is essential to avoid capsizing the craft. A sole survivor faced with a turtle whose size and weight make it impossible for him to roll it in on its back should try a different method, killing the turtle in the water. This appears never to have been tried. The first move is to pass round the turtle's neck the bight of a rope, using it like a lasso. It is worth noting that the head is not retractable. Rather than strangle the animal, which is theoretically possible but calls for exceptional strength if it is a large one, one might try drowning it by holding the rope with one hand and keeping the head under water with the other. This too calls for strength and patience, for after struggling for fifteen or twenty minutes one cannot be sure that the turtle is completely asphyxiated. Once it is dead and no longer struggling, it is easy to hoist the turtle on board. Cutting the carotid arteries under the water kills the animal in a few seconds but releases so much blood that no shark in the neighbourhood could resist it.

Killing and dismembering a turtle

With the turtle lying on its back on the bottom of the raft, the survivor has to play the role of butcher. To avoid being struck by the claws you have to kneel astride the turtle with your knees on the lower side of the front fins. You then cut its throat with a knife, using this like a saw, for it is probably not very sharp and the turtle's skin at this point is anything but tender. The vascular axes – the carotid arteries and jugular veins – lie to either side of and slightly behind the windpipe. When the knife gets through to them, the blood spurts out strongly and must be collected in a receptacle. It is an unsalted beverage[2] which must be drunk as soon as possible; it starts to coagulate in under a minute.

Dismemberment can then begin; in view of the nature and condition of the cutting instruments normally available to a survivor it can be a long and tedious business. You start by cutting right round the plastron (bottom) of the shell. You then remove this, severing all the tissue attached to its inner surface. This exposes the visceral cavity. Cut the intestine as far down as possible, squeezing it between two fingers just above the cut to stop the faeces escaping and fouling the rest of the offal. This operation is repeated as high up as possible, on the oesophagus, once again squeezing it to keep the contents in. The whole of this can then be thrown in the sea, where it will attract fish of every kind including sharks. Alternatively, just the contents can be squeezed out and the intestine itself preserved in a receptacle full of fresh or salt water to stop it drying out. It can then be prepared as a tripe dish or used as bait or, as we have already mentioned, it can be turned inside out to form a long tube with makes a very good container.

The next step is to cut away a kind of muscular diaphragm which masks the liver and the heart and respiratory system. Once these are removed, you can get at the major muscles which provide the largest

2. Not strictly, but somewhat hypotonic relative to the body fluids of a dehydrated survivor.

fillets of meat. These lie against the shell; they are attached both to it and to the pectoral and pelvic girdles, which have to be dissected out bone by bone. These large muscles converge on the fins they actuate, and this is why they are so large and powerful. This is a difficult stage in the dissection but it allows you to recover 25-30 per cent of the weight of the turtle in 'prime cuts' of meat. It is also essential to collect in a special container the fat which lines the shell and lies between the muscles. Melted in the sun, this gives a golden oil which has many uses.

Use and preservation of turtle meat

Even more than fish, turtle meat lends itself to numerous ways of preparation which also serve to improve the survivor's menus.

What is left of the blood, once thirsts have been quenched, will have coagulated very quickly. The clot soon divides into a globular mass and a liquid separation, the plasma. Both these can be eaten as ingredients or sauces to accompany raw or dried fillets of fish or turtle meat.

The Robertson family did not risk eating the liver, but it is, in fact, excellent. The only problem is that it must be eaten quickly and raw, for it cannot be dried and goes off more quickly than the flesh. The Baileys tell us that the livers of female turtles are larger and more succulent than those of males. One must remember to remove the bladder attached to the liver without puncturing it; otherwise, the liver will have a very bitter taste of bile.

Female turtles can most easily be identified by the absence of a tail or, rather, of a part of the tail protruding beyond the shell. The eggs may be of varying sizes and in varying states of development. They are rather like ping-pong balls and very nourishing. Turtle eggs can be eaten raw if it is impossible to make omelettes or to parboil them in a metal receptacle heated in the sun. When half-developed they are almost entirely made up of yolk, which is difficult to chew and swallow but particularly rich.

The oil obtained by melting the fat in the sun provides, along with the plasma, one of the best ingredients for seasoning fresh or dried turtle meat or fish fillets. The Robertsons also used it by rectal administration in their struggle against constipation, for lubricating various rusty instruments, for massaging stiffened joints and for dressing skin lesions and thus insulating them from salt spray. They had plenty of receptacles and were able to keep some oil for 'calming troubled waters'. As is well known, this is a time-honoured procedure which consists of dripping oil on to the water alongside the boat. It does not take large quantities to get good results – on an average 2.5-3 litres per hour (about 5 pints). To underline how useful this technique is it is worth recalling that in 1887 the Compagnie Générale Transatlantique's liner *Normandie* picked up two boats from the *Kjukan* with fourteen men on board. They had been adrift for seven days through a severe storm: 'We spread some kerosene round the boats,' the captain reported, 'and the waves came up to the boats without breaking.'

Even the bones of turtles are not without their uses. On chewing them one finds a delicious bone marrow which can be sucked out.

Finally the meat, as mentioned above, amounts to 25-30 per cent of the turtle's weight. The muscles can be cut into slices, making genuine steaks to be eaten raw. They are even better eaten half-dried, although digesting them then requires more liquid. Alternatively, they can be dried in the same way as fish fillets. It is a good general rule, however, to eat as much as possible of the meat raw or half-dried, because drying turtle meat is even more difficult than drying fish fillets. It would be a terrible pity to ration oneself only to find later that the dried meat was unfit for consumption because it was covered with mould. From raw turtle meat can be squeezed out what the Robertsons called 'turtle juice' – a mixture of blood, lymph and interstitial fluid which makes an excellent sauce.

To round off this gastronomic section I cannot resist quoting Lynn Robertson's recipe – two turtle's eggs beaten or pounded, sprinkled with turtle juice. This provides a sauce in which various bits of dried and fresh meat and dried strips of dorado can be marinated. When meat is in plentiful supply, it may seem unnecessary to catch a further turtle if, by chance, one comes along. Not knowing what the future may bring, one can then use the Bailey's technique: they simply kept their second turtle alive for the time being by putting a little seawater into the bottom of their dinghy to make it into a fishpond. They also let the turtle swim round the raft with a leash on one of its back fins.

4. Seabirds

In theory seabirds are doubly interesting to the survivor. They are a source of nourishment – in some stories the only one – and, depending on the species, they indicate the distance still to go to the nearest land. Only the first of these statements holds in practice; before examining it further, let us look at the second. Almost all survivors who have believed themselves to be near the end of their troubles from observing birds have been bitterly disappointed. We need only take the example of Alain Bombard who, since he made his crossing into a scientific experiment on all possible levels, equipped himself with the *Raft Book*. This is an American survival manual in which all seabirds are described with an indication of the distances they may fly out to sea. All the errors which Bombard points out at various points in his book *Naufragé volontaire* are worth recording:

When you see three tropic birds (*Phaëthon species*) together, you are not more than 80 miles from land – wrong.

When you see ten birds together, you are likely to be between 100 and 200 miles from land – wrong.

The frigate bird never spends the night at sea and is seldom found more than about 100 miles from land – wrong.

The northern gannet does not go more than 90 miles from the coast – wrong.

The false shearwaters[3] do not go more than 100 miles from land – wrong.

The tropical white-tailed sea eagle[4] shows that the coast is at most 60 to 80 miles away – wrong, wrong again!

On 27 November Bombard found a fly in his raft *l'Hérétique*. This was something the *Raft Book* did not mention, and he very naturally thought that land was not far away. He was to be the first to agree that his observations were just as wrong as those of the manual. On 4 December he was visited by a butterfly, but was proved wrong again, for he did not reach Barbados until 23 December.

These speculations provide little except disillusionment, so it is more realistic to talk of seabirds as a source of food and, as we have seen, of fishing tackle.

Birds which venture far out to sea do not behave in the same way as those we know on land. All sailors have known these visits from birds, exhausted or otherwise, which install themselves on the boat for several hours or days. It is the same with survivors – but for them these birds are not just companions but choice dishes. Apart from Gene Aldrich who shot an albatross with a pistol, all other birds reported have been caught by hand or surprised by having some kind of garment put over them. The second is certainly the safer method when the bird

3. I think this must refer to shearwaters other than those of the genus *Puffinus*.
4. Literally, 'white-tail of the tropics'; I think this must be the white-tailed sea eagle (*Haliäetus albicilla*).

in question, such as the brown or blue-footed boobies of the Pacific, has a sharp, dangerous beak.

In exceptional cases – although it did happen to Bombard with a shearwater – a bird becomes a victim of its own greed. This one swallowed the bait of a line that was being trailed and the hook was caught in its gullet. According to Bombard, shearwaters should not be plucked but skinned, the skin being very rich in fat. As for the meat, Bombard found it very good, with an aftertaste of seafood.

Like fish, all seabirds can be regarded as edible. Dougal Robertson was wrong to ignore a blue-footed booby, thinking that its flesh was 'leathery, salty and full of vermin' without even catching it and trying some. In any case, as we have already seen, the wing of a large bird dripping with blood can be a splendid way of fishing, providing line, hook and bait all in one.

5. Plankton

Thor Heyerdahl's interest in plankton started with the Kon-Tiki expedition of 1947. This is what he wrote:

More than once people have starved to death at sea because they have not found fish large enough to be spitted, netted or hooked. In such cases it has often happened that they have literally been sailing about in strongly diluted raw fish soup. If, in addition to hooks and nets, they had had a utensil for straining the soup they were sitting in, they would have found a nourishing foundation – plankton. . . . The marine biologist Dr A. D. Bajkov gave us the idea and sent with us a fishing net which was suited to the creatures we were to catch. The "net" was a silk net with almost three thousand meshes per square inch. It was sewn in the shape of a funnel with a circular mouth behind an iron ring, 18 inches across, and was towed behind the raft. Just as in other kinds of fishing, the catch varied with time and place. Catches diminished as the sea grew warmer further west, and we got the best results at night, because many species seemed to go deeper down into the water when the sun was shining.

If we had no other way of whiling away time on board the raft, there would have been entertainment enough in lying with our noses in the plankton net. Not for the sake of the smell, for that was bad. Nor because the sight was appetising, it looked a horrible mess. But because, if we spread the plankton out on a board and examined each of the little creatures separately with the naked eye, we had before us fantastic shapes and colours in unending variety.

Most of them were tiny shrimp-like crustaceans (copepods) or fish ova floating loose, but there were also larvae fish and shellfish, curious miniature crabs in all colours, jellyfish and an endless variety of small creatures. . . .

Where the cold Humboldt Current turned west south of the equator, we could pour several pounds of plankton porridge out of the bag every few hours.

The plankton lay packed together like cake in coloured layers, brown, red, grey and green according to the different fields of plankton through which we had passed. At night, when there was phosphorescence about, it was like hauling in a bag of sparkling jewels.... Our night's catch looked as nasty at close quarters as it had been pretty at long range. And bad as it smelt, it tasted correspondingly good if one just plucked up courage and put a spoonful of phosphorus into one's mouth. If this consisted of many dwarf shrimps, it tasted like shrimp paste, lobster or crab. And if it was mostly deep sea fish ova, it tasted like caviare and now and then like oysters. The uneatable vegetable plankton were either so small that they ran away with the water through the meshes of the net, or they were so large that we could pick them up with our fingers. . . . Two men on board thought plankton tasted delicious, two thought they were quite good, and for two the sight of them was more than enough.

Some years later Bombard too insisted on the value to a survivor of collecting plankton. He also showed that plankton was rich in vitamin C and thus enabled one to avoid scurvy, a deficiency condition much feared by sailors of old. Bombard collected it for only half an hour a day, which was just what was necessary to give him his vitamin C ration, since he felt he had enough fish besides to feed himself and therefore had no need to slow down his progress further. The whole point here is the need for a special net. It is true that silk or nylon stockings will do, but these must be provided in the survival kit on the raft. Few shipwrecked wives are likely to go on board the raft with their stockings on! In any event the diameter of a stocking does not provide a large collecting area.[5] So perhaps we should conclude by saying that, just like the solar still, a plankton net must be included in liferaft equipment. It could serve as a sea-anchor too.

6. Shellfish

Shellfish feature only to a very limited extent in survivors' diets. Of all the accounts we have analysed only Bernard Gilboy, Poon Lim and the Bourdens actually ate shellfish during a short period of otherwise complete fast. It did not occur to most of the others to lean over the edge of their raft and collect the little crabs which were swimming along with it or the barnacles attached to it. Certainly, these could hardly be called a staple diet, but those eaten are replaced by new ones and are enough to provide some energy at the height of a fast. The

5. Obviously, all sea-going girls should wear tights!

small crabs are chewed raw like shrimps. As for barnacles, the flat-shelled variety which is regarded as a delicacy in some places was not much to Gilboy's taste. He managed to chew them but never to swallow them!

7. Seaweed

We have already noted in the chapter on thirst that Wiktors Zvejnieks in 1954 survived for forty-six days by feeding almost entirely on floating seaweed. It is one of the few examples that can be quoted, but it is worth bearing in mind. What one survivor has done, others can do.

Unfortunately, the kinds of seaweed which float on the surface have little to do with the species so prized among some Far Eastern people, notably the Japanese. But even if they do not taste good, they have a certain calorie content which may make the difference between starvation and survival.

Last but not least, we have to consider the vexed question of cannibalism. A recent example of survival in the terrible climatic conditions of the High Andes has brought into the open all the philosophical, moral and religious factors involved in this. It was even aired before a large audience in a big television debate. I have recorded examples of cannibalism where they have been reported, from the *Méduse*'s raft to the St Helena deserters and John Dean's experiences. More recently, in 1972, Lucien and Catherine in the course of their twelve days' fast in the Mediterranean openly recognized that this problem often haunted their more or less conscious dreams.

34

The battle against fatigue

When survivors are picked up by a ship or manage to get ashore, they are without exception in a wretched state. The chronic lack of sleep, the permanent discomfort of their craft, and loss of weight and undernourishment are the three factors which combine to bring on, with varying degrees of rapidity, a state of physical debility. Closely bound up with this, difficult as it is to measure, is a fourth, purely psychological factor. These are the factors that we need first to examine and then to find remedies for.

Lack of sleep

Lack of sleep features in the accounts of all survivors at sea, except perhaps of those who had been adrift in their main boat and so remained in relative comfort. Lack of sleep is the normal outcome of what rapidly forms a vicious circle – continuous discomfort which itself sparks off other chain-reactions leading to physical exhaustion.

Blackburn, of course, fought against sleep with every means in his power, knowing that because of the cold he would never wake again. Fortunately, instances like this are the exception. In the great majority of cases it is the impossibility of finding a suitable position which favours falling asleep that is responsible for lack of sleep or at least for intermittent sleep, always quickly interrupted by the thumping of the bottom of the raft on the waves or blows from the fish lurking underneath it. In addition, there are the difficult moments when the survivor has to face dangerous seas that force him to keep a constant lookout to avoid a wave or breaker that might submerge or capsize him.

We know that sleep is as indispensable as water. It is even possible that certain organisms can withstand shortage of water for longer than they can a complete lack of sleep. We also know that the paradoxical type of sleep during which dreams take place is an absolute necessity for many living creatures and that reduction or elimination of it very quickly ends in a pathological condition of waking dreams leading to visual and auditory hallucinations. In a certain number of the older accounts what was attributed by the narrator to madness or delirium was very probably simply the result of these hallucinations.

Permanent discomfort

The problem of discomfort is directly related to the design of lifeboats and rafts. One recalls the acrobatic life in the *Juno*'s rigging that John Mackay and his companions experienced for twenty-one days, or again Romer's three months seated in his kayak. At the other extreme of relative comfort we might place Willis, Gilboy and the survivors of the *Marie-Jeanne* – in fact, all those who were adrift in their main boat. Most of the other cases lie somewhere between these two extremes, their key common feature being the tiny dimensions of the raft. In addition, rafts are very often occupied by a number of survivors having little relation to the capacity intended by the designer – who, for his part, does not always seem to give much thought to giving survivors enough 'living space'. To bring this point home one might recall that the US Navy itself provided for the crew of three of a torpedo bomber one inflatable raft of 8 by 4 feet. Despite owing his life to such a raft, Harold Dixon tells us with some humour:

One of our first discoveries was that it was almost impossible to sleep. To convince yourself of this, just try stretching yourself out on your back with your legs tucked under you – we had no room to stretch ours out. Then get a strong man to keep on tapping you on the head and shoulders with a board. If he gratifies your wish with a couple of taps every three seconds, he will just about reproduce the repeated impact of waves hammering the bottom of the raft. At the same time ask someone else to throw a bucket of cold water over you at regular intervals. Then, for the sound effects of this reconstruction, get a few empty tipper trucks to drive round and round you. After thirty-four days of this régime, you may find it the least bit boring.

This section on permanent discomfort can be summed up in one phrase – virtual immobility. This causes muscular atrophy, stiffness of joints and muscles, and pressure on the skin leading to ulcers, sometimes of the chronic bed-sore type. Immobilization also brings about a loss of bone calcium, just as is found in a fractured limb kept for three months in plaster. One might recall here the decalcification problems encountered by Alain Bombard. More recently this calcium loss has also been detected in cosmonauts.

Deprivations and undernourishment

Because of the wasting and deficiencies they bring about, deprivations are obviously an important factor in the fatigue which sooner or later overwhelms the survivor. Loss of weight during the experience of survival at sea is always considerable and serves to demonstrate this fact.

It is the relative effects of one or other of these three factors which end in physical breakdown, physiological deprivation as doctors call it; this is very likely to be the last phase of a victim's life, rapidly leading to semi-comatose prostration and death. In some instances physical exhaustion is present right at the start; this is almost always the direct result of shipwreck. It presents straightaway a threat of serious consequences, for it is very difficult indeed to regain strength. This was what happened with Lucien and Catherine in the Mediterranean when, over a period of thirty-six hours, they were subjected to dozens of capsizes which left them shattered to face the twelve days that followed. Luckily, it is more common for physical deterioration to set in much more gradually; it has its ups and downs, but is always insidious. So it is essential to make the first move and fight against this hazard right from the start.

However, before looking at the remedies that might be used against the symptoms we can group under the general term of fatigue, it is worth saying a few words about the psychological factors which are apt to influence the onset of fatigue one way or the other, to speed it up or slow it down. These are highly subjective elements, very difficult to extract from the accounts in the first part of this book, and one can hardly list them like the other factors; but even if they stay in the background, these psychological factors are clearly of first importance in every case. To try and quantify the imponderable one might say that every survivor's temperament is going to be tested. Some will submit passively to their lives as victims of shipwreck, while others will try to dominate the situation actively. This is the basic difference between those who fight against the onset of fatigue and those who accept it with resignation. The first of these attitudes leads naturally to consideration of the remedies which can be used to control or slow down this physical debility.

Methods of combating fatigue

To offset lack of sleep as much as possible the problems to be tackled are the cramped space and the incessant violent and painful movement of the bottom of the raft. All survivors agree that fatigue overwhelms them, but when they try to drop off to sleep they cannot. To overcome this some means of stretching out must be found, on one's side rather than one's back. All available textiles – sail, lifejacket, oilskins, etc. – should be used as mattress to ease the effects of blows on the bottom of the raft from fish or the continuous thumping of the waves. The ideal solution is to set watches and sleep in turn, the one whose turn it is to sleep being given every possible comfort so that he can relax completely. Those on watch must help him in every way possible, knowing that their turn will come. I know yachtsmen who follow Bombard's example and carry a plank for their liferaft. This is clearly an excellent solution which should be more widely used. It also has the great advantage of raising the sleeper above the inch or two of water which is often slopping about in the bottom of the raft, and thus plays a large part in countering discomfort.

Since it is impossible to convert a raft into a luxury craft, one has no choice but to submit to the discomfort, at the same time, however, fighting *the consequences of the virtual immobility that the raft imposes.* Bathing is by far the best way.[1] Everything said about bathing under the heading of countering the organism's fluid losses applies equally to countering immobility. Swimming around the raft on a line is the only real muscular exercise a survivor at sea can take. If the temperature of the water allows it, several bathes should be taken every day. It is quite wrong to think that the muscular fatigue induced by swimming will aggravate existing fatigue. They are quite different; it would make perfect sense to talk of healthy fatigue which will tend to bring bowel function, sleep and other things back to normal. The only disadvantage is that exercise sharpens the appetite a little.

When climatic conditions or the continuous presence of sharks prevent bathing, one has to resort to exercise and massage. Bombard forced himself to do flexing exercises every day. Lynn Robertson too imposed this discipline on her whole family, particularly her two young children. She also spent long hours massaging their stiffened limbs, using turtle oil as a lubricant.

It may seem paradoxical to talk about the struggle against undernourishment when survivors at sea spend most of their time in this condition. Nevertheless, a few small details may tip the balance in favour of an improved diet. I mentioned them in the preceding

---

1. Provided no significant heat loss occurs and plenty of fresh water is available (see page 136).

chapter. One is to vary the diet as much as possible by dreaming up day by day new recipes with whatever happens to be available; this prevents one lapsing insidiously into anorexia. Information from hunger strikers shows that the phase in which the feeling of hunger is acute, almost unbearable, is succeeded by a further period of indifference. It is probably the same for a survivor at sea. The more or less conscious revulsion at raw fish, bird and turtle flesh, together with an unvarying menu of them day after day, can easily end in anorexia.

One must therefore force oneself to eat, and to eat properly, with protracted chewing to ease the task of the stomach, which is, after all, not operating under ideal conditions. The secretion of gastric intestinal juices and of bile is in large measure triggered off by the appetizing appearance of a dish and the sensory stimuli it evokes. So putting pieces of meat on whatever will serve as a plate and seasoning them is better than tearing away with one's teeth at an unprepared chunk of fish.

35

The battle against climate

It is very rare for a survivor at sea to enjoy ideal climatic conditions, for this would presuppose a happy mean between four elements which, in their extremes, are always very hard to withstand – heat and cold, rain and drought. Either of the first pair may of course be combined with either of the second.

I dealt with two aspects of this problem in the first chapter of this part of the book. The ways of countering heat are in fact the techniques used to prevent fluid losses from the organism. Likewise, we have explored in depth the action to be taken against drought, which in the end adds up to the problem of getting fresh water. So we must now consider rain and cold.

Rain

Under this heading one is thinking of course of continuous, incessant rain, which can prove a very extravagant solution to the thirst problem. Rain like this gets in everywhere, reduces the raft's buoyancy, forces its occupants to bail frequently and, in a word, makes the survivor's immediate environment one of fresh rather than salt water.

The only real possibility of protection against rain is a sound tent of completely waterproof cloth or, if the raft is not equipped with one, a substitute in the shape of a sail stretched over a jury-rigged framework of paddles or oars. Good oilskins are clearly essential and should always be included in the survival pack or bag that goes with the raft. In fact, oilskins are really as important in surviving every kind of bad weather as the raft itself is in surviving shipwreck at all.

Cold

Here again one is not thinking of the relative coolness experienced by survivors in certain climates at certain seasons, but rather of the real rigours of Arctic cold of which we have seen some examples. Under moderate conditions it is simply a question of differences in day and night temperature giving an impression of cold – certainly very unpleasant and sometimes even intolerable. This was the case with Lucien and Catherine in the Mediterranean in September. On the other hand, we have the almost incredible accounts of Blackburn and his hands frozen on the oars, of Quirini and the eighteen days he and his shipmates spent in the waters of the Arctic Circle in mid-December, or, again, the odyssey of Houiste, whose liferaft was a drifting splinter of iceberg. Cases like this defy analysis; they simply show that the human race produces supermen capable of adapting to unimaginable climatic extremes.

A further point is that, in speaking of cold, temperature itself is not always the key factor. The wind that goes with it sometimes has just as serious consequences. As well as having a powerful effect on the sea state, an increase in wind speed lowers the temperature further. Humidity is an even more important factor; the chilling effect of water is twenty-three times greater than that of air. So it is clear that, at a given temperature, a victim of shipwreck in wet clothes will suffer much more severely from cold than one who is dry-clad.

I should like to quote the following passage from Dr H. Tanguy, whose excellent article in the April 1970 number of the magazine *Bateaux* was mentioned earlier. He gives an ideal summary of the methods of countering cold:

Resistance to cold depends:

on duration of exposure;
on the differing sensitivity of individuals in relation to the thickness of
    the fatty layer, and also to training and psychological resistance;
on the intensity of muscular effort called for (too much activity leads to
    exhaustion and increased sensitivity to cold; insufficient activity
    weakens the body's defence reactions);
on one's position in the raft – the greatest heat losses occur in the
    standing position;
the degree of fatigue and loss of sleep.

Prolonged immersion in the sea in conditions of extreme cold results inevitably and rapidly in death. This apart, various measures can be taken to improve resistance to cold:

Rafts must be enclosed. The ideal is that the survivor should be
    surrounded by a virtually heat-insulated environment – an inflatable

or cellular floor providing a buffer of gas against the cold of the water, and a double-walled tent to protect against the cold of the atmosphere. (This is another way of producing the insulating qualities of an igloo.)

If wet clothing cannot be replaced by dry, it must be wrung out, and the bottom of the raft then bailed dry.

The best materials for protection against cold are wool and mesh, as in string underclothes; plastic materials and oilskins give protection against wind and moisture.

For physiological reasons digestion helps raise body temperature. It is therefore best to eat little and often.

Alcohol increases heat losses by causing dilation of the capillaries near the surface of the skin; the immediate sensation of warmth is illusory and rapidly succeeded by a feeling of intense cold.

Sleep and reduced muscular effort increase the ability to resist cold.

The seated position and being packed closely together maintain body heat.

Survival rations must contain fatty foods for moderate cold, and sugar or glucose-based foods for extreme cold.

36

The battle against panic and despair

Of all the shocks to which the victim of shipwreck is subjected, panic is surely the most dangerous, the one that has chalked up the greatest number of deaths. Indeed, anything that can be said about a subject like this applies not only to shipwreck but as much, if not more, to every kind of circumstance in which a human being is brutally confronted with unexpected hardship.

The examples are without number. Those that first come to mind are events in everyday life – fire in overcrowded public premises, an electricity failure in the underground, the derailment of a train, and so on. In every case the number of victims increases in direct proportion to this factor of panic, which is so difficult to hold in check.

In the area with which we are concerned, apart from the pathetic story of the *Méduse*'s raft, panic does not seem to have had too much adverse effect on the thirty other heroes whose stories we have examined. The explanation is simple enough: none of those who allowed themselves to be overcome by sustained panic has lived to tell the tale.

We know that for Alain Bombard the starting-point for the celebrated application of his theories was prolonged contemplation of the paradox that 90 per cent of the victims of shipwreck die in the three days following the event, yet it takes much longer than that to die of hunger or thirst. In the introduction to his book *Naufragé volontaire* he expounds the arguments which led him to risk his life to prove that his theories were right. He recalls the story of the *Titanic*:

On 15 April 1912, the liner *Titanic* hit an iceberg in the North Atlantic and sank in a few hours. When the first relief ships arrived, three hours after the liner had disappeared, a number of people had either died or gone mad in the lifeboats. Significantly, no child over the age of ten was included among those who had paid for their terror by madness and for their madness by death. The children were still at the age of reason.

Bombard goes on to analyse the feelings of the majority of the victims:

When his ship goes down a man's whole universe goes with it. Because he no longer has a deck under his feet his courage and reason abandon him. Even if he reaches a lifeboat he is not necessarily safe. He sits, slumped, contemplating his misery, and can hardly be said to be alive. Helpless in the night, chilled by sea and wind, terrified by the solitude, by noise and by silence, he takes less than three days to surrender his life.

The introduction to Bombard's book closes with this question which should be inscribed on every liferaft:

How many castaways through the ages have become stiff and sudden corpses, killed, not by the sea, not by hunger or thirst, but by their own terror?

These few lines say it all. All that we can do is try to analyse this psychological aberration and find remedies for it, even though we know that panic, itself very often irrational, may show little response to reasoned solutions.

Littré defines panic as 'a sudden and groundless terror'. Littré could never have been shipwrecked, otherwise he would probably have given the word a different definition. 'Sudden terror' is the least one can say of a man's passing in a few moments from the situation of a sailor to that of a victim of shipwreck. But the word 'groundless' is surely exaggerated. As one reads the tales of every kind of suffering in the first part of this book, every kind of 'ground' leaps from the pages. It is precisely the more or less unconscious knowledge of all these 'grounds' which is bound to trigger off the unreasoning process of panic. Once panic sets in, imagination nurtures it and makes it contagious. The result is then compulsive acts which are almost always ill-starred and catastrophic.

The question of what the remedies for panic are is an extremely difficult one to answer. None the less, certain rules emerge from the experience of those who have been hit by panic or known it for a few seconds. The first point is that the responses are completely different depending on whether the victim of shipwreck is alone or in a group.

For both cases there is, however, one common cure. This is thorough knowledge of the survival equipment and the confidence which this brings. It presupposes that every member of an ocean-going crew is briefed on the safety equipment, is given a demonstration of the handling and use of the raft, and knows the contents of the main survival packs and what to put in the personal survival kit that every good sailor should have prepared for himself. Briefly, it is preparation and conditioning for the possibility of life under survival conditions that make people accept this without panic when it suddenly happens. Observation of this first principle would surely have spared Lucien and Catherine their odyssey in the Mediterranean. One recalls that Lucien 'panicked' for the simple reason that he had no confidence in his inflatable liferaft, being convinced that it would not inflate at the moment he needed it.

A second rule is never to abandon ship, even if the boat looks as though it will certainly be lost, as long as there is the remotest chance of its staying afloat. It is really much better to be shipwrecked on a drifting wreck, as in the cases of Gilboy, Vidot and Corgat, than in a pneumatic raft – which of course then remains as a last resort. The story of Lucien and Catherine illustrates this second rule too; their boat, the *Njord*, was found, still afloat, long before they were.

Other remedies are more closely tied to the situation of a sole survivor and a group.

For a sole survivor the very fact of resisting the clutches of panic is an achievement which augurs well for the future. If, by mischance, one of its claws, one of the ramifications which nurture panic, gains a hold in the victim's mind, no rules will help much. One can indeed prescribe constant occupation of mind and body, recall all those who have experienced equally dramatic situations – even perhaps find examples of still worse conditions – and one can appeal to religious feelings, faith and prayer; but all this is useless if the victim does not have within himself the qualities and the temperament that will enable him to break the hold of panic on his own.

The conditions under which panic appears and thus may be cured in a group of victims of shipwreck are very different. Because of its contagious nature panic, having once infected a single member of the group, can gain a hold on all. However, if just one personality remains free of this psychological cancer, there is every chance that the others will be cured of it too. The answer lies, then, in whether or not the shipwrecked group contains a man with nerves of steel who succeeds, at the critical moment, in crushing once and for all the spirit of madness which inspires panic. There is no lack of examples. I think the best of all is that of Captain Bligh and, nearer our own times, that of Teehu, the pearl-fisher of Manihiki.

The role of a leader like this is by no means easy. All the sang-froid he possesses must be given over to the maintenance of a serene calm which serves as an example and is, on its own, enough to calm the others' minds.

On other occasions violence may help. The classic double slap, the old cure for hysterical crises, may also be the remedial gesture which drives the demon panic away. Alternatively, the point of the chin is the best target for a knock-out blow to produce the saving grace of unconsciousness – just as the rescuer of a drowning man knocks him out so as not to be dragged down with him. After this first stage come reasoning and the allocation of activities, of permanent duties and clear-cut roles, producing a sense of responsibility towards the group as a whole. These can provide a measure of psychological support.

Within the scope of this chapter despair should also be examined. One can see that the onset of despair is easy to explain when living conditions or the duration of the survival experience cross a certain threshold, clearly very variable from one individual to another, beyond which the victim feels he has no more chance of pulling through. Despair can also be the result of a major disappointment – a ship which passes and takes no notice, a shower which falls just beyond reach. a tasty fish which gets away, and so on. It was despair that drove Commander Denny, up to that point a real leader of men, to throw himself overboard and make a quick end of it. It was despair which made Lucien and Catherine drink up all the rest of their water at once. It was really despair too which drove McCannon to talk of sacrificing one man to allow the others to survive.

Every survivor has known those terrible moments when the 'frenzy to survive' contends with the longing to have done with it all. Almost all of them, or at least of those who have lived to tell the tale, have succeeded in overcoming this feeling and sometimes discovering in their struggle a new reason for continuing the fight.

It is also in these times of despair that many victims of shipwreck have gone back to the prayers of their childhood, put themselves at peace with God and, as a result, regained a serenity they thought beyond them. The pages which the Bourdens, the Robertsons and the Baileys have written on this are deeply moving, as is Barry Wynne's account of the indestructible faith of Teehu Makimare.

37
The battle against drowning

Along with panic, drowning kills most people. Alain Bombard quotes the statistics for the 1950s. These amount to some 200,000 victims of shipwreck per year, a staggering figure which can be divided into about 150,000 drowned and 50,000 who survived at least for a few hours or days with the help of lifeboats or liferafts.

The drowning problem should be examined in terms of the two times when it normally occurs – the shipwreck itself and the capsize of a lifeboat or raft.

On abandoning ship

The risks of drowning are greatest at the time of the shipwreck itself. There are various circumstances which tend to increase the risk.

The absence of lifejackets, or at least of a sufficient number of them, is very common, bearing repeated witness to the negligence of the master or owner of the boat. Even if it is accepted that all shipwrecked people can swim, something which is becoming increasingly the rule,[1] the absence of lifejackets is a major handicap resulting in a number of secondary risks.

Sea state is another key factor. Heavy seas encourage panic and may very rapidly exhaust a person in the water who has lost sight of his shipmates and/or the raft that means safety. This emphasizes the need to do everything possible to ensure that the raft is launched close to the side, made fast securely with the warp slack or taut depending on the extent to which the disabled ship is rolling. Each person must enter the lifeboat or raft in turn, settle down, bearing in mind that he must act as a counterweight to those who follow, and stow as securely and quickly as possible all the precious cargo passed down to him.

---

1. This may be true of France, but is certainly not true of the UK, where the number of non-swimmers remains astonishingly and alarmingly high.

Water temperature is another important factor in drowning, once it falls to levels where human resistance is rapidly exhausted. The American Navy has published the following table which explains, far better than discussion, the result of cold and exhaustion acting in conjunction:

Water temperature 0°C (32°F), time of survival well below 1 hour.
Water temerature 5°C (41°F), time of survival between ½ hour and 3 hours.
Water temperature 10°C (50°F), time of survival between 1 hour and 6 hours.
Water temperature 15°C (59°F), time of survival between 2 hours and 24 hours.
Water temperature 20°C (68°F), time of survival between 3 hours and 40 hours.
From 25°C (77°F) upwards, time of survival can be regarded as unlimited, so that it is physical exhaustion which leads to drowning.

Another factor is the *weight of clothing*. Many victims of shipwreck who abandon ship as she is sinking drown because they are dragged to the bottom by the weight of all the clothing they want to take with them. This clothing soaks up the water and quickly gains weight. One needs, therefore, to know how to undress in the water, empty one's pockets, take off one's shoes, and so on. On the other hand, shirt and trousers, thanks to air bubbles trapped in certain positions, may aid buoyancy. It is worth recalling the story of Arne Nicolaysen who kept afloat by swimming for twenty-nine hours and took his socks half-off to give himself warning of attack from sharks. His story, together with that of Tice, also shows that, even if the liferaft disappears from view, the person in the water must at all costs resist despair and wait for those who have managed to reach the craft to come and look for others.

Capsizing of lifeboat

Drowning when a lifeboat or raft overturns is rarer. In the accounts we we have studied it arises only in cases where the craft could not be righted and the survivors became exhausted and soon let go. This is what happened to Armstrong's companions. In the other stories featuring capsize, particularly that of Lucien and Catherine who turned over dozens of times, the survivors have managed to right their boat at the cost of more and more exhausting physical effort and the loss of most of their provisions and equipment. Admittedly, there must be many who failed to right their craft and have not lived to tell the tale; for people such as Gilboy and Teehu Makimare, who are capable of righting or refloating a large boat, are exceptional. Rather than explore the ways of righting a lifeboat or raft further, I would refer the reader to the accounts which deal with this problem, those of Gilboy in the Pacific and Lucien and Catherine in the Mediterranean – and especially of Teehu Makimare.

38

The battle against not being spotted
and the dangers of going ashore[1]

In the first part of this book it was not possible in all cases to cover the physical and psychological problems posed by what, in theory, amounts to the end of the survivor's suffering. I say 'in theory', for the two ways which can bring a period of survival at sea to a successful conclusion, appearance of a ship or reaching shore, are full of pitfalls.

A key point is that of the thirty-one accounts we examined only one, Teehu Makimare and the *Tearoha*, involved an active search. The study also showed reaching shore to be the more usual occurrence. Eighteen out of thirty achieved this, admittedly sometimes to find living conditions there scarcely better than those they had just left. Twelve were rescued by ships which crossed their paths. To balance this account one must add, however, that of the eighteen who finally found safety on terra firma most had also seen ships but had been unable to attract their attention. This, in fact, seems to be the whole problem.

The obvious sometimes bears repeating: the fact is that modern navigational aids have radically changed the life and mentality of sailors. Radar systems, gyrocompasses and, most of all, autopilots and self-steering gears have provided many boats, including some yachts, with a new order of safety. A side-effect of this has been the almost complete abandonment of the good old rule that every boat must keep a sharp lookout. Only among navies, with their high standards of discipline, can a visual lookout still be counted on. This makes the future very black for victims of shipwreck; they can no longer rely on that kind of tacit solidarity that lookouts on every ship once provided.

---

1. In this and some subsequent chapters I have left the detail of the original, corresponding to French regulations practice, as it will provide English-speaking readers with an interesting comparison.

It is more and more illusory to place one's faith in the traditional distress signals. In my opinion the problem is to try and find other means better suited to today's maritime practices.

It may help to divide distress signals into three categories: traditional methods by day and night; do-it-yourself methods when conventional means are lacking; modern methods, not yet specified in detail or laid down in regulations, which every thinking sailor should do something about.

1. Methods of indicating position at sea

The traditional methods, distress signals, are many in number. We might look first at those which are most valuable at night. All in all they are highly effective but their success relies on the eye of a watchkeeper on the ship. Having myself spent some 1500 hours on night watch on the bridge, I can say with some confidence that it is by night that these devices are most likely to be seen.

The most effective signals are *red parachute flares*. French law requires every craft cleared for coastal, offshore or ocean use to carry four of these. Class I, II and IV liferafts must carry two. Incidentally, the four flares required by law will fit very nicely into the container that every good sailor prepares against the possibility of shipwreck, so he will in fact start life as a castaway with six flares. These flares reach a height of 600 ft and can be seen at fifteen miles in average visibility.

On this topic Jacques Vignes has made a penetrating analysis of the case of Lucien Schitz:

The purpose of the parachute flare is to give the alert. Once it has been launched, the rescuers' efforts must be guided by another distress signal – hand-held automatic red flares (the sticks of phosphorus mentioned by Lucien are not approved in France).[2]

. . . The first flare may not be noticed. Generally, that happens because the flare has been quite wasted by being launched too far from the coast and without first determining whether there was a reasonable chance of anyone seeing it. Yet, sometimes, as we have seen, the flare goes unnoticed even by those to whom it is directed. In other cases, also, it may be necessary to send off a second flare before being able to make worthwhile use of the red hand flares.

And giving the alert does not necessarily mean being rescued. We have seen,

---

2. I think this must be simply loose terminology. A hand-held phosphorus flare would be incredibly dangerous, and I cannot believe they were on the market in Europe in the 1970s.

as in the case of the *Njord*, rescuers looking for survivors for hours, not finding them, and these survivors being saved subsequently by other rescuers. The main piece of advice to give about using distress signals is not to be hasty. One must launch them only on the basis of reasonable expectation, when, in one's opinion, the most favourable conditions are united to provide for them the maximum effectiveness. Using them during the day is usually a needless waste.

Vignes continues his analysis:

Incidentally, using them is not always without dangers. . . .

There are many cases of burns caused by distress signals. In my opinion, there are two factors responsible for the occurrence of this type of accident. First, although many flares are manufactured, they are (happily) seldom used. Most of them end their short-lived careers at the bottom of the sea (where they are required to be thrown once their expiration dates have been reached). We are talking, therefore, about things which are seldom if ever handled. If it were otherwise, the manufacturers would soon redesign them to make them much safer to handle.

Next, the person using one is not only sure to be under stress but also nearly always a novice in the matter. Usually the person has just read the instructions for their use for the first time or, if he has read them before, is sure to have forgotten them. As things stand now, such a predicament is virtually inevitable. For obvious reasons, it is strictly forbidden to set off distress signals without cause, which at once rules out any experimentation. Would it be possible to do things differently? To authorize experimental launchings in certain areas and under certain conditions? This question has been asked several times. Until now there has been no official reply.[3]

Red hand-held flares, as we have just seen, take over from parachute flares. Class I liferafts carry six and Class II and IV rafts only three. Their range is five miles in very good visibility. If the seas are high, they can be seen only intermittently; being held at arm's length while burning, their light is inevitably masked by the wavecrests.

Here we might turn once again to Jacques Vignes:

The risk of burning one's hand is less great than with rocket flares, but the heat of the casing may become so great as to force one to let go before the flare has fully burned. . . .

But even if the hand is relatively protected, the same does not hold true for the surroundings. Blown back by the wind, sparks may burn faces, damage sails or, worse still, the rubber raft in which one has taken refuge. Therefore, one must position oneself so that the wind carries the smoke seaward.

---

3. This is not the case in the UK, where demonstration firings are arranged from time to time, usually by clubs affiliated to the Royal Yachting Association, acting in conjunction with the Coastguards and other authorities concerned.

By day these two main types of distress signal are of very little use. The accounts of Part 1 demonstrate this. On the eighth day of their life as survivors the Baileys saw a ship just over a mile off; they fired three flares which functioned correctly but did not attract the ship's attention. It was the same with their fourth flare on the twenty-fifth day. The Robertsons used two red parachute flares and three illuminating flares[4] on their seventh day; these were directed at a ship which passed by about three miles off without seeing anything. In the Mediterranean Bombard too experienced this kind of setback. At 6.00 p.m. on 6 June he fired two flares to no effect. The following day, 7 June, fourteen days out from Monaco, he fired three flares for a ship three miles off. Again no result. He then used a smoke signal which was quickly spotted.

In broad daylight the *smoke signal* is the most effective device. Here is what Vignes, our specialist on this topic, has to say about it:

There is no danger of burns with smoke signals. Once the pin has been pulled and they have been thrown into the sea they give off a thick red smoke for at least four minutes.[5] Yet there is another risk: that they do no good at all unless used during a dead calm. The slightest breeze blows the smoke along over the sea and dissipates it. Apparently, floating smoke canisters are useful for attracting the attention of an aeroplane. I have never had any personal experience with them and have never met anyone who could give me any actual information on that point.

In fact, I can answer Jacques Vignes's question myself. In the Pacific I had the opportunity of working with our Naval Aviation on some experiments on this precise point. The aim of our study was to compare the conspicuousness of buoyant smoke signals and coloured fluorescent-type products spread on the surface in a large patch contrasting strongly with the blue of the ocean. In the absence of a victim we dropped the devices ourselves, flew off around the Tuomotu atolls and then tried to find the smoke and coloured patches again. I can say that, provided we did not have the sun in our eyes, both were clearly visible at our flying height of 5000–10,000 ft. I must also, of course, point out that the experiment was invalidated from the start by the fact that we set off these distress signals ourselves and thus had a better idea where to find them. However, this does not alter the fact that they are very easily seen in good weather.

4. i.e., white anti-collision flares, which are not in fact a distress signal.
5. On the British market there are two types of smoke signal, hand-held and buoyant, associated with the standard coastal and offshore flare packs respectively.

When there are no conventional distress signals or they have been used unsuccessfully, one has to resort to much less orthodox methods of signalling. Once again the distinction must be drawn between day and night methods.

At night the whole problem is to set up a light source intense and long-lasting enough to attract attention. Many modern survivors have had a torch with the bulb and batteries still working. The Baileys used theirs on their twenty-fifth day to no avail. For the Robertsons, on the other hand, a torch brought rescue on their thirty-eighth day, after they has used a hand-held illuminating flare and a second which hung fire as night fell. A torch can also be used to give indirect light. Bombard did this by shining it on his sail for the completely different reason of making up for his lack of navigation lights.[6]

There is no evidence of the use of an electronic or magnesium photographic flash. In fact, apart from the Baileys, the victims of shipwreck who have thought of taking their camera with them as they abandoned ship have been few; and the Baileys had no flash. The following advice may be helpful. For any sailor who has with him a large number of flash bulbs, or better still an electronic flash, it is well worth while to take them with him – not to provide a photographic record of his hardships but to use as a distress signal. The light of a flash is visible over long distances, and repeated flashes can be used to guide the rescue boat. It is worth pointing out that complicated apparatus of this kind does not take kindly to damp and spray, so it must be kept in a completely waterproof plastic bag.

A third solution by night is to light a fire. This presupposes that the survivor has fuel, paper, cloth, plastic or pieces of wood, and of course matches or a lighter. All these objects are treasures, and it takes great strength of mind to burn them with the thought at the back of one's mind that the lookout on the passing ship is probably non-existent. The Robertsons even tried, luckily for them without success, to set their sail on fire. This was on their seventh day when they saw their first ship.

Apart from the traditional shirt waved in the hand, daytime methods add up to mirror or smoke. Only Class I liferafts are equipped with a signalling mirror. The smaller ones do not have this in their standard equipment – an omission in the regulations which the buyer would do well to remedy. Properly handled – that is, so as to reflect the sun or a

---

6. This is, of course, also recommended practice for yachts under sail at night in areas of heavy traffic, when ships are sighted in heavy weather or as a preliminary to firing an anti-collision flare.

bright light towards the ship whose attention is to be attracted – and used with perseverance, the mirror has proved a successful method. Continuous or intermittent mirror flashes on the surface of the waves, which look quite different from the sparkle of the waves themselves, will catch the attention of a keen eye – if, of course, there is one. When a survivor knows a sea or air search for him has been mounted, mirror signalling is most useful.

The second method, a substitute for smoke signals, is also an excellent one. The Baileys used it on their thirty-ninth day, when they sighted their fourth ship. After the first three disappointments, they had prepared a small stove in a turtle-shell; on this they raised and lowered a damp towel to make the kind of smoke signals so beloved of Red Indians. This could well have succeeded. The ship evidently saw this unusual smoke; she stopped and turned through 180° but resumed course without spotting them. The Baileys themselves provided the explanation – the relative positions were such that the lookouts on the ship, however vigilant, had the sun in their eyes. This was the time they most of all regretted not having a mirror for making signals.

We must now turn to modern methods. Unlike the ones already discussed, they owe little to do-it-yourself techniques but are highly sophisticated methods which must be provided for well in advance. Like every aspect of survival, this must be foreseen and organized before having to be put to eventual use.

The first possibility springs from the existence, known for forty years or more, of what is termed by international agreement as the SOFAR channel (Sound Fixing and Ranging). This is a layer of water in the ocean through which sounds are transmitted almost perfectly and over virtually unlimited distances. This layer lies roughly between depths of 600 and 1200 m (roughly 325-650 fathoms). Sound waves released within it strike the layers of water above and below whose properties are sufficiently different to reflect the waves and thus channel them onwards almost without interruption. The detonation of an explosive charge can be 'heard' at 15,000 miles. It is even thought that whales, using the SOFAR channel, can communicate at distances calculated in thousands of miles. This has a practical application for survivors. If they have available suitable alarm systems, monitoring stations which already exist all over the world can locate their position in the open sea to within about one square mile.

The second method takes into consideration one of the most basic facts for all survivors: in more and more cases the watch on ships is now kept on a radar screen. The problem of being spotted by day and by night might thus be partially solved by liferafts having the means of giving a clear signal on these screens. To this end I suggest that the tent or superstructure and the inflatable rings of all liferafts should be coated with metallic paint to improve the radar echo. Knowing the difficulties of interpreting the kind of echo that might be produced by a small liferaft in the midst of the clutter produced by the surface of the sea, I would further suggest that all rafts should be equipped with, say, two or three large balloons made of strong foil or thin rubber and, once again, coated with metallic paint. If a ship were in sight, the survivor would reach for his balloons and blow them up hard – or, better still, use small canisters of compressed hydrogen (which must also, of course, be in the survival kit) to get good lift. Secured to the raft, these balloons could then rise to heights of 50 to 75 feet or more. This would produce an echo on the radar screen that would be much more conspicuous and would catch the eye at once. In addition, these balloons would also have the opposite effect to a sea-anchor and significantly increase the raft's windage and thus its rate of drift.[7]

At the beginning of this chapter I pointed out that in the case of thirty of our survivors and their numerous companions there had been no active search. Apart from the *Tearoha*, the other exception may have been the *Central America*. We have no information on this, but it seems very probable that a mayday signal was made, since several ships appeared on the scene rapidly both before and after the ship went down.

So we have to consider the possibility of a search, fortunately an increasingly common one, as more small boats become equipped with two-way RT. An excellent solution would of course be to have a battery-powered RT set which could easily and, above all, quickly be picked up at the moment of abandoning ship and taken on board the raft in a large waterproof plastic bag. In these circumstances – with the possible exception of rare cases like that of the Robertson family who had only four minutes to get clear of the *Lucette* – a mayday signal could be made before transferring to the liferaft. The possibility imposes two requirements – knowing the exact position of the wreck and staying there.

The first of these presupposes that the navigator has taken a daily fix. A quick dead-reckoning calculation (distance made good and

7. This is an excellent idea; so far as I can establish neither balloons nor kites are provided for in any leading British liferaft/survival pack. There seems no reason why they should not be inflated and deployed automatically when the raft is deployed, with spares provided in the pack.

course since the fix) would then allow an estimated position of abandoning ship to be sent. Should the survivors be fortunate enough to have taken a battery-powered RT set with them on the raft, they might be able to maintain contact with the rescuers and thus greatly improve the probability of their being spotted and picked up.[8]

The second requirement is to stay near the position of the wreck. This requires use of the sea-anchor – and a great deal of patience, for searches almost always take a long time. It hardly needs emphasizing that water and food rationing should be started straightaway, just as if no search had been launched.

Methods of signalling to be used will obviously be those discussed above. They are all the more effective because the searchers will be keeping a diligent and unwavering lookout for them.

2. The dangers of getting ashore

On 8 July 1810 the St Helena deserters reached the coast of Brazil; they still numbered five. That day the breakers swept the bodies of three drowned men on to the shore. For them, as for many others before and after them, the land had not given them a very warm welcome.

A coral reef that tears the raft and its occupants to pieces, a cliff too steep for the exhausted survivors to climb, huge breakers which capsize the raft and swallow up the men, inshore currents which relentlessly drive them out to sea again – these are some of the hazards that may have to be faced in getting ashore.

I should like to quote again from Alain Bombard:

Once in sight of land, the worst seems over, but remember the danger of being killed by the very land which promises salvation. Take your time. Impatience can ruin everything. Stop the boat, observe the coast closely and choose your point. Never forget that 90 per cent of all accidents occur on landing. You must choose a stretch where the sea beats less violently, where there is sand or beach and not some murderous rock. The way to determine this is by observing the colour and nature of the sea; little white caps probably hide a reef, so take care. Make only for smooth stretches without turbulence or breaking waves.

---

8. There are, of course, a number of sets in the EPIRB (Emergency Position Indicating Radio Beacon) category which are waterproof and start to function automatically when immersed. There are also emergency battery-powered AM (medium wave) and VHF RT sets working on Channel 16 only – see Royal Yachting Association Booklet G22/78 and manufacturers' catalogues.

Using local currents, Bombard succeeded in catching a breeze parallel to the shore and running along the coast in search of a sandy beach. His story is instructive and his experience is unique:

I was by this time 300 yards out, and had made up my mind that this was the point to land; it took me three more hours to get there. Now I had found a stretch of sand, my life was no longer in danger. The dinghy was undamaged and all its equipment intact, but I took special care to protect my precious log notes, with all the details I hoped would help to save the lives of so many future castaways.

The final manoeuvre was exhausting for anybody as worn out as I was. As on most of the African and Caribbean surf beaches, the waves did not break with equal force, but with a clearly defined rhythm which differs from place to place. The seventh and the sixteenth are usually the most dangerous and must be met with extreme care. At this point, every seventh wave seemed the strongest. The wind was abeam and I turned the dinghy to present the stern to the shore. At the third wave in each series I turned about to gain some distance towards the shore. After the fifth I faced out to sea again to take the force of the seventh wave by the bow. Laboriously, I covered a few yards at a time, but each successive seventh wave became more and more dangerous. The fishermen who had seen me did not yet seem to realize that there was anything unusual in my arrival or that any boat coming from my direction must hail from the far off lands of their ancestors.

Suitably adapted for each type of coast, Bombard's advice always holds good: 'Stop, look and choose.' In this crucial moment of getting ashore the sea-anchor or local currents may prove an invaluable addition to the survivor's experience of handling his raft.

39

The battle against illness

All the prevailing factors in survival at sea are themselves contributory causes to what one might call the pathology of the victim of shipwreck. It seems clear that a large number of the conditions from which every survivor suffers sooner or later can really be explained by one of three things: the climatic conditions which he must withstand without any real shelter and usually without suitable clothing, with the common factor – regardless of latitude and season – of humidity and the corrosive action of salt; the conditions of food and water intake, usually a meagre and unbalanced diet, which affect most of the metabolic processes and consequently all aspects of the survivor's health, notably by weakening all the organism's defences; and the conditions of life on a tiny raft which lead to lack of sleep and virtual immobility.

This is clearly rather a generalized treatment, for many other factors play a part too, but if we stick to these three main causes we shall not, in my opinion, miss very much that affects the survivor's condition. Let us now examine them in detail: for the sake of clarity and to avoid putting the reader off with a dry pathological treatise I shall look at the conditions and their symptoms and treatment organ by organ, or rather system by system. I have placed them in an order matching their frequency of occurrence according to the accounts in the first part of this book.

1) *The locomotor system* is statistically the most often affected; one might even say that it is always impaired. The absence of physical activity puts the survivor at sea in the same category as an injured person – for instance, someone with a fractured limb who has to spend three months in bed. The bones decalcify, the muscles atrophy and the joints stiffen. There is only one treatment for these three elements in the disorder of the locomotor system – movement in the form of exercises, massage, bathing, and so on. Here I would refer the reader to Chapter 34 on the battle against fatigue.

2) *The skin, teeth, nails and hair* come a close second. Most survivors' accounts tell of a whole host of skin troubles: boils, which begin as small sores but are aggravated by the action of salt water until they become real ulcers which show no sign of healing; and pressure on the skin from a skeleton with less and less protection from wasting muscular tissue, once again resulting in ulcerations, mainly on the buttocks and the sacral region, which may also become increasingly inflamed.

Since even Class I liferafts do not carry a proper emergency medicine chest, one must assume that the victim of shipwreck has not thought to put one in his survival bag either. The question is then, what can be done to relieve simple discomfort before it turns to real suffering – in other words, to stabilize or even cure skin conditions before lack of treatment makes their aggravation almost inevitable? I suggest that the following preventive measures should be taken by survivors at all costs:

Movement to prevent compression and resulting tenderness of the skin.

Every kind of precaution to avoid the small injuries which are of no concern in normal life – use of a rag or piece cut from one's trousers to protect the hands when fishing, preparing a fish, dissecting a turtle, and so on.

Avoidance of sunburn in the tropics, when the skin may undergo twelve hours a day of intense heat, further increased by reflection from the surface of the water.

Use of every shower of rain to wash away all salt from the body and all available clothing and cloths, so as to limit skin irritation.

Drying in the sun of small pieces of cloth for use as sterile dressings (the sun's ultra-violet rays having high sterilizing power).

When the first skin lesions appear, as they are almost bound to, despite the advice on prevention given above, everything must be done to stop them developing. Pieces of cloth washed free of salt in a shower of rain, or with fresh water if there is enough to spare, can be made into bandages and applied to the area to be treated as protection against the sun and salt spray. As a healing agent, one might use a slice of fish liver or soft roe – the kind of fish does not matter – placed between the lesion and the improvised dressing. One should try to renew this with fresh liver or soft roe every day. When turtle oil is available, fatty dressings are indicated because of their excellent insulating effect. Periods of exposure to fresh air – but with protection against sun and spray – must be alternated with these two types of dressing to speed up the drying of the sores.

The nails, in particular, may undergo changes. On this point it is worth quoting the findings of Surgeon-Captain John Duncan Walters, of the Institute of Naval Medicine of the Royal Navy, who studied the Baileys' case:

Why Maralyn's finger nails lost their natural coloration is an interesting problem. The normal translucent pinkish colour of the finger nails was maintained for the first month in the raft and then, over a period of about two weeks they changed from pink to pale pink and, finally, pearly white. They did not become unnaturally brittle or deformed, and, now the nails are growing out, a distinct transverse line of demarcation between pearly white and the normal colour may be seen on each nail. Although the feet were equally exposed to the elements the toe nails did not show the same discoloration, and, whilst various suggestions and explanations for this phenomenon have been offered, no final conclusions have yet been reached.

(Bombard, however, completely lost his toe nails.)

With regard to the teeth, Bombard suffered, from the fifth day of his experiment, an abscess which collected pus much more quickly than usual – according to him, because of the organism's weakened defences. (At that point he had had nothing to eat and only seawater to drink.) He lanced the abscess himself with the point of his seaman's knife, sterilized in a flame, and it then cleared up very quickly.

3)   *The digestive system* is also an early victim of survival conditions, even if the results are less spectacular.

One of the first problems may be seasickness. For all victims of shipwreck the movements of the raft are completely different from the familiar movements of their boat, to which they have become fully adapted. Vomiting and the resulting dehydration and loss of electrolytes from the digestive juices may, right from the start, put the occupants of a liferaft in a worse physical condition to tackle the rest of their time adrift. The equipment of Class 1 rafts provides for six seasickness pills a head, while Class II and IV rafts have only six tablets in all. This is inadequate for getting one's sea legs in a strange craft, and those suffering from seasickness must be given priority for stretching out on the bottom of the raft. If the reserves of water allow, their ration should be increased. The addition of a small quantity of seawater may restore the levels of sodium chloride in the organism because, of the electrolytes contained in the gastric juices and bile, chlorine and sodium are the two most frequently lost by vomiting. Another way of fighting seasickness is to occupy oneself permanently with a demanding task such as bailing or rowing. Everyone, in fact, has a patent remedy that will relieve him with varying degrees of success.

During the first few days the sensation of hunger may be succeeded by stomach pains in the form of abdominal cramps spreading towards both shoulders. These usually cease on the third or fourth day of fasting.

It is worth repeating here that the digestive problems, vomiting and diarrhoea, formerly said to be the consequence of drinking seawater, do not occur if it is taken in strict accordance with the rules stated by Bombard – 800 ml per day, a little at a time, for not more than seven days and, above all, provided that the diet is started before any degree of dehydration has set in.

Constipation is inevitable on board liferafts; for most survivors it lasts for weeks. Fortunately, it is not painful, as wind continues to be released, and has nothing to do with an intestinal stoppage. It must be partly attributable to lack of physical activity and the imbalance caused by a violent change in diet, notably the absence of vegetable fibres.[1] We have already seen that enemas of salt water or turtle oil have been found effective in treating this complaint.

On the other hand, few accounts mention bouts of diarrhoea. These are much more serious because, like vomiting, they cause major losses of fluids and electrolytes. Diarrhoea calls for an increase in the intake of water and sodium chloride in the form of small quantities of seawater. Maurice Bailey produced a full-scale dysentery syndrome, perhaps from poisoning by bad fish or turtle fillets. Bombard suffered the same, a month before reaching Barbados. His attack went on for fourteen days and was accompanied by massive rectal discharge and bleeding which left him gasping with weakness and twice almost made him lose consciousness.

To conclude this section I should like to mention a condition which is never reported but which must be present in some survivors – gastric or duodenal stress ulcers. We know that all major, repetitive stress may result in the rapid formation – over a period of days – of a gastric ulcer. Clearly, no kind of life could be much more stressful than that of the survivor at sea. One of the main causes of these ulcers is constant anxiety, nervousness and mental distress – in fact, all the elements of panic. This is yet another reason why it is so important to fight panic in the ways suggested in Chapter 36.

1. According to British opinion, low food and water intake is the sole reason for this type of constipation. It is of no medical significance and thus requires no treatment.

4)   *The sensory organs* also have a place in this review of the pathology of life adrift. Those mainly affected are the eyes which have to cope with the powerful reflections of ultra-violet rays from the surface of the water. The reader will recall that Jean de Léry thought he had gone blind and that one of Houiste's shipmates did go blind for forty-eight hours after landing, having spent fifteen days on the drifting ice-floe. Ophthalmia (inflammation of the eyes) is therefore a problem which must be tackled by preventive action. The best way is, of course, to make sure you take with you sunglasses with very heavily tinted lenses.[2] Without these the survivor must rig himself an eyeshade and do his best to live with the sun on his back, keeping his eyes as nearly closed as possible. He should withdraw under his tent, if he has one, or put an opaque cloth over his face when he does not need to use his eyes for some specific purpose. If, ophthalmia still occurs, he must make himself an opaque bandage and remain for at least forty-eight hours in darkness before trying to recover the use of his eyes. The eyes will still be in a very delicate state, and prophylactic measures must be applied even more strictly.

Conjunctivitis has also frequently been reported. All one can advise, in the absence of eye lotion, is bathing of the eyes with the purest possible rainwater to clear the conjunctiva of its secretions of serum and pus.

Hearing problems are mentioned only by Jean de Léry who suffered a pronounced loss of aural acuity on landing and feared, wrongly as luck would have it, that he had gone deaf.

5)   *The respiratory system* seems to pose few problems, apart from the cases of Sandy Robertson, who had broncho-pneumonia, and Maurice Bailey, who suffered for a long time from shortness of breath, complained of pain in the side of his chest, and had several bouts of spitting blood.

The infrequency of bronchial and lung conditions among individuals who have to face so much bad weather may seem surprising. Even those who experienced the worst cold – Blackburn, Houiste and Quirini, for instance – suffered terrible frost-bite or amputations of their extremities but never mentioned a word about chest troubles. Life in the open air must have at least one salutary side to it!

6)   *The urinary system* adapts well to conditions of survival at sea. It

2. The problem is reflected ultra-violet light, just as it is in snow blindness. It is therefore important to have side-shades on the glasses or a 'wraparound' visor.

even attempts to limit dehydration by reducing the amount of urine passed when the fluid intake is insufficient. However, it can only tolerate so much, and it is the kidney which plays a large part in the deterioration of general health, once a certain tolerance threshold is exceeded.

Clearly, the kidney has to work harder when the survivor is forced to drink seawater. The limited quantity of 800 ml per twenty-four hours introduces about 28 g of sodium chloride, which the kidney cannot excrete over long periods without risk of becoming inflamed. The puffiness of Bombard's face when he arrived in the Balearics after ten days out of fourteen on seawater (albeit not ten consecutive days) was symptomatic of this tendency towards salt water retention. Nevertheless, the kidney is an organ which recovers very quickly, and the technique recommended by Bombard is completely valid.

7) *The cardiovascular system* also stands up very well to life adrift. The only exception, after a few weeks, is a fall of blood pressure and a permanent speeding up of the heart-beat, probably linked to the almost universal anaemia which will be examined later.

8) *The genital system.* In the accounts we have studied only Maralyn Bailey reported cessation of her periods for three months after the first one, which itself came six days late. This is not a worrying symptom, for it is well known that women often suffer menstrual irregularities when under stress, whatever the cause.

The universal modesty of survivors leaves us uninformed on the subject of sexual activity during their lives adrift. However, for those interested in the problem the reader may refer to the account of the ACALI Expedition organized in 1973 by Santiago Génoves, a sociologist and anthropologist, who wanted to study the scientific and human aspects of relations between individuals faced with major survival problems. He built a raft, 40 feet long and 23 feet wide, and, by numerous psychological tests, carefully chose ten other people to accompany him. The composition of this crew was interesting: apart from Génoves himself, a Mexican, there were a female Israeli doctor, a female Swedish naval officer, a male Greek radio operator, a black American mother, a white American waitress, a French frogwoman, a female Algerian librarian, a Uruguayan father and a male Japanese photographer. They left Las Palmas on 12 May 1973 and, after a crossing of 4,632 miles, reached the isle of Cozumel off the Yucatán Peninsula 101 days later. The press reported the expedition in detail at the time, provocatively christening the raft the 'Sex Raft'. A major part of Santiago Génoves' work develops all the psycho-sociological factors involved in an adventure of this kind, but these cannot be examined here.

9)   *The major metabolic processes* are nearly all affected. One of the main reasons for this is the almost total lack of carbohydrates in the diet of a survivor who is living by fishing. In this way the survivor at sea undergoes the kind of slimming diet so favoured these days by women's magazines. Loss of weight among survivors is therefore always considerable – 55 pounds for Bombard's sixty-five days, 22 and 33 pounds for the Robertsons' thirty-eight days and 44 pounds each for the Baileys after 117 days adrift. Figures are lacking for many of the others, but the descriptions and the difficulties encountered by doctors in restoring survivors to health give rise to quite incredible suppositions. This was the case with Zvejnieks, with Widdicombe and Tapscott, and with Antoine Vidot and Selby Corgat, for example. These men had virtually no success with fishing, and their loss of weight was essentially like fasting – the organism using up its own reserves. In cases like these all metabolic processes are affected, and in particular those concerned with proteins, the lack of which is responsible for the deficiency oedemas (swellings) so often reported in survivors' accounts.

Anaemia too is always present. On arriving at Barbados, Bombard's red corpuscle count was down to 2,500,000 per cubic millimetre, but in his case massive and repeated rectal haemorrhages were added to the other causes of anaemia. These are not really fully understood; lack of certain vitamins, especially B12, are most probably a factor, together with wasting of the body and some perturbation of the kidney function. All these conditions are normally accompanied by anaemia, and in this case their effects are combined.

As we have already seen, phosphorus and calcium metabolism is impaired by the lack of physical activity. Scurvy, the lack of Vitamin C, has only occasionally been reported, for in most instances of sea survival the time adrift falls far short of the long months endured by sailors of a few centuries ago. Nevertheless sub-clinical symptoms of scurvy appear in some accounts, such as that of Teehu Makimare. To prevent it Bombard collected a small quantity of plankton every day, and the Baileys treated themselves to the eyes, brain and pancreas of fish – organs which have a high concentration of Vitamin C.

With regard to problems arising from varying degrees of toxicity in fish, I would refer the reader to Chapter 33 on the battle against hunger.

10) Finally we come to that vital organ, *the brain*, and all the emotional states, of anxiety, despair or panic, that it represents. In the pathology of the castaway panic is not only the most difficult condition to overcome but also the one that governs and determines, in one way or another, all other organic and functional conditions. We have already discussed the battle against panic and despair in Chapter 36. In conclusion, however, I should like to quote from Surgeon-Captain Walters's study on the Baileys:

Evidence regarding the mental and emotional state of Maralyn and Maurice during and immediately following their voyage is difficult to evaluate in retrospect but it does not seem that they have suffered any permanent incapacity in this regard. The difficulties arise not only because of the lack of objective evidence but also because mental deterioration can occur in association with dietary deficiencies as well as with prolonged isolation in a hostile environment. Nevertheless, the story as it has been told shows that it is possible to survive in the face of apparently insurmountable odds without irreversible mental deterioration.

At the time of the sinking both Maralyn and Maurice were sufficiently calm for them to stock the raft with a very sensible assortment of water, food and oddments which were subsequently to prove immensely valuable. This confidence at a time of great stress derives largely from good training in survival techniques and confidence in one's knowledge so that panic, with its possibly fatal results, is minimized. Under the stimulus of such danger the body reacts with an increase in physical and mental activity which subsequently gives way to a period of adaptation to the survival situation. If the survival period is prolonged there will be a degree of mental deterioration dependent upon individual reaction and to physical circumstances. Irritability, aggressiveness, selfishness and day-dreaming are common. Especially when water and food are in short supply there appears a preoccupation with drink and food. Sometimes suicidal or homicidal tendencies occur or delirium but complete madness is unusual unless the castaway has been drinking sea water or is suffering from severe wounds or illness.

In the case of Maralyn and Maurice there were periods of depression, anxiety, tenseness and self-reproach but they overcame these difficulties extremely well. They fished, played games with improvised equipment, wrote a great deal and discussed the future, all of which activities must have assisted in maintaining morale and thus their chances of survival.

I should also like to include a phenomenon dependent on man's mystical powers and too frequently ignored – premonition. Our accounts contain three (that is, one in ten) examples, which should not be ignored. These premonitions were so accurate that those who had them subsequently found the courage to speak of them at the risk of seeing themselves ridiculed by a large number of people. The first example is that of Bombard himself, who certainly suffered the whole gamut of experiences. On 23 November he felt an inexplicable and unforeseen sense of disquiet growing in him. In his own words:

Before the storm clouds started to gather on the horizon I had begun to feel curiously uneasy. Perhaps that is not the right word, but I felt a strong compulsion to flee, to get away from where I was. I could not tell why, but I would have liked to have found myself somewhere else, and quickly at that. There was little to distinguish my situation from that of the creatures in the sea round me, and I must have acquired some part of their instincts. I took out my Pilot Book to read the section dealing with indications of a typhoon. I scrutinized every point of the compass and saw only gold flecks on the sky and a few black patches gathering on the horizon, nothing alarming, but I still felt that something unpleasant was going to happen. I felt quite unable to escape what I was sure was some impending catastrophe making straight for me. Some time after I arrived in Barbados I discovered that in a number of ships a hundred miles or so to the north, the crews had experienced the same feeling of disquiet.

Here the rational, logical minds will say that meteorological changes, most probably a fall in barometric pressure, act on the cerebral cortex by processes which they are totally unable to explain. Undoubtedly, they are right, but let us turn to the two other examples.

Josée Bourdens had a genuine premonitory dream. Several days before leaving the Island of Bathurst, where life was becoming a living death for her and her husband, she had dreamt that they would be rescued on 1 April. The reader will remember that after four days adrift on a raft which, hour by hour, was sinking deeper into the water they were finally rescued with Henri Bourdens semi-comatose. It was 1 April.

Catherine Plessz underwent the same experience. She dreamt that she would be rescued on the twelfth day of her time adrift in the Mediterranean. She believed it at the same time disbelieving it, as the conditions of life she shared with Lucien grew worse day by day and reached the point of drama. On the twelfth day, however, they were picked up.

Those who see only pure coincidence in this should make an honest attempt to take a little more interest in such astonishing phenomena. On the other hand, the survivor at sea who has a premonition should not attach too much importance to it in case it results in serious disillusionment.

In conclusion I should like to draw attention to the problems raised by the return to normal diet when the survivor is rescued. Paradoxically, this is a new trial for him; he has one last battle to fight, the battle against refuelling himself. In numerous instances this battle is in fact fought in a hospital by a whole team of medical experts. In the case of Zvejnieks, Widicombe, Tapscott and others almost on the point of death, the only possibilities in the first few days were rehydration and nourishment by intravenous drip, carefully regulated by a number of biological tests. Consumption of food under any other conditions would most probably have had fatal results. There are numerous examples of this in the accounts we have studied – notably that of Jean de Léry who tells us: 'A score died ashore from having sated themselves too quickly.'

In addition, there is the extraordinary phenomenon of Poon Lim who, before going into Belém hospital for a fortnight, had eaten his fill – notably a dish piled high with peppers – before the incredulous eyes of the fishermen who had just rescued him. Most survivors have brought this battle against gorging to a successful conclusion. The key to it is to impose maximum restraint on the longing for food and the urge to make up for lost time, to eat as little and as often as possible, and to take only liquids (drinks with plenty of sugar) for the first few days before progressing to a solid diet.

40

Preparations ashore against shipwreck

(Practical advice based on the experience and views
of recent survivors)

Apart from what the victim of shipwreck finds in his raft, it is
absolutely essential that he takes with him additional provisions, water
and items of every kind. Only this additional equipment will give him
some trump cards in what is, unfortunately, always a game of life or
death.

Every skipper worthy of the name should therefore have thought
about the actions to be taken if forced to abandon ship in the following
circumstances: calm sea or storm, and all conditions in between; day or
night and, in the latter case, lights working or failed; length of time
available before the ship goes under (to be estimated as soon as
possible); and the actual causes of shipwreck (storm, collision, explosion, fire on board).

The various terms of these four possibilities can interact, giving an
infinite variety of conditions of shipwreck with, clearly, an equal
variety of practical situations. Here are examples taken from among
the most recent cases: ship sinks very quickly, by day, calm sea
(Robertsons); ship sinks more slowly, by day, calm sea (Baileys);
abandonment in heavy weather, by night (Lucien and Catherine, who,
of course, had all the time in the world because the *Njord* did not sink).

It is in the light of these various situations that the following
precautions must be taken:

Posting of a notice of actions to be taken by each person in case of
abandonment.
Posting of a checklist showing what must be taken if time allows.
Last but not least, preparation of a plastic bag or container in which the
items that are essential and, unfortunately, are not included in the
raft's equipment are permanently kept. I would imagine that skip-
pers who are punctilious about keeping their boat shipshape will not
want this bag permanently stowed on deck; but it must be in a place
known to all and readily accessible whatever the conditions – even
the most unfavourable, such as storms by night.

Let us now look at the practical applications.

1. The choice of a liferaft

There are, of course, three classes of liferaft (I, II and IV, Class III not being used for pleasure craft). These three types of raft differ in structure, which is very difficult to alter, and in equipment, which is much easier to improve. *When choosing a raft, it is therefore the structure which matters.*

To sailors who are concerned not only with keeping on the right side of the law but also about safety, the only advice one can offer is to buy a Class I raft, at all events, whatever the difference in cost, the size of boat and the kind of sailing. This is the only raft in which the tent has a double skin or even several thicknesses of waterproof cloth and is fitted with a device for collecting rainwater; in addition, it is the only raft with a double bottom, which improves both buoyancy and insulation.

It is really very difficult to argue that only ocean-going boats in Category 1 are liable to shipwrecks, the only boats for which a Class I raft is obligatory. Examples of shipwrecks not far from the coast of boats in other categories are proof to the contrary. Ruled by the action of currents or winds, survivors at sea are very quickly apt to break the law – equipped only with the liferaft that the law requires!

In spite of the disproportionate additional cost, it is always wise to buy a raft designed for a larger number of occupants than it is intended for in reality. So for two people a six-man raft would not be extravagant – 'six' is merely the number specified by the regulations.

Finally, one cannot really discuss the choice of a liferaft without giving some thought to countering its main drawback – the virtual impossibility of navigating with a device that, by definition, is exposed more than any other to the whims of wind and water. Here it is worth quoting the views of David Lewis who in 1972-3 was the first to make a single-handed crossing of the Antarctic Ocean in the worst conditions imaginable, all the more so since he capsized and was dismasted twice:

But how *can* he help himself when even the most expensive circular covered-in inflatable that he can buy, though it may keep him alive for a long time in mid-ocean, cannot be sailed or directed towards land? It is perhaps unreal to expect to produce a *sailable*, *steerable*, covered-in inflatable for a minuscule market (though the passive rescue philosophy would often be inapplicable to service personnel in wartime), the immediate problem is one of improvisation. Several possible solutions present themselves.

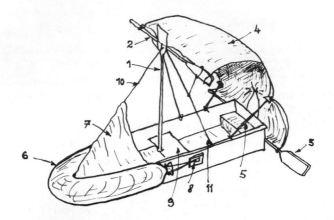

The Robertson family's dinghy.   Before even being aware of Lewis's proposals, Dougal Robertson put them into practice in converting his dinghy.

1. Oar used as a mast
2. Paddle used as cross trees
3. Second oar
4. Sail
5. Sheet
6. Inflatable ring of damaged raft
    mounted forward as a float
7. Tent
8. Lee-board support with inflat-
    able section attached
9. Midships thwart
10. Forestay
11. Backstay

David Lewis's first proposal.   A large inflatable boat, easier to steer than a
circular raft, contains a small circular or oval liferaft which serves as a 'cabin'.

David Lewis's second proposal. An inflatable dome incorporated in manufacture into a large inflatable dinghy.

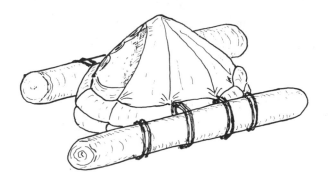

David Lewis's third proposal. Two inflatable cylindrical floats are attached by the crew at either side of the inflatable liferaft, forming a kind of catamaran.

Variant on David Lewis's third proposal. Here the floats are replaced by two air mattresses doubled along their length.

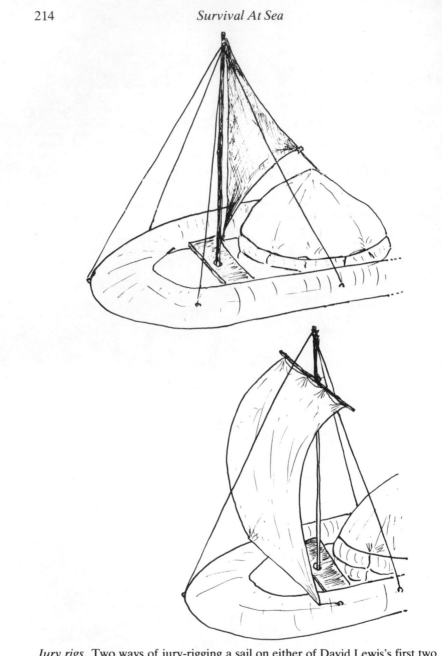

Jury rigs. Two ways of jury-rigging a sail on either of David Lewis's first two proposals. Lewis himself called for a mast, sail and sheet, and a steering oar (not shown here).

One: Any of the larger models of inflatable boat (Avon, Zodiac, Gemini, etc.) could carry one of the smallest of the circular (or preferably oval) covered-in rafts inside it. A tiny protective cabin would thus be provided.

Two: More satisfactory, would be the incorporation of an inflatable enclosed canopy in the manufacturing stage of an otherwise standard large sized inflatable boat. Obviously, some 'outside' space would have to be left for 'working ship'. This would be an excellent and not too expensive solution.

Three: Longitudinal cylindrical inflatable pontoons could be attached along either side of an inflatable life raft, so providing it with hulls of a sort, rather after the manner of a primitive catamaran. Again this modification would ideally be carried out during manufacture, but the contraption could be assembled when afloat (in Arctic waters by a wet-suited crew) at leisure, once the original storm had been ridden out.

Rigging a mast, sail and steering oar to any of the above would be a relatively simple matter, provided the necessary equipment had been collected beforehand.

The reader may ponder on David Lewis's various proposals and I hope he will find applying them to his own case a valuable exercise. Should any manufacturer put them into practice, I should like to suggest that the resulting craft should carry David Lewis's name.

2. Liferaft equipment

We might start by assuming that a liferaft is bought complete with the equipment included in the price. In France this equipment is laid down by the Order in Council published in the *Journal Officiel* on 24 January 1967.[1] Equipment of the three classes of raft which concern us is set out in the table on the next page.

1, These classifications have now in fact been superseded (see pages 222 *et seq.*).

Equipment	Class I	Class II	Class IV
Small marker buoy	1	–	–
Light buoyant line	100 ft	(length not specified)	
Floating knife	1 or 2 depending on capacity	1	1
Collapsible bailer	as above	1	1
Sea-anchor	2	1	1
Pair of paddles or oars	2	1 or 2	1 or 2
Sponges	2	2	2
Repair kit	2	1	1
Air pump	1	1	1
Instruction book	1	1	1
Fishing tackle	1	–	–
Signalling mirror	1	–	–
Whistle	1	–	–
Waterproof torch	1	1	1
Spare batteries	1 set	–	–
Spare bulbs	1	–	–
Parachute flares	2	2	2
Hand-held red flares	6	3	3
Tables of distress signals	1	–	–
Food rations (per head according to capacity)	2,250 calories	–	–
Water (per head)	1,500 ml	600 ml	–
First-aid kit	1 for 12 people	–	–
Seasickness pills	6 per head	6 in all	6 in all

This table calls for only one comment: whatever the class, it is inadequate and must therefore in all instances be supplemented. In the first place owners of Class II and IV rafts must bring their equipment up to Class I standard and, secondly, once the three classes of raft have the same equipment, the remaining deficiencies must be overcome.

We now arrive at the key moment when the skipper prepares his survival bag or container – the one he will snatch up if the boat goes down very quickly by night and in heavy seas. My suggestions are drawn from advice given by recent survivors, but the list is naturally not exhaustive.

Equipment

  i) A portable bilge-pump, which some people consider essential for emptying a raft of water quickly.

ii) A more suitable repair kit than the one normally provided with the three classes of raft. Having used them myself, I suggest the plastic patches and adhesives used by the owners of swimming pools with a plastic liner inside the concrete basin. They can be put on under water without having to drain the pool and seem to be completely satisfactory.

iii) One or two air mattresses of dimensions matching those of the raft. There is nothing like them for comfort, and they will help prevent multiple skin problems; if necessary, they can also be used as water-tanks or floats to improve stability.

iv) For the most far-sighted the survival bag should also contain the inflatable cylindrical floats, small mast, sail and steering oar described by David Lewis. It must, however, be appreciated that these ideas cannot be put into practice by jury-rigging and must be provided for in advance.

v) Finally, cordage, plenty of buoyant rot-proof lines of the kind used to tow water-skiers. There is always a shortage of these on board rafts, and they have many daily uses. Equally useful is a roll of sailmaker's or whipping twine; it takes up little space and is very versatile.

Distress signals

i) It is important to keep the parachute flares, required by law to be carried on board, in a side pocket of the survival bag; they will then be available in addition to those normally included in the raft's equipment.

ii) The two or three rubber balloons I suggested earlier; these should be covered with several layers of metallized paint to make them act as radar reflectors. It is worth while inflating them with compressed hydrogen and securing them with some nylon line, like fishing line, to the raft once inflated.

Water

i) The emergency plastic containers (only part-filled to ensure buoyancy) cannot be put in this survival bag.

ii) On the other hand, one or more solar stills must be included. They represent a very small outlay, considering their enormous value as aids to survival.

Food

i) An amount of canned food, depending on the skipper's tastes and appetite, will weigh the survival bag down. It is important to include foods composed mainly of carbohydrates, which retain water in the organism and are almost entirely lacking in the basic fish diet.

ii) These provisions must be used up now and then and immediately replaced.

iii) As examples of a few of the many items that might be included in these supplementary rations one might mention dried fruit, chocolate, boiled sweets and candies, cold dessert mixes, sweetened condensed milk and powdered milk, cans of jam, cans of fruit juice.

iv) A small solid-fuel stove and some boxes of matches in sealed packets, which may have many uses besides cooking.

Fishing tackle

The fishing tackle provided with Class I rafts should be supplemented.

i) It is easy to increase the number and size of hooks and the amount of line – plenty of the latter because it has so many other uses.

ii) It is most important to include a few large hooks, 2-3 inches across, which can be fixed to a wooden handle to make a gaff. As we have already seen, this is one of the best ways of catching the large fish which escort the raft.

iii) It is also essential to include a can of mussels – one of the best baits, and one which will keep almost indefinitely.

iv) A special plankton net is strongly recommended. If you have a large enough one, it will also serve as a second sea-anchor.

Medicine chest

Here again it is a matter of adding to the first-aid kit included in the equipment of Class I rafts. The possibilities are infinite, but the following are probably the bare minimum:[2]

---

2. It is important to ensure that the survival bag contains sufficient quantities of any special medicament an individual member of the crew may require. Insulin and tablets for heart conditions are obvious examples, but any allergic condition – particularly skin allergies – could become extremely serious under survival conditions.

i) Skin creams and sunscreens.
ii) Eye lotions.
iii) Antiseptics, and sulfa drugs for disorders of the alimentary tract.
iv) Antibiotics of the tetracycline type, in tablet form.
v) Suppositories against seasickness (the tablets included in the equipment being highly likely to be brought up before they have had time to act).[3]
vi) Inflatable plastic splints, one for upper limbs and one for lower. These are in no way superfluous, for they will serve many other purposes, such as containers or floats.
vii) Dressings, bandages and compresses.

Most of the items mentioned above have to be used before the date marked on the package; they must therefore be renewed from time to time.

Miscellaneous

i) Plenty of plastic bags in different sizes. They must be strong such as the type used for carrying exotic fish.
ii) *Stainless-steel scissors* which greatly simplify the dissection of fish, turtles or birds.
iii) *One or two good multiple-blade knives*, well greased, in waterproof plastic sleeves. These provide a complete kit of miniaturized tools, allowing one to work on wood, the tinplate of food cans and other materials.
iv) *An underwater mask* greatly increases safety when bathing. It also allows one to check the submerged part of the raft for leaks or small tears and makes the repair of these much easier. It is also very useful for gathering the shellfish and seaweed which soon colonize the bottom of the raft, and for harpooning or otherwise catching fish by sight; for this one need only lean over the inflatable ring with one's face under the water. The mask can also be converted into a sun visor by covering the inner surface of its glass with fish or turtle blood, diluted to give the degree of tinting required.

---

3. As readers who have lived in France will know, no self-respecting French doctor ever fails to prescribe a suppository. The point the author makes is a good one, but I would not think suppositories advisable for those unfamiliar with them, unless there is a doctor or nurse in the crew.

v) *Heavy cloth gloves,* like gardening gloves, are useful for avoiding
injury when preparing fish or handling flares; they are also useful
for keeping the salt out of a hand injury which will not heal.

vi) *A lemon-squeezer* for extracting 'fish juice'.

vii) *Several large towels, or an old sheet.* Experience shows that on
many occasions every scrap of cloth is valuable; in fact, accounts
often tell of sacrificing a shirt or a pair of trousers.

viii) *A 'housewife'*, with some needles and strong thread.

All the small items can be packed in a Tupperware plastic container,
which will subsequently have many other uses.

3.   Checklist for abandoning ship

I am thinking here of the list of everything which has to be collected in a
matter of seconds when abandoning ship. Experience shows clearly
that, even when there is no panic, most victims of shipwreck forget
major items while taking less important ones. The best example of this
is perhaps the Baileys, who forgot all their fishing tackle but took time
to take a photograph of their boat *Auralyn* as she sank. A checklist
should therefore be put on display in the wheelhouse or at a convenient
point near the main hatch.

i) *Reserve water containers* come first and foremost. Many far-
sighted sailors carry them in the survival bag. Personally, I prefer
to think in terms of several 20-litre plastic jerricans (*partly* filled,
of course) tied together with a strong line, whose free end can be
caught whatever the conditions and quickly secured to the raft. A
compromise is to put two 10-litre containers in the survival bag in
addition to the large jerricans. If there is no room for these on
board the raft, they can be left in the water and towed like a train
of barges.

ii) *A food container.* In harbour, when the skipper is ordering and
stowing provisions for his next passage, he would be wise to put
some of them – an assortment of four non-perishable items – into
a bag which is easily accessible. At sea these will be the last
reserve rations to be consumed. To take foresight to its extreme
one should lash the sack between two large empty jerricans which
will serve as floats, so that the major reserve of provisions it
contains does not sink if, in case of emergency, it has to be thrown
overboard and recovered later.

iii) *A navigator's bag.* For readers who follow David Lewis's advice
and arrange in advance to equip their liferaft to sail, they clearly

need to take with them, when they abandon ship, a minimum of instruments and documents which will enable them to make the best of their raft. This navigation checklist must include a sextant, charts of the area (those lying on the chart table which can be snatched up in an instant), almanac and reference books, compass, chronometer, pencils, etc. Since it is out of the question to double up on all this equipment, it is worth having, by the side of the chart table, a little wooden box with compartments into which the sextant in its case, the compass, charts and so on can quickly be fitted. Here again a large plastic bag will be needed to keep everything dry.

iv) *Clothing.* This is very often forgotten, most survivors seeming to end up in the raft in whatever garments they happened to be wearing at the time. This is all very well for those wearing oilskins, as they can pick up some extra clothes if they have time; but for those who are not wearing oilskins, it is vital that they take a set along with them. At least one set per person is essential, for this is the best clothing for all kinds of bad weather.

v) *An underwater gun with one or more harpoons.*

vi) *A snorkel* to go with the mask. This provides unequalled comfort in the water, which in many cases has saved people from drowning.

vii) *Photographic flash equipment* (along with the camera of course).

viii) *Books, paper and pencils.* When one realizes the moral consolation certain books have brought to many survivors, it seems well worth while taking some. Everyone must decide for himself the authors who will keep him company during his life as a survivor.

ix) *A battery-powered RT set.* If there is one on board, it is clearly essential to find room for it on the raft.

x) The same rule applies for any *battery-powered radio beacons.*

---

4. This operation may prove difficult while attempting to abandon ship in a hurry, and I think it *is*, in fact, entirely practicable to keep one's 'emergency cover' charts and some spare dividers and pencils in the survival bag, along with a spare tidal atlas. Similarly, the plastic sextants and compasses now available are very cheap and adequate for this purpose. Many yachtsmen now wear a waterproof quartz watch on their wrist anyway, thus leaving only the almanac to be flung in at the last moment.

41

Updating in the light of the new standards for makers and users of liferafts[1]

(Order in Council of 12 December 1975)

While I was writing this study on survival at sea, the French Ministry of Transport was also active. Their work – in particular, the part which interests us – took shape in the Order in Council of 12 December 1975 on the subject of the *Conditions of carriage, approval and inspection of pneumatic liferafts for pleasure craft up to 25 m in length*.

This Order was first published in the *Journal Officiel* of 25 February 1976 and the main points are as follows:

Terminology

i) The Class I raft disappears from the nomenclature.
ii) It is replaced by the Class II raft which must be carried on pleasure craft cleared for Categories 1 and 2 (ocean and off-shore).
iii) A 'light Class II' raft is specified.
iv) This or the Class IV raft, whichever is preferred, must be carried on pleasure craft cleared for Category 3 (coastal).
v) Finally, a Class V raft is specified for use in Category 4 (sheltered waters).

Equipment

As far as the equipment of these liferafts is concerned, there is, unfortunately, no significant change.

i) The equipment of the Class II raft (now the most sophisticated) is exactly the same as that of the old Class I with the sole addition of 'three devices for opening, if necessary, food and fresh water containers, and a stainless-steel graduated drinking cup'.

1. See footnote on page 191, and Appendix.

ii) The Light Class II raft has the same equipment except for the graduated cup and the three openers mentioned above.

iii) The equipment of the Class IV raft corresponds to that of the former Class II (see table, page 216), with the addition of a signalling mirror, a whistle and a table of distress signals; but the 600 ml of drinking water per head and the six seasickness pills have disappeared.

iv) Finally, the equipment of the Class V raft corresponds to that of the former Class IV, with the addition of a signalling mirror, a whistle and six red flares instead of three, but again with the disappearance of the six seasickness pills.

Since this new legislation really changes only the terminology, the proposals I made about the former standards still apply. It is worth repeating here the expensive but prudent advice on carrying a (new) Class II raft, whatever kind of sailing you do. Since the equipment of this raft is virtually unchanged, everything said concerning the deficiencies of the former Class I raft and the conclusions drawn still hold for this new Class II raft. It is essential to prepare a survival bag and a checklist for abandoning ship, and to provide oneself with the extras needed to give the raft some degree of navigability.

Specifications

It is in the specifications of liferafts that some progress has been made. Although these specifications are aimed at manufacturers, I shall quote them in full from the *Journal Officiel*, so that the owner of a new Class II raft may become more familiar with its characteristics without having to deploy it in the water. The reader should also appreciate that the specifications for the other rafts are progressively less exacting as one moves down to the new Class V.

Here, then, is the whole of Article 2 of the annex to the Order in Council of 12 December 1975:

A Class II inflatable liferaft shall meet the following specifications:

It should be constructed so that when thrown into the sea its shape and characteristics are developed automatically by the release of gas stored under pressure or any other equivalent means.

It should have a shape and proportions which will give it a high degree of stability in the sea when it is fully inflated and floating with its tent in place. The stability of the raft shall be improved by the addition, in the most appropriate place, of one or more water pockets or any other effective device, provided that it can be quickly and easily attached and fills with water when the raft is in the sea in a laden condition; and can be effectively put out of action so as not to hinder progress under tow.

It should be equipped with a tent which is set up automatically when the raft is inflated; if the device used contains inflatable structural elements, these shall be automatically isolated from the other inflatable elements of the raft.

This tent shall effectively protect the occupants against bad weather and be equipped with a device for collecting rainwater.

The tent shall consist of one thickness of waterproof cloth.[2]

Two electric lamps with a rating of at least 0.25 watts and an intensity of at least 0.20 candelas, supplied by one or more batteries activated by seawater, shall be fixed at the top of the tent, one inside and one out.

The outer surface of the tent shall be orange-red in colour.

The tent shall carry on its outer surface sheets of material reflecting light and radar waves; these sheets shall be properly distributed in such a way as to facilitate detection from all directions. The light reflecting elements shall have an area not less than that of rectangles of 30 by 5 centimetres (12 by 2 inches); their overall surface shall be equal to whichever is the higher of the following two figures: 3200 square centimetres (500 square inches) or 2 x N x 150 square centimetres (24 square inches), N being the number of persons authorized to be carried. The radar reflectors shall present an overall surface of at least 7500 square centimetres (1150 square inches); the area occupied by these reflectors shall not exceed half that of the surface of the tent, any excess being located on the flotation compartments. The raft shall be fitted with a mooring rope and surrounded by two lifelines, one on the inside and one on the outside.

The minimum breaking strain of the mooring rope and the lifelines, which shall be of polyamide (nylon) or equivalent material, and of their attachment points shall be at least 500 kilograms (700 pounds).

The length of mooring line shall be related to the location of the raft on board the boat and shall in any case not be less than 10 metres (33 feet). The inflated raft, when floating upside down, shall be capable of being righted by one person. Two openings opposite one another shall be provided for access and ventilation. These openings shall be capable of being effectively sealed. To the right of each opening shall be fitted a ladder or other device allowing a person in the water wearing a lifejacket to get on board without assistance.

The raft shall be accessible from above decks and carried in a strong waterproof cloth bag, fitted with carrying handles, enclosed by a device which will break under pressure when the raft is inflated. The raft shall be kept on board on the deck or in a locker which will effectively protect the equipment against shocks, vibrations and rubbing; this locker must be sheltered from seawater, vented and completely accessible at all times at sea, so that the raft can be deployed

2. I think the French must be incorrectly quoted, omitting the words 'more than'.

instantly. Alternatively, the raft may be carried in a rigid casing designed to withstand the most severe conditions of use at sea. This will be located with the same accessibility as stipulated above.

The casing or bag of the raft shall be white. The raft, packed in its bag or container, shall remain afloat for at least thirty minutes on the surface of the water.

The buoyancy of the raft shall be achieved by an even number of separate compartments, so that inflation of a number of compartments not exceeding half the total will support the authorized number of persons clear of the water without their having to move. The inflation system of the buoyancy compartments shall be designed so that each compartment shall be automatically isolated from the others as well as from all other inflatable elements of the raft. Further, a device shall be provided to allow the correct inflation pressure to be maintained under changing ambient conditions.

Any other effective means that guarantees equivalent buoyancy when the raft is damaged or partially inflated shall be acceptable.

The total weight of the raft, including the bag or casing and equipment, shall not exceed 90 kilograms (200 pounds).

The number of persons the inflatable raft is authorized to carry shall be equal to: (i) the largest whole number obtained by dividing by 96 the volume of the main air compartments in the inflated condition, measured in cubic decimetres (or dividing by four the volume in cubic feet). This calculation shall not include the arches of the tent, nor any thwarts that may be fitted, nor the volume of air enclosed within the double bottom; or (ii) the largest whole number obtained by dividing by 3720, the surface of the floor of the raft in the inflated condition, measured in square centimetres (or dividing by 576 the area in square inches). For this calculation any thwarts fitted may be included; (iii) the smaller of these two numbers shall be accepted; (iv) the capacity of the raft so calculated shall be not less than six and not more than ten.

The floor of the raft shall be waterproof and adequately insulated against cold. It shall be formed by a double bottom filled with gas or any other suitable contrivance. Inflation shall be automatic and shall make use of one or more cylinders of gas under pressure; it shall be actuated by pulling a line or any other simple and effective means. The gas used shall not be harmful to the occupants.

The containers holding the gas used for inflation of the raft shall be made of steel or of a material considered to offer equivalent assurance of reliability. They shall be in accordance with national regulations in force. The stamping of these containers shall be carried out by the government agency authorized to carry out regulation tests.

The containers must be fitted with a device ensuring that they remain fully gas-tight up to a pressure corresponding to a temperature of 65°C (149°F). The raft shall be capable of functioning in a temperature range of -15°C (5°F) to $+65$°C (149°F). It shall be so constructed as to be able to resist all weather conditions and any sea state for a period of thirty days.

To simplify movement and securing when in the water the raft shall be equipped with two diametrically opposite securing patches or any other suitable device. These shall be strong enough to withstand the forces involved in a short tow in the laden condition.

The coated textiles and other materials used in the construction of the raft against the effects of seawater, heat, cold and accidental contact with hydrocarbons (fuel) shall in all respects match the requirements of this regulation.[3]

To conclude this survey of the *Journal Officiel* of 20 February 1976 I shall quote Articles 3 and 4 of the Order in Council of 12 December 1975:

Article 3 – This Order in Council and the attached regulations shall apply in full to inflatable liferafts installed on board French pleasure craft of an overall length below 25 m from 1 January 1976 for Class V rafts, and from 1 October 1976 for Class II, II (Light) and IV rafts.

Article 4 – Rafts installed on pleasure craft in commission on 30 September 1976 and operating in Categories 1, 2 and 3 may be kept in service until they are no longer usable.

3. See Appendix page 229

42
Conclusion

I should like to conclude this work, which leaves much ground still to be explored, with the following story. A friend of mine, Dr P. Chevailler, read my manuscript, while he was preparing for an Atlantic crossing. He telephoned me the next morning and told me that his sleep had been disturbed by a long nightmare. All night he had dreamt that he was shipwrecked, and it had made such an impression on him that he sat down and wrote an account of it:

It was not without some difficulty that I managed to cut the lashings holding the container on its cradle, and I lost a few precious seconds going back to the cabin to look for a knife, the one which was normally within reach of the raft having mysteriously disappeared. Unfortunately, when leaving harbour the night before in an alcholic haze I had forgotten to take off the metal anti-theft cables by which the raft was padlocked to the deck. I had to go back a second time for the pliers. The water was rising rapidly; by now it was up to the berths. With the raft at last free, I lifted it out of its cradle with a series of heaves – my God, it was heavy! As I moved it near to the toe-rail, I saw to my despair that it would not go under the lower lifeline, and I should never have the strength to heave it over the top. Groping in the dark, I found the pliers which must somehow have slid to the other side of the boat. I cut the damned lifeline. At the last minute, just as I was going to put the raft over the side, my heart sank as I realized I had not secured the deployment line. God! There it was in the water. I got hold of it as quickly as I could and gave a sharp tug, as the pictures in the instruction book show. A moment of suspense – and it inflated.

Without wasting time – I must have been struggling for at least five minutes no, surely only four, I said to myself – I turned to the saloon. Let's see. Survival bag? On the right in the navigator's berth. The water was up to my thighs. She'd be gone in no time. I grabbed the bag, which stayed put. Yes, of course, the shock-cords. Quick! One, two, and it was free. I heaved it up, put it on the companionway and shoved it into the cockpit.

Now the jerricans. Where were the jerricans? Ah yes, two ten-litre ones just beside the bag. I pulled at them, but they were jammed. Hell! Their securing line was fouled in a hook. With my arms in the water I managed to get them out. Up they came with a bump to go the same way as the bag. Not much time left. Now let's see, my checklist. What was there on my checklist? No question of reading it in the dark. Ah yes, the waterproof bag tied to the fenders in the sternsheets. Good. From below what should I take? Clothes? They were all wet by now. My oilies were in the locker. Quick! Navigation? To hell with it, what was the use! My hand found the torch. I lit it and swept the cabin with its beam. My binoculars were floating there and, for some reason, I put them round my neck. The electronic flash I'd promised myself to take was already under water. Feverishly, I opened the drawers to let as many things as possible float out and snatched a half-empty bottle of cognac which came to the top. There was nothing more to be done; it was time to get out – and quick.

Above decks, I heaved the provisions bag from the sternsheets. The fenders jammed. Inevitable! In passing I cleared away the paddles of the inflatable dinghy. I was now in the cockpit – with water up to my knees and everything I had thrown there around me. The raft was floating a few metres away on its painter. I opened the sail locker, cleared away a bag and pulled out some more fenders which I tied on to the survival bag, knotting the sleeves of my oilskins round the lines. God, I hadn't even got a life-jacket on! It was no good now, they'd all be up forward.

I went up on deck, gropingly undid the knot by which the raft was made fast, and pulled it to the stern, hard alongside. Luckily, the sea was relatively calm. What should I do in a storm? The bag, quick! She was going down! My God, it was heavy to heave and tip into the raft. I was out of breath and my pulse must have been up to 200. The jerricans were already floating in the cockpit; I threw them over. One fell in the raft, the other floated to one side. Luckily, they were tied on. One paddle drifted away. The water was up to the deck – it was time to say goodbye. I just had time to grab the fenders and the other paddle and jumped into the raft.

There I was. I drew breath; then suddenly I thought of the painter? Cut the painter! Quickly, my knife. There was a knife provided in the raft for this purpose, but where? The painter started to drag. Was I crazy, I had something to cut it with in my pocket. The right-hand one? The left? No . . . ah yes, the right one. Now to open the knife. My hands were shaking and my thumb nail was torn. How did that happen? I used the other hand and it was done. I groped for the painter and slashed it. That was all. Now, I said to myself as I collapsed on the bottom of the raft, now I could get my breath back. . . .

I shall have achieved the aim I set myself in making this study if, on closing this book, every reader lives as intensively through this nightmare – unpleasant, it is true, but packed with lessons.

Appendix

Liferafts

Extracts from the International Convention for the Safety of Life at Sea, 1974. Inter-Governmental Maritime Consultative Organization.

Regulation 15

Requirements for Inflatable Liferafts

(a)   Every inflatable liferaft shall be so constructed that, when fully inflated and floating with the cover uppermost, it shall be stable in a seaway.

(b)   The liferaft shall be so constructed that if it is dropped into the water from a height of 18 metres (60 feet) neither the liferaft nor its equipment will be damaged. If the raft is to be stowed on the ship at a height above the water of more than 18 metres (60 feet), it shall be of a type which has been satisfactorily drop-tested from a height at least equal to the height at which it is to be stowed.

(c)   The construction of the liferaft shall include a cover which shall automatically be set in place when the liferaft is inflated. This cover shall be capable of protecting the occupants against injury from exposure, and means shall be provided for collecting rain. The top of the cover shall be fitted with a lamp which derives its luminosity from a sea-activated cell and a similar lamp shall also be fitted inside the liferaft. The cover of the liferaft shall be of a highly visible colour.

(d)   The liferaft shall be fitted with a painter and shall have a line securely becketed round the outside. A lifeline shall also be fitted around the inside of the liferaft.

(e)   The liferaft shall be capable of being readily righted by one person if it inflates in an inverted position.

(f)   The liferaft shall be fitted at each opening with efficient means to enable persons in the water to climb on board.

(g)   The liferaft shall be contained in a valise or other container so constructed as to be capable of withstanding hard wear under conditions met with at sea. The liferaft in its valise or other container shall be inherently buoyant.

(h)   The buoyancy of the liferaft shall be so arranged as to ensure by a division into an even number of separate compartments, half of which shall be capable of supporting out of the water the number of persons which the liferaft is permitted to accommodate, or by some other equally efficient means, that there is a reasonable margin of buoyancy if the raft is damaged or partially fails to inflate.

(i)   The total weight of the liferaft, its valise or other container and its equipment shall not exceed 180 kilogrammes (400 lbs.).

(j)   The number of persons which an inflatable liferaft shall be permitted to accommodate shall be equal to:

(i)   The greatest whole number obtained by dividing by 96 the volume, measured in cubic decimetres (or by 3.4 the volume, measured in cubic feet) of the main buoyancy tubes (which for this purpose shall include neither of the arches nor the thwart or thwarts if fitted) when inflated; or

(ii)   the greatest whole number obtained by dividing by 3,720 the area measured in square centimetres (or by 4 the area, measured in square feet) of the floor (which for this purpose may include the thwart or thwarts if fitted) of the liferaft when inflated whichever number shall be the less.

(k)   The floor of the liferaft shall be waterproof and shall be capable of being sufficiently insulated against cold.

(l)   The liferaft shall be inflated by a gas which is not injurious to the occupants and the inflation shall take place automatically either on the pulling of a line or by some other equally simple and efficient method. Means shall be provided whereby the topping-up pump or bellows required by Regulation 17 of this Chapter may be used to maintain pressure.

(m)   The liferaft shall be of approved material and construction, and shall be so constructed as to be capable of withstanding exposure for 30 days afloat in all sea conditions.

(n)   No liferaft shall be approved which has a carrying capacity calculated in accordance with paragraph (j) of this Regulation of less than six persons. The maximum number of persons calculated in accordance with that paragraph for which an inflatable liferaft may be approved shall be at the discretion of the Administration, but shall in no case exceed 25.

(o)   The liferaft shall be capable of operating throughout a temperature range of 66 °C to minus 30 °C (150 °F to minus 22 °F).

(p)   (i)   The liferaft shall be so stowed as to be readily available in case of emergency. It shall be stowed in such a manner as to permit it to float free from its stowage, inflate and break free from the vessel in the event of sinking.

      (ii)   If used, lashings shall be fitted with an automatic release system of a hydrostatic or equivalent nature approved by the Administration.

     (iii)   The liferaft required by paragraph (c) of Regulation 35 of this Chapter may be securely fastened.

(q)   The liferaft shall be fitted with arrangements enabling it to be readily towed.

Regulation 17

Equipment of Inflatable and Rigid Liferafts

(a)   The normal equipment of every liferaft shall consist of:

    (i)   One buoyant rescue quoit, attached to at least 30 metres (100 feet) of buoyant line.

    (ii)   For liferafts which are permitted to accommodate not more than 12 persons: one knife and one baler; for liferafts which are permitted to accommodate 13 persons or more: two knives and two balers.

    (iii)   Two sponges.

    (iv)   Two sea-anchors, one permanently attached to the liferaft and one spare.

    (v)   Two paddles.

    (vi)   One repair outfit capable of repairing punctures in buoyancy compartments.

    (vii)   One topping-up pump or bellows, unless the liferaft complies with Regulation 16 of this Chapter.

    (viii)   Three tin-openers.

    (ix)   One approved first-aid outfit in a waterproof case.

    (x)   One rustproof graduated drinking vessel.

    (xi)   One waterproof electric torch suitable for signalling in the Morse Code, together with one spare set of batteries and one spare bulb in a waterproof container.

    (xii)   One daylight-signalling mirror and one signalling whistle.

(xiii) Two parachute distress signals of an approved type, capable of giving a bright red light at a high altitude.

(xiv) Six hand flares of an approved type, capable of giving a bright red light.

(xv) One set of fishing tackle.

(xvi) A food ration, determined by the Administration, for each person the liferaft is permitted to accommodate.

(xvii) Watertight receptacles containing 1½ litres (3 pints) of fresh water for each person the liferaft is permitted to accommodate, of which ½ litre (1 pint) per person may be replaced by a suitable desalting apparatus capable of producing an equal amount of fresh water.

(xviii) Six anti-seasickness tablets for each person the liferaft is deemed fit to accommodate.

(xix) Instructions on how to survive in the liferaft; and

(xx) One copy of the illustrated table of life-saving signals referred to in Regulation 16 of Chapter V.

Extracts from Offshore Rating Council Regulations

5.0 *Categories of Offshore Events*

5.1 The International Offshore Rating rule is used to rate a wide variety of types and sizes of yachts in many types of races, ranging from long-distance ocean races sailed under adverse conditions to short-course day races sailed in protected waters. To provide for the differences in the standards of safety and accommodation required for such varying circumstances, four categories of races are established, as follows:

5.2 *Category 1 race.* Races of long distance, well offshore, where yachts must be completely self-sufficient for extended periods of time, capable of withstanding heavy storms and prepared to meet serious emergencies without the expectation of outside assistance.

5.3   *Category 2 race.* Races of extended duration, along or not far removed from shorelines or in large unprotected bays or lakes, where a high degree of self-sufficiency is required of the yachts but with the reasonable probability that outside assistance could be called upon for aid in the event of serious emergencies.

5.4   *Category 3 race.* Races across open water, most of which is relatively protected or close to shorelines, including races for small yachts.

5.5   *Category 4 race.* Short races, close to shore in relatively warm or protected waters.

Race Category
 1   2   3   4

				11.0 *Safety Equipment*
x	x	x	x	11.1 *Life jackets,* one for each crew member.
x	x	x		11.2 *Whistles* (referee type) attached to life jackets.
x	x	x		11.3 *Safety belt* (harness type), one for each crew member.
x	x	x		11.41 *Life raft(s)* capable of carrying the entire crew and meeting the following requirements:

> • Must be carried on deck (not under a dinghy) or in a special stowage opening immediately to the deck, containing life raft(s) only.
> • Must be designed and used solely for saving life at sea.
> • Must have at least two separate buoyancy compartments, each of which must be automatically inflatable. Each raft must be capable of carrying its rated capacity with one compartment deflated.
> • Must have canopy to cover the occupants.

• Must have been inspected, tested and approved within two years by the manufacturer or other competent authority.

• Must have the following equipment appropriately secured to each raft:

    1 Sea anchor or drogue
    1 Bellows, pump or other means for maintaining inflation of air chambers
    3 Hand flares
    1 Repair kit
    1 Signalling light
    1 Knife
    1 Baler
    2 Paddles

x   11.42 Provision for emergency water and rations to accompany raft.

        x   11.51 *Life ring(s)*, at least one horseshoe type life ring equipped with a waterproof light and drogue within reach of the helmsman and ready for instant use.

x x x   11.52 At least one horseshoe type life ring equipped with a high-intensity water light and a drogue within reach of the helmsman and ready for instant use.

    x x   11.53 At least one more horseshoe type life ring equipped with a whistle (referee type), dye marker, a high-intensity water light, and a pole and flag. The pole is to be attached to the ring with 25 feet (8 m) of floating line and is to be of a length and so ballasted that the flag will fly at least 8 feet (2.45 m) off the water.

x x x x 11.61 *Distress signals* to be stowed in a waterproof container.

x   11.62 Twelve red parachute flares.

x x   11.63 Four red parachute flares.

x x x x 11.64 Four red hand flares.

Index